THE ART OF PUNK

THE ART OF PUNK

RUSS BESTLEY & ALEX OGG

OMNIBUS PRESS

London / New York / Paris / Sydney / Copenhagen / Berlin / Madrid / Tokyo

Copyright © Elephant Book Company Limited
www.elephantbookcompany.com

Cover, book, montages and title font designed
by Paul Palmer-Edwards, www.gradedesign.com

Editorial director: Will Steeds
Project editors: Chris Stone, Laura Ward
Copyeditor: Magda Nakassis
Colour reproduction: Pixel Colour Imaging Ltd.
Picture administration: Katie Greenwood
Index: Christine Shuttleworth

ISBN: 978-1-78305-736-8

Order No: OP56056

Exclusive Distributors
Music Sales Limited
14/15 Berners Street
London, W1T 3LJ

Macmillan Distribution Services
56 Parkwest Drive
Derrimut, Vic 3030
Australia.

Every effort has been made to trace the copyright
holders of the images in this book but one or two
were unreachable. We would be grateful if the
copyright holders concerned would contact us.

Printed in China

A catalogue record for this book is available
from the British Library.

Visit Omnibus Press on the web
at www.omnibuspress.com

CONTENTS

Celebrating a wide range of punk art and design in posters, flyers, record covers, fanzines, and ephemera, *The Art of Punk* highlights the evolution of the punk movement within graphic design and print, while also considering its impact on fashion and popular culture. It charts a chronological narrative running from the US and UK proto-punk scenes of the late 1960s and early 1970s through to a contemporary global punk arena that operates as both an established genre of the music industry and a still vital and antagonistic underground movement.

A Punk History

Following early developments in New York and London, punk began its migration, and mutation, as it traveled across the UK regions, the US Midwest and West Coast, Australia, Europe, and beyond, reaching as far afield as the Nordic countries, Eastern Europe, South America, Asia, and Africa. In the process, it cross-fertilized with allied genres including new wave and powerpop, post-punk experimentation, the "do-it-yourself" DIY underground, hardcore, anarcho, Oi!, and street punk. *The Art of Punk* charts some of that progress, highlighting the visual development of a movement that now encompasses all forms of media and artistic practice.

Given that scope, one volume cannot, obviously, be comprehensive, and many of the themes touched upon here could easily form the basis of a library in themselves. However, we have attempted to establish a critical position and employ a narrative arc that highlights crucial developments and interventions, and their consequences. Equally, as Gang Of Four so correctly intoned, history is "not made by great men," and it is important to recognize the role played by less established figures in punk's historical fabric. It is in some ways symbolic of the genre that punk has a huge legacy of what might be termed minor players—its whole ethos took Andy Warhol's "fifteen minutes of fame" theme to its logical conclusion, though in many cases we should perhaps make that three minutes at breakneck speed.

The contemporary received version of punk history, centered on certain key individuals in a few major cities in the US and UK and lasting two years from 1976 to 1978, has become widely accepted as an authentic account, and this has led to a stylized and inaccurate summary of what was, and is still, a disparate and fragmented movement. Many participants, be they musicians, designers, writers or fans, have deeply felt personal views and memories of events that touched their lives and placed them within the collective consciousness of the subculture, on a more or less visible level, and their recollection is bound to be affected by

personal taste and experience. Furthermore, the nature of punk as an ephemeral, diverse, and popular form that flies in the face of authority and rejects intellectualization means that writers and historians have had a difficult time documenting developments beyond a simple chronology of its major themes and events.

Nor have historians been particularly successful in building a social history of punk, beyond the repetition of usually exaggerated stories culled from press releases and interviews of the period, or the application of sociological theories and a tendency to extrapolate meaning and intention through an often heavily distorted philosophical or political lens. It should also be emphasized that the notions of personal direct action and autonomy that are strongly associated with punk automatically produce a widespread distrust of what might be seen as "outsiders" attempting to pin down and locate the subculture. Gang Of Four once again lead by lyrical example here—"history's bunk!" This, then, is not an attempt to capture and contain the vitality and essence of an amorphous and radical subculture—it is instead an attempt to trace influences, connections, and patterns while charting a course through some of the visual and graphic elements that have come to constitute "punk."

A Punk Definition

A definition of "punk," along with its primary aesthetic elements, or "art," is something particularly difficult to pin down. Even within the context of youth subcultures and popular music, punk occupies its own unique space—underground *and* commercial, antiauthoritarian *and* traditional, nihilistic *and* forward-looking; its breadth, depth, and diversity seem tailor-made to defy historical narrative. Its visual art is equally resistant to categorization—covering dress styles, fashion, graphic design, fine art, illustration, film, publishing, marketing, and packaging— though perhaps a thematic undercurrent in the deliberate defiance of convention or authority might allow these disparate disciplines to be seen as interlinked.

When compared with other contemporary forms of popular music, punk offers some interesting contrasts. In particular, a significant strand of the movement can be seen to have engaged in a constant battle with the music industry to remain underground, avant-garde, and strictly uncommercial. As the industry invested in what would be termed new wave, for instance, other punk subgenres sought to distance themselves from any such acquiescence to commercial acceptability. The development of individual subgenres of punk, from Oi! to anarcho and hardcore in the early 1980s,

demonstrates that punk style was never static; rather it was subject to radical and continual change and renegotiation.

The terms "punk" and "new wave" have always been adopted and used in a very loose manner by the music press, and even by record labels and the bands themselves, and a notion of a pure or authentic punk style is difficult to justify. The increased fragmentation of the genre often demonstrates a clear development in both musical and visual styles, with groups citing influences within the earlier punk canon and what might be termed a punk "heritage." New styles and subgenres can be seen in part as a reaction to the co-option and cultural acceptance of earlier punk styles. This "back to basics" ideology took what participants saw as the original spirit or intentions of punk and revitalized it, emphasizing those core principles that had been neglected as punk gained commercial stature. These increasingly aggressive, abrasive, and deliberately awkward punk subgenres splintered and mutated, often in direct antithetical relation to shifts in "popular" punk styles. Such evolutionary steps can be observed in the way that waves of acceptance and opposition played out over time.

These patterns can be seen as both political and aesthetic—from the lyrics and public statements of the groups involved to the musical and visual styles of their records, posters, flyers, and graphic identities. This trend identifies punk as distinct from other contemporaneous forms of popular music that can be seen to enjoy a close allegiance with the music industry's commercial imperatives. In particular, the close fit between the punk subculture and a wide range of radical political and cultural groups meant that the genre was to become widely successful *in spite* of the mainstream, and punk record sales and events remain buoyant in a largely independent and underground market.

Following the initial impetus provided by first-wave punk, many existing groups became associated with the movement. Though their attitudes, music, or fashion sense may have been at odds with bands such as the Ramones, the Sex Pistols, or the Clash, they possessed elements that marked them out as fellow travelers in some crucial regard. In the UK, the music press, keen to promote a new scene, was quick to identify (sometimes quite tenuous) links between groups. This did lead to some confusion, with many bands branded "punk" by promoters and agents quick to spot a new trend—though this tactic could often be self-defeating once venues began to reject punk acts in light of bad publicity in the national press, and audiences became more familiar, and discerning, with the recognized (musical and visual) codes of the new movement.

I WANNA SEE SOME HISTORY

Punk was always based on immediacy—shock-tactical assaults on culture and an often inspired amateurism drawing on underground, close-knit communities that were not intended to extend beyond the gig, the event, the scene, the moment. Songs have a tendency to be short, fast, and aggressive, and the widely repeated credo of the early punk progenitors that ". . . if it can't be said in three minutes, it's not worth saying" was adopted as standard practice. Punk celebrated a lack of musical prowess, and the skill, dedication, and discipline necessary to pursue more traditional routes into the established "entertainment industry" was beyond the reach of many participants in the movement.

It is ironic, then, how many have survived the long haul, either as part of what might be termed a career in punk (the Damned, Buzzcocks, UK Subs, Bad Religion, NOFX, Stiff Little Fingers, et al.) or through periodic revivals of fortune (the Sex Pistols, Cock Sparrer, the New York Dolls, Devo, Wire, Misfits). A newer generation, taking its cue from punk's legacy, has seen the subculture grow and expand—geographically, musically, and philosophically—far beyond anything those early pioneers might have thought possible. Punk's global history extends across a period of more than forty years and its attitudes and aesthetics continue to thrive and prosper—and evolve.

A Punk Aesthetic

Often regarded as the lowest and cheapest rung on an increasingly sophisticated advertising and marketing ladder, few appreciated the worth of punk graphic material during its early phase of development—particularly the wide range of work produced outside of the heavily publicized scene leaders. The value of such groundbreaking artwork, which continues to have an impact on music, fashion, design, and media to this day, is even now only becoming fully apparent. The visual legacy of punk is extensive and its graphic codes—

symbols of struggle and resistance, but also a complex subcultural visual vocabulary and, more cynically, a means to tap into deeply held antiauthoritarian consumer sentiments by lifestyle branders—still have resonance.

Like the music that accompanied it, punk art and design cannot be tied down to one set of processes or concepts. Equally, it cannot make claim to a clear sense of originality, and the "year zero"—punk's "virgin birth"—so often claimed at different points on the punk time line, remains disingenuous. Its graphic strategies tapped into long-established practices and countercultural crafts—in some cases knowingly, as with Malcolm McLaren and Jamie Reid's Situationist rhetoric, Malcolm Garrett and Richard Boon's overt references to modernist design, Adam Ant's homages to Eduardo Paolozzi, or Winston Smith's reinterpretation of the subversive potential of collage—although it would equally be an oversimplification to extrapolate from this a kind of shared intentionality in relation to the wider range of punk material.

Punk's musical and visual identity was at least in part about solidarity, although it was often expressed in a language that proclaimed individuality and autonomy. Graphic design styles relating to the movement also follow similar patterns—the need to be recognized as part of the subculture is counterbalanced by the desire to stand out as an individual or to display an originality of intent. Punk's graphic language needed to be identifiable to potential audiences—to be effective, record sleeves or posters generally have to connote their connection to "punk"—but at the same time designers often strove for an individual identity for the band or label within that context.

It is important to question the notion of a direct association between work by prominent early punk designers and the emergence of a radical new visual language of parody or agitprop. To an extent, the techniques adopted

01   01 02

01
_"Gabba gabba, we accept you, we accept you, one of us." The Ramones live onstage, Manchester Apollo, December 21, 1977. Johnny Ramone (guitar, left) and Joey Ramone (vocals, right). Photography by Howard Barlow.

02
_Sex Pistols press conference to announce their signing to A&M Records, March 10, 1977, featuring new bassist Sid Vicious alongside Paul Cook, Steve Jones, (manager) Malcolm McLaren, and Johnny Rotten. The group would be fired within a week. Photography by Peter Gravelle.

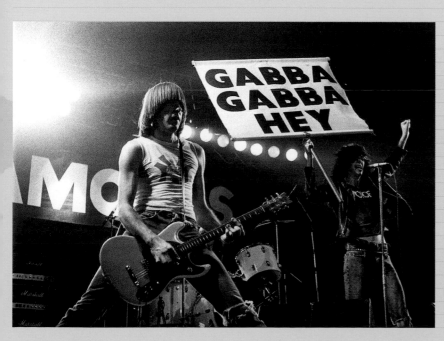

by Jamie Reid, for instance, were already widely accepted as the natural graphic languages of anger and protest. The samizdat tradition of subversive, lo-tech graphic material disseminated through personal networks—originally a feature of the Russian underground where the term denoted the clandestine copying and distribution of government-suppressed literature or other media—led to the evolution of a particular visual style, largely driven by necessity. The natural limitations of simple tools and materials, as well as the quick production of graphic work by untrained designers, led to a repetition of certain graphic conventions: simple black-and-white or two-color artwork, stencil or relief printing, hand-folding and binding techniques, and hand-rendered or simple letterpress or typewritten text.

Formal "punk" graphic conventions during its initial explosion—ransom note or aggressive typography, heavy halftone photographic treatments, dynamic angles and hard lines—can all be traced back to this tradition, together with earlier movements in art and design, particularly constructivism, Dada, surrealism, the Lettrists, and the Situationist International. As such, early punk art and design has been reappraised in design histories as a formative influence within postmodern visual culture, drawing eclectically on what came before to create a new "bricolage" of disparate elements.

Punk's visual style, like the music, was often aggressive and contemporary, reflecting and commenting on its surroundings. A number of thematic design methods can be associated with the movement, though they should not be seen in isolation from other forms of design with similar messages to convey. The use of parody and pastiche, for instance, has been a common design strategy in political satire for hundreds of years, while certain visual codes to denote disposability or the quick dissemination of polemical ideas have been a feature of political propaganda and art

throughout the twentieth century. Jamie Reid's awareness of the work of the Situationist International and the late hippie underground in Europe and the US may have led him toward more "informed" interpretations of agitprop graphic material, but many subsequent punk designers made no such historical allusions—the look was simple, dirty, and aggressive, and it meant "punk."

It should also be noted that the visual styles of record covers, fanzines, and graphic ephemera surrounding punk did not stand still—there is no one standard punk visual language—but did in fact undergo an evolution in terms of both the creation and use of imagery and in typographic style. Techniques for reproduction and manufacture of a range of punk graphic material have also undergone change, partly because independent producers of fanzines and sleeves could build upon innovations and good practice developed by their peers and the benefit of collective knowledge. In other words, a good idea can be copied.

The growth of the independent DIY scene in the late 1970s also resulted in graphic design for record sleeves, posters, flyers, and fanzines that could be targeted to specific, often small-scale, markets. Many of these could be regarded as strongly noncommercial in terms of the mainstream record industry, either in their uncompromising use of text and imagery, or in the handmade, labor-intensive nature of the packaging itself. Their designs often involved strategies that, although based on limited budgets, were inventive and sophisticated—incorporating alternative production processes, the adaptation of available, lo-tech materials, and simple, often handcrafted, printing techniques.

Certain design strategies later became established more widely within the field of music packaging and proved influential within the wider practice of graphic design, while

many others were ad hoc adaptations of more traditional design skills relating to the branding, marketing, and promotion of popular cultural artifacts. The growth in small-scale DIY punk outlets, labels, and distributors also helped to establish an effective "alternative" marketplace that continues to thrive to this day.

A Punk Product

Each subcultural group, particularly in the field of youth culture, has its own outlet for the graphic expression of its identity and values. For the rock 'n' roll generation of the 1950s, that visual field of operation was largely centered around the nascent technologies of television and color film, while the hippie era saw an explosion of color in the form of psychedelic light shows, live events, and poster art. Punk's visual vitality was largely expressed through record sleeves, fanzines, and flyers, together with hairstyles, clothing, and other outward signs of fashion and dress.

The traditions of music promotion were still important to punk, of course, and large-format posters were produced for many of the leading groups, clubs, and labels, following industry conventions stretching back over thirty years. However, the grassroots nature of punk activity, and particularly its widespread desire to provoke a counter to those traditions and conventions—to reject the past—determined a shift in material as well as aesthetic output. Why go to the trouble—and expense—of producing a large piece of printed material to promote a small event at a tiny club, when word of mouth within a close-knit scene and a few simple flyers could do the job just as effectively?

The physical format most associated with punk, particularly during its early period but also still highly relevant today, is the 7-inch, 45rpm single, or EP, packaged in a suitably genre-defining picture sleeve. Traditionally viewed within the industry

as disposable, attention-grabbing promotional items for the "real" business of selling (more expensive) albums, the 45 had largely fallen out of favor by the mid-1970s. Packaged in generic sleeves branded with the company logo, these "pocket money" items were fine for the teen pop market, but offered little of substance or material value. Pioneering early proto-punk and punk labels such as Skydog, Chiswick, and Stiff Records saw the potential for the format, and particularly the picture sleeve, early on. Cheap, simple, user-friendly, and perhaps more importantly a perfect mirror to the short, sharp shock of the music itself, no other "product" epitomizes punk more effectively.

Many of the leading figures in punk art and design have a personal heritage in the creation of 7-inch picture sleeves, along with many more who disappeared just as soon as they arrived, but left a legacy of imagination and innovation behind them. Along with the flyer (a simple but effective form of street-level marketing and publicity) and the fanzine (the equivalent model applied to journalism and publishing) the picture sleeve forms the foundation of a punk graphic design aesthetic.

The Art of Punk features early work by Jamie Reid, Chris Morton, George Snow, Malcolm Garrett, Peter Saville, Linder Sterling, Gee Vaucher, Winston Smith, Jello Biafra, Raymond Pettibon, Brian "Pushead" Schroeder, Mad Marc Rude, and Shawn Kerri, much of it establishing the influential visual codes of punk through the format of record sleeves and flyers. Others, such as Gary Grimshaw, Arturo Vega, John Holmstrom, Gary Panter, Paul Henry, Hipgnosis, Barney Bubbles, Jo Mirowski, Jill Furmanovsky, Michael Beal, David Jeffery, Bill Smith, Jill Mumford, Russell Mills, and Peter Christopherson brought their graphic skills to the service of the punk subculture, while those within the scene including David Byrne, Richard Meyers, Nicholas De Ville, Sebastian Conran, Poly Styrene, Savage Pencil, Adam Ant,

Mark Perry, Phil Smee, Steve McGarry, Bob Last, Mike Coles, Nick Lant, and Spizz took control of their own version of punk graphic style. It is also important to recognize the output of a host of other designers, many of whom have remained unsung and unacknowledged, who each contributed to an evolving punk aesthetic.

Today, historical examples of punk posters and flyers, record covers, fanzines, and pins are collected and admired by a new generation who appreciate the validity of punk's revolutionary, anticommercial, "anti-design" ethos. Those values, at the heart of punk identity throughout the past forty years, refuse to be contained, boxed, packaged, and sold as "just another fashion trend." This book is an attempt to draw a thread through that story, and a reminder that punk is still very much alive, active, and kicking.

01   01 02 | 03 04

01
_ Anarcho punk scene-leaders Crass at the Mayflower Club, Manchester, October 1981. Steve Ignorant (vocals, left) and N. A. Palmer (guitar), with Penny Rimbaud (drums) in the background. Photography by Kevin Cummins.

02
_ Punks salute the local constabulary: Rebellion Festival, Blackpool, August 2008. Photography by Karen Duckworth.

03
_ Punks at the Rebellion Festival, Blackpool, August 2008. Photography by Karen Duckworth.

04
_ Circle Jerks live: Keith Morris faces the moshpit. Photography by Ben DeSoto.

Punk's "year zero" rhetoric resounded through the music press in 1976 and 1977, proclaiming the obliteration of everything that had gone before it. But the genetics of punk belie the virgin birth narrative.

By definition, "proto-punk" exists only through the lens of what came after. Punk's various bloodlines were seldom acknowledged as exceptional or evolutionary at the time, and—crystal balls being in short supply—these groups had no sense of themselves in terms of musical descendants. Their critical or cultural importance was often invisible until much later in the story. Still, many of the first names in punk, both in the United States and Britain, had been formulating ideas, negotiating positions, and claiming their cultural space for some time, often with more of an eye to the past—and what had gone wrong with it—than to the future. Others were simply taking chances with their sound—louder, artier, edgier, sloppier, less melodic—which only later influenced the many strands of punk. The pantheon of proto-punk can stretch absurdly (the elasticity of the term is unsurprising given its posthumous coinage) but the simple roots of pose, antifashion, and excessive volume are obvious enough in 1970s superstars like David Bowie, Mott the Hoople, Slade, and AC/DC. Likewise, the simplified song structures of beat and glam offered at least partial templates for punk's three-chord hymnody, though the most important factors in punk's genesis were musical only as an afterthought.

Amateurism . . .
In the mid-'60s, the garage rock boom saw teenagers attempt to emulate the new pop sounds of the "British Invasion," serendipitously alighting on something far more visceral in the process, reminding listeners that enthusiasm and attitude are essential rock elements in themselves—counting for more, when the time is right, than song craft or technical prowess. This in turn led to an explosion of low-key, local label 45 releases that frequently spun hometown success into the national charts at rates without parallel before or since. Just a handful of years after the fact, the seminal Nuggets album was compiled in 1972 by Jac Holzman of Elektra Records and collector/musician Lenny Kaye, who himself went on to do pioneering work with Patti Smith. Kaye's liner notes used the term "punk rock" to refer to featured groups like Count Five, Shadows of Knight, and the Castaways.

"Musicians Wanted: Decadent 3rd generation rock 'n' roll image essential. New York Dolls Style."

Advert for London SS placed in *Melody Maker* by Mick Jones (later of the Clash) and Tony James (later Generation X)

In a better world, Nuggets should have opened teenage minds by the thousand to the garage band's glamor-free raw power, but under the crushing, multiplatinum weight of the Eagles, Lynyrd Skynyrd, Pink Floyd, ELP, Yes, and hordes of pretty-haired "singer-songwriters," Nuggets stiffed (i.e. flunked, commercially). Horribly. Fortunately, thousands of the Day-Glo double LPs soon populated the US's plentiful bargain bins, where at $2.99 they awaited discovery at a more favorable time.

. . . noise . . .
The American counterculture had become increasingly self-critical following the Woodstock and Altamont festivals of 1969, both of which had exposed serious fissures within the hippie dream. The Manson "family" murder spree of August 1969 had also proved to be a wake-up call, while the Vietnam War remained an open sore.

At the trailing edge of the garage bands, and in gleefully brutish defiance of major, label-sanctioned "flower power," Detroit's MC5 began to forge a new sonic template that, in the words of rock critic and tastemaker Lester Bangs, was "intentionally crude and aggressively raw," while at the same time presenting a politicized vision of the hippie ideal. Nearby, the Stooges, led by Iggy Pop, brought outrage and confrontation to the rock stage, drawing hostility from audiences but setting the scene for what was to follow. Together with the Velvet Underground in New York, these groups began to garner critical praise on both sides of the Atlantic, though wider commercial acceptance was hardly forthcoming.

. . . and revolution
In the UK, the Deviants, Pink Fairies, Here & Now, and Hawkwind were leaders of a new "underground" music scene, drawing on ideological and political principles from the Paris student riots, radical scenes in the US (through the likes of the MC5's manager and activist John Sinclair), and the wider hippie movement. In Europe, civil unrest during the spring of 1968 had spread from France to neighboring countries, and underground protest groups such as Dutch Provos in the Netherlands and King Mob and the Angry Brigade in the UK adopted more proactive strategic positions in an array of nonmusical media. Many of punk's first generation were active during this period, such as Mick Farren of the Deviants, Malcolm McLaren, Bernie Rhodes, and Jamie Reid, together with some of those who would change its later course, including Penny Rimbaud and Gee Vaucher.

Blitzkrieg Bop
All these strands began to coalesce around a number of low-key scenes in the mid-'70s, particularly in London and New York. Television, formed in New York in 1973 by aspiring poets Richard Hell and Tom Verlaine, became central to the punk vanguard based around Hilly Kristal's CBGB club at 315 Bowery in the Bowery district. They were soon followed through the same doors by the Ramones, Patti Smith Group, the Fast, Blondie, and Talking Heads. Fifteen blocks uptown, Max's Kansas City had hosted the Velvet Underground, Silver Apples, the Modern Lovers, the New York Dolls, Wayne County, and was, initially, more receptive to out-of-town bands like Cleveland's Pere Ubu. Minimalist art thugs Suicide, veterans of the Mercer Arts Center scene, employed prehensile onstage electronics and inspired many of punk's first families.

While much has been made of the transatlantic influence of Richard Hell, the Ramones, and the New York Dolls (the latter band briefly and disastrously stewarded by future Sex Pistols' manager Malcolm McLaren), the London pub rock scene was of equal import in shaping what was to come. Stripped-down rock 'n' roll from Dr Feelgood, Ducks Deluxe, and, later, Eddie & the Hot Rods was a regular attraction at small pub stages in London such as the Hope & Anchor in Islington, Tally Ho in Kentish Town, the Red Cow in Hammersmith, Nashville Rooms in West Kensington, and Dingwalls in Camden. Others such as Kilburn & the High Roads and the 101'ers provided developmental shelter for future punk scene leaders, while the Stranglers successfully crossed over from pub rock to punk as exemplars of a subculture in transition. This back-to-basics live music scene, with groups often playing for tips, was the antithesis of the prevailing trend for large venues and spectacular shows by rock stars, while at the same time providing a ready-made circuit for the hastily assembled punks of '76.

NO ELVIS, BEATLES OR ROLLING STONES

"Malcolm McLaren didn't invent punk overnight. 'I invented punk!' 'No, you didn't, Malcolm!' People in the punk bands were going to see bands like the Count Bishops and Feelgoods. Because what they copped from that was the attitude. The attitude was quite tough and heavy, quite punky in their approach. The other thing was, they were playing '50s/'60s styles of music, but at twice the speed. People used to describe the Count Bishops' first EP as the Rolling Stones played at 45rpm, or even 78rpm! It was totally revved up '60s R&B."

Roger Armstrong, Chiswick Records

01

_ Windsor Festival, 4th People's Picnic, August 23, 1975. After problems at the previous Windsor Free Festivals, the event in Windsor Great Park was banned and moved to a vacant airfield near Watchfield, Berkshire, UK. In addition to performances by British underground regulars including Hawkwind, Traffic, Gong & the Edgar Broughton Band, the lineup included early performances by the 101'ers (led by Joe Strummer) and the Stranglers (this was keyboard player Dave Greenfield's first gig with the group).

02

Artist The Ramones
Title S/T
Format LP, 12-inch
Label Sire, USA, 1976
_ Photography by Roberta Bayley.

03

_ The first two albums by the Patti Smith Group, *Horses* and *Radio Ethiopia*, were released by Arista Records in November 1975 and October 1976. Smith's androgynous image is highlighted in the album cover photographs by Robert Mapplethorpe and Judy Linn respectively, and in the strong central portrait on this promotional poster by Lynn Goldsmith.

02

01 **03**

Kick Out the Jams, Motherfucker!

The Velvet Underground's initial notoriety came as the house band for Andy Warhol's Factory art lab and Exploding Plastic Inevitable touring show. Their 1967 debut album *The Velvet Underground & Nico* was banned from many record stores and radio stations who were horrified by subject matter concerning prostitution, sexual deviancy, drug dealers, and pharmaceutical come downs. Front man Lou Reed's subsequent fame as a solo artist led to a critical reappraisal of the group, but during their nine-year career their renown always far exceeded their record sales.

Detroit's MC5—an abbreviation of Motor City Five—built a sizable local following through their explosive live shows, leading the Detroit rock scene through a renaissance alongside the Stooges from nearby Ann Arbor. Both groups were signed to the fledgling Elektra label in September 1968 by later Ramones manager Danny Fields, with the MC5 recording their debut live album *Kick Out the*

Jams at the Grande Ballroom, Detroit, a month later. The group's unconventional manager, John Sinclair—founder of the White Panther Party—encouraged them to engage with radical left-wing politics and to use their platform to promote countercultural revolution.

The Stooges, meanwhile, were gaining a reputation for increasingly incendiary live performances, with vocalist Iggy Pop baiting audiences, lacerating himself, and stripping naked on stage, but drug addictions and increasingly erratic performances eventually led to the group's demise. Like the Velvet Underground and MC5 before them, the Stooges were not to gain critical or commercial success until long after the group ceased to exist, but all three are now considered part of a critical triumvirate of American rock bands that propelled punk.

01
_MC5 and the Chosen Few at the Grande Ballroom, Detroit, October 7–8, 1966. The Chosen Few split up before the gig, and were replaced at short notice by local group the Wha?, though the posters had already been produced. Design by Gary Grimshaw, who was asked by promoter Uncle Russ to produce a poster "in the San Francisco psychedelic style."

_ Andy Warhol's Exploding Plastic Inevitable Show featuring the Velvet Underground and Nico, at Poor Richard's, Chicago, June 1966. In what could be called a multimedia road show, the Velvet Underground provided a soundtrack to 16mm film projections and installations set up by pop artist Warhol. The show toured the US and Canada in 1966 and 1967.

03
Artist The Stooges
Title S/T
Format LP, 12-inch
Label Elektra, USA, 1969
_ Photography by Joel Brodsky.

04
Artist Alice Cooper
Title Pretties for You
Format LP, 12-inch
Label Straight, USA, 1969
_ Led by singer Vincent Furnier, who later changed his name to that of the group and established a successful solo career, Detroit's Alice Cooper established

a reputation for controversial and bizarre performances featuring staged fights, torture scenes, and mock executions.

05
_ Advertisement placed by the MC5 in the *Ann Arbor Argus*, February 1969, attacking Hudson's department store in Detroit for refusing to sell the album *Kick Out the Jams* due to concerns about its obscene content. The group included the logo of their label Elektra on the ad, and in response the store withdrew all Elektra products from its shelves. The resulting controversy saw the group and label part company. Design by Robin Sommers.

06
_ MC5 at Grosse Pointe Hideout, Michigan, May 31, 1968. Design by Gary Grimshaw.

07
_ MC5, Congress of Wonders and Clover at the Straight Theatre, San Francisco, March 14–16, 1969. The Star-Spangled banner, often used as a live backdrop by the group, makes another appearance here in suitably adapted form, while the symbol of the White Panthers holds center stage. Design by Gary Grimshaw.

01 02 | 05 06 07
03 04

KICK OUT THE JAMS, MOTHERFUCKER!

and kick in the door if the store won't sell you the album on

FUCK HUDSON'S!

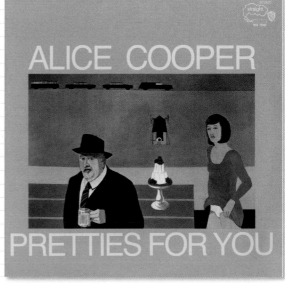

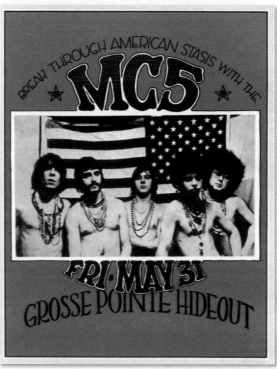

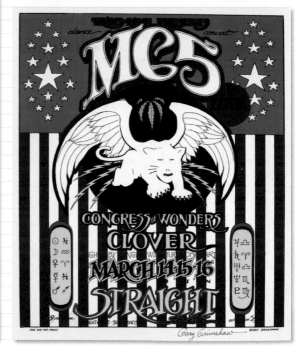

Mick Farren's Deviants existed somewhere on the periphery of the hippie subculture, but always retained an anarchic spirit and more defined political agenda. To many, the Deviants were the UK's missing link between '60s countercultural activism, psychedelia, garage rock, and the explosion of punk, while Farren also coauthored songs for fellow travelers Hawkwind, Lemmy, and Pink Fairies. A prolific writer, his prose appeared in underground press publications *International Times* and *Nasty Tales*, the first issue of which was subject to a protracted Old Bailey obscenity trial over its inclusion of a Robert Crumb cartoon. He was a staff writer at *NME* when punk's shockwaves first hit and was an advocate long before it became fashionable to be so. Later, relocated to the US, he would write for the *Village Voice* and *Trouser Press* and author a number of fictional and nonfictional books, including his autobiography, *Give the Anarchist a Cigarette*. Mick Farren elaborates on the hidden links between Brando and the new Wild Ones:

The Hippies Won't Come Back, You say?

So much of hippie art was a product of Pre-Raphaelite, Aubrey Beardsley stuff; a kind of elegant decadence that didn't even fit those times. It certainly didn't fit the coming of Thatcher and the potential for the miner's strike and the three-day week and unemployment. Hippie was not some unilateral movement. If they put the Deviants on with the Incredible String Band on the same bill at a club in Sunderland—which actually happened—it was bit of a mess. The Incredible String Band fans would be sitting cross-legged on the floor, drifting away on whatever drugs they could get hold of, while in the back there would be a load of gibbering speed freaks waiting for us to come on. It was not a happy marriage.

But we knew there were a few of us out there who were not quite conforming to the hippie concept. There was Blue Cheer in San Francisco, the Velvets, I had a personal relationship with Wayne Kramer and John Sinclair of the MC5, I knew Iggy quite well. We knew they were getting up to all this mayhem in Detroit. The Deviants didn't go down well in some places, but we sure as shit went down well in Coventry or Dagenham on a Saturday night. We knew, just like the MC5, what a car factory crowd was like. Or the people who sold pills outside the car factory gates. They were our demographic, and we knew 'em well. They were like Who fans who'd taken acid.

Notes from the Underground

There were two very important things that helped the underground press happen. The Underground Press Syndicate first—if you put UPS on your masthead, you could take material from any other underground paper. We were taking stuff from Ann Arbor, as the MC5 and the White Panthers were getting off the ground, and running it in *International Times*. That was backed up by the Liberation News Service in New York. They would send a package out to UPS members once a fortnight or so, full of clippings. We were getting bits and pieces from Detroit, New York, etc. It was, in a nutshell, anarcho-syndicalism with drugs. Which is essentially what McLaren was pushing behind the Sex Pistols. If you pinned him down to a philosophy, that's what it fucking was.

Shake Some Action

Malcolm McLaren and I are contemporaries, although I didn't know him at the time. So the 1968 Situationists and the comics and things that came out of Paris were an influence. But jumping further back, when I was fourteen, I was wearing a leather jacket and a coalman's hat and pretending to be Gene Vincent or Marlon Brando in *The Wild Ones*. When I saw Jamie Reid's ransom notes and Vivienne Westwood using Bruce Weber homoerotic photography and Tom of Finland and Irving Klaw/Bettie Page bondage stuff—that was the *Forbidden Planet* of the 1950s! Back then we kind of knew about it and were anxious to learn more, like we knew about drugs but couldn't get any. And then you get the Clash wearing the same "great coats" that Elvis and Eddie Cochran had, and the Ramones dressed up like Marlon Brando or Lee Marvin. There's Richard Hell being quite open that he stole the whole idea of the ripped T-shirt from that great scene in *A Streetcar Named Desire*. Hey, I know this shit! It's the underground of my early youth suddenly being incorporated into what you might call mass bohemian culture. That "year zero" thing was bullshit. There wasn't a punk band on the planet who didn't play "Sweet Jane" and "I'm Waiting For The Man." There's an easily traceable Bohemian thread from the '50s to '60s to punk, and the bridging entities like Patti Smith and the New York Dolls.

I always had a really good relationship with John Lydon, because I knew where he was coming from and he knew where I was coming from. And all the "Never Trust A Hippie" stuff was as much bollocks as us saying "Don't trust anyone over thirty." It was a grim, hard world and we'd been in the trenches over a decade when those guys got started. The rhetoric really didn't matter.

History's Bunk

I grew up in Brighton in the '50s. There were a couple of dirty bookshops. If you wanted to get hold of Kerouac or Burroughs, or pornographic pulp fiction like *I Was Backseat Dynamite*, with those great lurid covers, it was all there. If you wanted to find a copy of *Naked Lunch*, it would be there on the shelf

next to Tom of Finland shit, or Irving Klaw's Bettie Page stuff. It was all part and parcel of some weird underworld that hadn't quite formed yet. Then you had mass murderers like Charlie Starkweather and you threw all that into a blender. That was what was influencing me and Wayne Kramer and Iggy and Lou Reed and everyone. And it never came to fulfilment until the New York Dolls took that weird drag queen approach and Patti Smith really crystallized it with her early recordings like "Piss Factory." Suddenly this shit is happening in CBGB and then you turn around and McLaren's getting the Sex Pistols moving and the 101'ers and the London SS have combined into the Clash and they're down the Elgin. And you go—OK! I see!

I use the enemy

Nick Logan was reorganizing *NME* to keep it in business. He cherry picked Charlie [Shaar-Murray] and Nick Kent, and then me and I brought Edwin Pouncey [cartoonist Savage Pencil] in and Ray Lowry. Essentially the *NME* for a long time was being run by a team of former underground press veterans, getting drunk every lunchtime in order to force themselves to continue to work for IPC. At which point the "Young Gunslingers required" advert got hundreds of applications and the winners were Tony Parsons and Julie Burchill. Burchill was a very good idea, I never had any time for Parsons. At least Burchill is good for a laugh.

Shot by Both Sides

If you went into the dirty bookshops I mentioned earlier, you could learn about sadomasochism in the Weimar Republic and George Grosz. Then some arsehole like Siouxsie starts wearing swastikas—a cheap shot to annoy the squares. I have arguments with Lemmy about it, because I don't think it's terribly healthy. Kids get the wrong idea, start reading *Mein Kampf*, and before you know it you have to take them out the back of the shed and shoot them. Before the first Rock Against Racism show, Jimmy Pursey basically had to be stood up against a wall and asked "What you going to do, Jimmy?" Cause he was still playing to fascist skinheads. He wanted it both ways. "Either you're with us or against us." Go join the fucking National Front, otherwise give it up. There was a defining moment where people had to make up their minds which side they were on.

LET'S LOOT THE SUPERMARKET

It's the New Thing

A lot of art is molded by the technology available. In punk visual art the two pieces of technology that were utilised really well were the Canon 5000 copying machine and the spray can, in the same way the hippies had the silkscreen press. The first issue of *IT* was printed on old-fashioned, movable type—letterpress. That was a real fucking pain in the arse. By issue ten we were using web offset. *Sniffin' Glue* was using the fast-run Canon 5000-style copiers. We had to have enough of an organization and a support system, an art department and enough readers, to support a web-offset tabloid. Mark Perry just had to have enough money to pay the photocopying shop. The same with records. To put out records with the Deviants cost a lot of money. Ten years later you could do it much cheaper, plus you had geezers like Ted Carroll (of Rock On!/Chiswick) around to help you. Someone who had been through the mill and seen how it worked. Doing that was now economically viable, because you'd taken out of that equation the whole of Decca Records and their profits and shareholder system. It was workers controlling the means of production, while the technology moving on to allow Mark P. to turn out *Sniffin' Glue* on a photocopier, that was the technological seizure of the means of production of the media.

Brand New Age

Were the Deviants proto-punk? Wayne Kramer said to me, "What is punk? I thought punks were guys who took it up the ass in prison?" Punk was a word coined by Legs McNeill. It worked, it caught on. Legs was a great advocate of the "year zero" theory, so he could get more grandiose about what was coming out of CBGB. But we knew Dave Johansen [the New York Dolls] from way back, and a lot was glossed over. Just as it was in the UK. There was a history and it had to be

> "The Deviants didn't go down well in some places, but we sure as shit went down well in Coventry or Dagenham on a Saturday night. We knew, just like the MC5 knew, what a car factory crowd was like."
>
> Mick Farren

recognized, otherwise you can't deal with Patti Smith. You can't get too Khmer Rouge about all of this, so, what came before? Oh, it was proto-punk. It's like asking Stephen Hawking what came before the big bang. It's semantics in terminology, really. As far as I'm concerned, it's all the same fucking revolution, all the way back to Wat Tyler. You know what started the revolution? The black death killed so many people that labor suddenly came at a premium, and the working man ceased to be a serf and became a commodity. Market forces!

You Dirty Old Icon

The true godfathers of punk? Marlon Brando and Eddie Cochran, even if we all knew that Ian Dury and Johnny Rotten were students of Wilfrid Brambell, too! Brando because his visuals are so primal, and Eddie Cochran simply because as a songwriter he really did invent a lot of the structures we know as punk rock. To the extent that the Deviants and Nick Lowe and the Stiff guys—if someone was playing "da-da-da, da-da-da" it became known as "an Eddie." "Stick an Eddie in there, that'll make it perfect!" That's how [Deviants' song] "Let's Loot the Supermarket" was written. Yeah, Marlon Brando and Eddie Cochran, you can quote me on that. Joe Strummer and Mick Jones stole that image from that great photograph of Gene Vincent and Eddie Cochran coming off the plane, starting the tour on which Cochran was killed. Right down to the sideburns and gel-grease job on their hair. The same rebel chic.

01
_ Cartoon by *IT* illustrator and designer Edward Barker, from the book *Watch Out Kids*, a 1972 collaboration with Mick Farren.

02
_ Gummed flyer showing a robotic Nazi stormtrooper burning the *Oz Skool Kids Issue*. The flyer was designed to raise awareness in support of the Oz Obscenity Trial, summer 1971.

03
Artist Mick Farren
Title Play with Fire
Format Single, 7-inch
Label Ork, USA, 1976

04
_ *The Trials of Nasty Tales* magazine, 1973, featuring the work of cartoonist Robert Crumb. This edition was a posttrial publication (like the editors of *Oz*, the *Nasty Tales* team were also the subject of a court case).

05
_ Hawkwind *Astounding Sounds, Amazing Music* poster, 1976. Design by Barney Bubbles.

_ *Oz* magazine Special Pig Issue, number 35, 1971. The piq on the cover, wearing a policeman's uniform, is depicted holding a copy of the *Oz Skool Kids Issue*, number 28, at the time subject of an obscenity trial in the UK High Court.

....

07

Artist Warsaw Pakt
Title Needle Time
Format LP, 12-inch
Label Island, UK, 1977
_ Warsaw Pakt featured musicians with connections to a number of high-profile underground and proto-punk groups, including Motörhead, Pink Fairies, and the Zips. The gimmick behind *Needle Time* was to record, press, package, and distribute an album within twenty-four hours. The album "cover" was simply a card-mailing envelope decorated with stickers and rubber stamps.

Artist Third World War
Title A Little Bit of Urban Rock
Format Single, 7-inch
Label Polydor, Germany, 1971
_ A British proto-punk rock band who gigged regularly through the early 1970s, their second album track "Hammersmith Guerrilla" provided the original name template for London pub rock stalwarts the (Hammersmith) Gorillas.

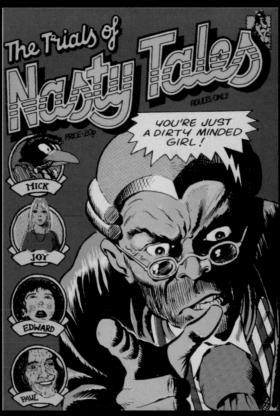

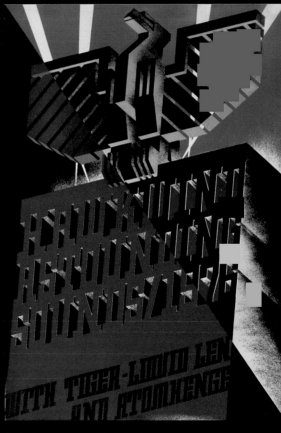

The Blank Generation: American Roots

As the beat and psychedelia booms of the 1960s gave way to a new decade, a number of disparate local scenes in the US can be seen, at least with the benefit of hindsight, to have had a formative influence on the coming punk explosion. In New York, Greenwich Village, center of the '60s hippie dream and home of the Mercer Arts Center, provided a liberal environment for the New York Dolls to develop their chops and try out their makeup. Another small club with a big reputation, Max's Kansas City—situated in the East Village and long frequented by artists and the bohemian set—became a center of attention through the patronage of Andy Warhol and the Velvet Underground, before closing at the end of 1974 and being reborn as a bonafide proto-punk venue a year later.

Meanwhile things were also heating up across the country. In the Midwest, Detroit's MC5 and Ann Arbor's Stooges had paved the way

for the new sounds of Cleveland's short-lived but subsequently influential Electric Eels and Rocket from the Tombs—the latter splitting in 1975 to spawn Pere Ubu and the Dead Boys. On the West Coast, producer Kim Fowley found his (wet) dream partnership in the teenage Joan Jett and Cherie Currie, gaining equal parts fame and notoriety with the Runaways. From 1974, New York's then crime and poverty ravaged Bowery district provided the backdrop to the birth of a distinct scene based around Hilly Kristal's CBGB club. *PUNK* magazine was on hand to lend the new zeitgeist a name, and within the next eighteen months virtually the entire US punk vanguard—Patti Smith, the Ramones, Television, Talking Heads, Blondie, and the Heartbreakers—would burst out into the world from that tiny, ten-square-foot stage.

01
Artist Flamin' Groovies
Title Grease
Format EP, 7-inch
Label Skydog, France, 1973
_ Cover designed by noted underground comix artist Vidal Angel.

02
Artist The Modern Lovers
Title New England
Format Single, 7-inch
Label Beserkley, USA, 1977

03
Artist Ramones
Title The Blitzkrieg Bop
Format Single, 7-inch
Label Sire, UK, 1976

04
Artist The Runaways
Title S/T
Format LP, 12-inch
Label Mercury, USA, 1976
_ Debut album by the Los Angeles all-girl group that launched the careers of Joan Jett and Lita Ford. Manager Kim Fowley had been a successful producer during the '60s and he saw a potential market for a raucous all-girl rock group, establishing the Runaways lineup in 1975. "Joan [Jett] was totally influenced by the punk and new wave direction. The band were all into glam rock and Deep Purple and Led Zeppelin as well—but the punk thing opened up a new world for her. She became quite friendly

with them and she loved the simplicity and the rawness and directness, because that was very much her style." (Toby Mamis, the Runaways' manager following their split with Fowley in 1978.) Guitarist Joan Jett would later produce the Germs' first and only album, and find fame fronting her own group the Blackhearts in the 1980s. Design by Desmond Strobel.

05
Artist The Dictators
Title Search & Destroy
Format Single, 12-inch
Label Asylum, UK, 1977
_ Cover version of the opening track from the Stooges' *Raw Power*, issued to promote the Dictators' second album *Manifest Destiny*.

06
Artist Pere Ubu
Title 30 Seconds Over Tokyo
Format Single, 7-inch
Label Hearthan, USA, 1975
_ Design by Jon Luoma.

07
Artist Patti Smith
Title Hey Joe (Version)
Format Single, 7-inch
Label Sire, USA, 1977
_ Reissue of the debut single release, backed by "Piss Factory," by New York poet/performance artist Patti Smith, originally recorded in 1974 and issued on the Mer label without a picture sleeve.

08
_ Poster promoting the eponymous debut album by the New York Dolls, released by Mercury Records in 1973.

09
_ Television plus the Ramones at the Truck & Warehouse Theatre, New York, November 22, 1974. Design by Richard Meyers aka Richard Hell.

10
_ Patti Smith plus Television at Max's Kansas City, New York, six-day residency starting August 28, 1974. Design by Richard Meyers aka Richard Hell.

11
_ Poster promoting Iggy and the Stooges live album *Metallic K.O.*, released by Marc Zermati's influential Skydog label in 1976. The album was recorded in Detroit on February 9, 1974, at the group's final show, and features a riotous performance in the face of a hostile audience. Designed by Michael Beal, photography by Joseph Stephen.

01 02 03   07 08
04 05 06 | 09 10 11

PATTI SMITH
HEY JOE (VERSION)
PISS FACTORY

SRE 1009

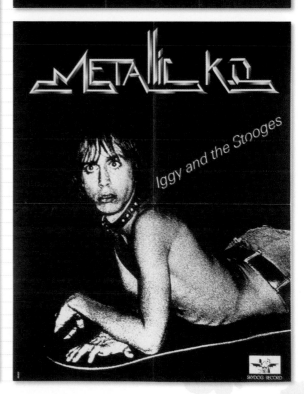

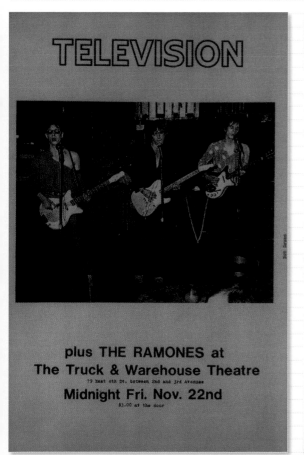

TELEVISION

plus THE RAMONES at
The Truck & Warehouse Theatre
79 East 4th St. between 2nd and 3rd Avenues
Midnight Fri. Nov. 22nd
$3.00 at the door

PATTI SMITH
with Lenny Kaye, guitar, and Richard Sohl, piano

TELEVISION
Richard Lloyd   Tom Verlaine   Richard Hell   Billy Ficca

At Max's Kansas City
213 Park Ave. South at 27th St. 777-7870 shows at 9:30 and 11:30
Wed. Aug. 28th-Mon. Sept. 2nd

METALLIC K.O.
Iggy and the Stooges

To what extent do you think PUNK *marked out its own territory in terms of graphic language? Or was it really part of the continuum of Crumb and comix culture that just happened to collide with what was bubbling up at the time?*

Although I was very influenced by the 1960s underground and especially Robert Crumb, I was also aware that for *PUNK*, we needed to create a new look and break away from the flowery graphics that were so dominant back then. It was a similar position, I think, to how Johnny Ramone viewed prog rock. He couldn't match the virtuosity of ELP or Led Zeppelin, etc., and I could never be the next Maxfield Parrish or use an airbrush and I didn't like art nouveau so I went for more of the EC comics, early Marvel comics, early Mad magazine look—the stuff I liked.

I think once I realized we had to hand-letter the magazine because we couldn't afford typesetting and I didn't like the typewriting from the IBM typewriter we stole from the office, I established a radical look that, like you said, marked our own territory. A lot of graphic design people were impressed—there's a story that someone showed *PUNK* to Milton Glaser, who was the top graphic/magazine designer at the time, and he was told that this was the future of magazines. He just shook his head in disbelief.

How much did the advent of PUNK *"reflect" what was happening in NYC, and how much did the magazine serve as an energetic, or contributor, to events?*

There was a punk scene of sorts in New York, but except for the Ramones, we weren't reflecting what was going on here. *The Aquarian*, New Jersey's answer to the *Village Voice*, did a cover story on "Punk Rock," which featured a photograph of a guy in a big floppy hat, bell-bottom jeans, a flannel shirt, and a big-ass mustache. I had a different idea of what punk should look like, and I think the magazine did that.

I think the biggest influences on punk from the art scene were minimalism and pop art. Most punk bands tried to strip rock down to its basics—and here's where a band like the early Talking Heads were considered punk. Blondie were like an early '60s band, and were pop art influenced. But really, punk rock was already happening all over the country—and the world. So at first I thought we were just contributing to the rock 'n' roll scene, but our immediate success within that culture suddenly made us large and in charge.

When did you first become aware of the way the musical temperature was changing?

I think by 1974 glam rock had run its course and you could see the new directions bands were going in. I think the Little Hippodrome show where Television opened for the New York Dolls reflected it best. The Dolls had a new manager (Malcolm McLaren), dressed in tight red patent leather outfits, and performed their new songs in front of a huge communist flag. Television played their last shows with Richard Hell, but you could see and hear that something new was going on. After the show, someone told me about CBGB, and she made it sound like the most exciting place on Earth.

As well as strips and cartoons, PUNK *also used photo-fumetti (for example, the one with Debbie Harry and Joey Ramone). Where did that influence come from?*

I created a Cartoon Concert in 1972 while going to the School of Visual Arts with Batton Lash, and we did several photo comics for it. The next year, Harvey Kurtzman was hired to teach cartoons and comics, and he'd show us these amazing fumettis from Europe, where the "graphic novel" had been well established. Comics were published in hardcover editions and read by adults—which was a bizarre concept in the States back then. You know, comic strips were for children only! That was something the underground tried to change, and something I tried to change.

Did people sometimes overlook the obvious humor in your pages (for example, Punk of the Month*).* Punk *is taken very seriously these days, isn't it?*

Punk of the Month was Joey Ramone's idea, you know . . . He was always suggesting stuff for us and telling us which bands we should cover. Joey and Chris Stein were like our contributing editors.

Most of the work I do now is for Japanese punk bands, who have a wonderful sense of humor and are nothing like any of those dismal punk bands that take themselves too seriously. They are entertaining, hilarious, and popular! Anyhow I think most punk bands still have a sense of humor. I could list a bunch of them . . . Ever heard of Endangered Feces?

I'm not too interested in the partisanship/territorial pissings that go on with regard to whether punk was primarily a UK or US phenomenon. But I am interested in how you viewed the arrival of the Sex Pistols, the Clash, et al. from an American perspective.

Well, we know Legs has fairly firm views on this . . . but that wasn't necessarily reflected in the magazine?

The one band I always point out when people bring up the UK vs US thing is the Saints. They were one of the earliest and best punk bands; "I'm Stranded" was one of the first punk songs to make the charts, and they were from Australia. Punk was something the Stooges spawned, and it happened worldwide after they broke up.

As far as the Sex Pistols, the Clash, and also the Damned and Eddie & the Hot Rods (I think they're punk and not pub rock), I loved those bands, all of them. I was blown away by the Pistols' first single, I enjoyed meeting Joe Strummer, and I always call the Damned/Dead Boys double bill the best show I ever saw at CBGB. Going on the first Sex Pistols tour of the US was the greatest experience of my life. Legs didn't have a lot to do with the magazine, by the way, he was more like a cartoon character than an editor or writer.

When *PUNK* magazine first came out, we got a lot of attention from England, and we heard a lot about their punk bands: the Stranglers, the 101'ers, the Count Bishops, and the Hot Rods. I think when the Ramones appeared they all realized that they had to up their game, which they did, and the competition between the scenes is another reason there was so much great music being made back then.

Do you see any echoes of PUNK *mag's work in any of the subsequent incarnations of punk itself?*

I've seen a few. In the 1970s, *The Next Big Thing*, a zine published in Scotland, was also hand-lettered, and they stood apart from the English scene and supported US punk. I enjoyed London's *Ripped and Torn*; they seemed to echo our sense of humor. There were many other zines that I liked and took inspiration from, thinking: "YES! Someone understands what we're trying to do!" Which was to publish a zine that wasn't only about the music and the pop stars but dealt with a bit of real life, and was entertaining.

Mostly what I was trying to do with *PUNK* was to make rock 'n' roll on paper. Bands could play rock 'n' roll on a record or live in

WATCH OUT, PUNK IS COMING!
—JOHN HOLMSTROM

concert, but magazines were always so boring. It was like reading a newspaper or a trade magazine with stories about musicians instead of movie stars or business executives. I liked comic books, but they were almost always kid stuff, or stories about superheroes who wore long underwear. Music was so creative and inspiring, so I wanted a magazine to be like the music instead of other magazines. I like to think that once in a while we succeeded.

Because I am a cartoonist, I think people do not think of me as a "serious" artist . . . And I'm not! But serious artists are terrible bores and usually inflate their contributions to the culture, while cartoonists are more subversive and use visuals as a weapon . . .

01
Artist Ramones
Title Rocket to Russia
Format LP, 12-inch
Label Sire, USA, 1977
_ Reverse of cover,
illustration by John
Holmstrom.

02
Artist Ramones
Title Road to Ruin
Format LP, 12-inch
Label Sire, USA, 1978
_ Cover illustration
by John Holmstrom.

03
_ PUNK magazine, number
1, January 1976,
featuring a cartoon of
Lou Reed drawn by John
Holmstrom, cofounder
of the magazine with
publisher Ged Dunn and
"Resident Punk" writer
Legs McNeil.

04
_ PUNK magazine, number
3, April 1976, featuring
a cartoon of Joey Ramone
drawn by John Holmstrom.

05
_ PUNK magazine, number
6, October 1976,
featuring a cartoon of
Judy LaPilusa, Richard
Hell, and Debbie Harry
by John Holmstrom.
The issue was entirely
devoted to a twenty-four-
page photo-fumetti
entitled "The Legend of
Nick Detroit," featuring
characters from the CBGB
scene. The photographers
were Roberta Bayley and
Chris Stein.

01 02
03 04 05

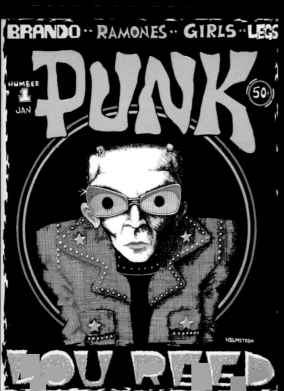

01

_ Poster promoting the debut album by Richard Hell and the Voidoids, *Blank Generation*, released by Sire Records in 1977, and their accompanying UK tour with the Clash. Hell had been a key member of New York proto-punk groups Neon Boys, Television, and the Heartbreakers.

02

_ Poster promoting the UK issue of the eponymous debut album by Suicide, released at the end of December 1977. Suicide, a New York electronic music duo comprising Martin Rev and Alan Vega, had formed in 1970, but it wasn't until 1977 that they committed material to vinyl, through the Red Star label in the US and Bronze in the UK. The group opened for the Clash on their UK tour the following year, meeting some resistance from UK punk audiences in the process. Design by Timothy Jackson and Alan Vega, photography by Michael Robinson.

03

Artist Richard Hell
Title Another World
Format EP, 7-inch
Label Ork, USA, 1976

04

_ Poster for Dead Boys with Toronto bands Viletones and the Poles at the New Yorker theater, Toronto, Canada, October 14, 1977.

05

Artist Dead Boys
Title Young Loud And Snotty
Format LP, 12-inch
Label Sire, USA, 1977
_ Debut album by key US punk originators Dead Boys, formed from the ashes of proto-punk outfit Rocket from the Tombs, which also spawned Pere Ubu. Originally from Cleveland, Ohio, the group relocated to New York in 1976 and signed to Sire—a label keen to capitalize on the nascent punk rock movement. Design by John Gillespie.

06

_ Poster promoting the *Blatantly Offensive* EP by Wayne County & the Electric Chairs, released by Safari Records in the UK in 1978. The EP included the notorious "Fuck Off," originally released as a single on the Sweet F.A. label in 1977. County had been a key figure in the New York proto-punk scene based around Max's Kansas City club in the early '70s, and relocated to London in 1977.

03
04
01 02 | 05 06

ALBUM SUICIDE BY SUICIDE / BRON 508
SINGLE CHEREE BY SUICIDE / BRO 57

RICHARD HELL
81976
ANOTHER WORLD
BLANK GENERATION
YOU GOTTA LOSE
EXTENDED PLAY STEREO 45 RPM
ORK RECORDS

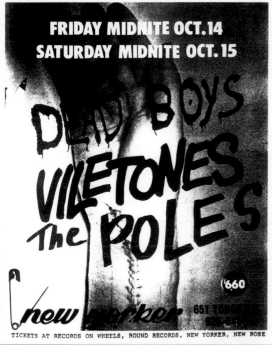

FRIDAY MIDNITE OCT. 14
SATURDAY MIDNITE OCT. 15
DEAD BOYS
VILETONES
The POLES
'660
new yorker 651 TONGE ST. 926-9010
TICKETS AT RECORDS ON WHEELS, ROUND RECORDS, NEW YORKER, NEW ROSE

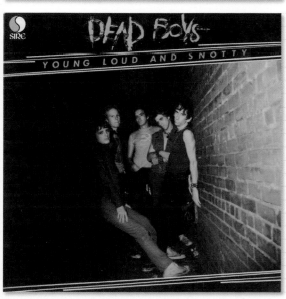

SIRE
DEAD BOYS
YOUNG LOUD AND SNOTTY

max's

SAFARI RECORDS
in association with Colonel B
presents
WAYNE COUNTY
AND THE ELECTRIC CHAIRS
Blatantly Offensive

First 1,000,000 in gold vinyl.
Second 1,000,000 in platinum vinyl.

99p
RETAIL PRICE

RECORD NUMBER WC2

An E.P. of an event from Wayne
County and the Electric Chairs.
In which County and his boys explore
those areas of depravity once reserved
for tom cats and over-sexed goats.
Yes, it does include THE track.

They ought to be ashamed of themselves

DISTRIBUTED EXCLUSIVELY BY Lightning 841 HARROW ROAD, LONDON NW10   SAFARI

Artistic director for the Ramones since 1974, Arturo Vega is responsible for, alongside their stage lighting and backdrops, supervision of all artwork, all merchandise including T-shirt designs, and the distinctive crest logo that has become a staple of fashion lines worn by everyone from David Beckham to Sly Stallone to Woody Allen.

Probably the prime outside influence on the development of both the sound and spirit of UK punk and much else besides, the Ramones' influence was always as visual as it was musical. The skintight jeans, T-shirt, and leather look was as brute minimalist and lacking in frippery as the band's sound. And that aesthetic was all conceptualized in a logo that emphasized both a gang mentality and that this was very much an American band—albeit from an America that didn't, and doesn't, appear in tourist brochures.

Arturo's time with the Ramones spanned twenty-two years, and 2,261 of the 2,263 shows the group played. Both Joey and Dee Dee moved into his loft which became Ramones Central. Arturo designed the T-shirts which kept the band afloat financially and served as their 'guardian dog'—a role that has shifted to that of keeper of the flame since the sad procession of fatalities, with Joey, Dee Dee, and Johnny all passing within a few short years of each other.

It is the Ramones logo that continues to ripple through popular culture, however. There's no real accounting for the symbol's reach or commercial appropriation, from A-through D-list celebrities to main street fashion chains.

Where Eagles Dare:
The Making Of Punk Rock Iconography

'Hi, I'm Dee Dee,' said the boy in the peculiar page boy haircut who had just opened the door of my loft to introduce himself.

'I come to see the girl that lives above you,' he continued, 'and every time I pass by your door I listen to the music you are playing and I like it.' It was the fall of 1973 and I was doing paintings that looked like supermarket posters. Dee Dee kept coming back. We always talked about music and bands and one day he said that he and a good friend were going to start a band and since he was Dee Dee Ramone and it was his band they would be called the Ramones. In early 1974, he invited me to their first show and from that day on I only missed two of the thousands the Ramones performed, becoming their roadie, lighting director, T-shirt guy, artistic director, etc.

By 1976, they already had an album out and had gone to London to ignite the rocket that would become punk rock, but something was bothering me a lot and that was the cartoon image tag that a lot of people were hanging on the band. I like comic books and I think cartoons are cool, but I wanted people to look up to the Ramones, not to look at them and laugh. I decided to design a logo that would do justice to the power I saw and heard in the Fast Four and enhance their image. We went to Washington, DC, to perform for the first time there in October of 1976. We walked for hours because their manager Danny Fields wanted to take photos of them all over the place. I was very impressed with the atmosphere of classical architecture, the grandiosity of the buildings, and the fact that there were eagles everywhere. We went to the White House but the lines were so long we decided not to go in. But as we walked by I saw the presidential seal and it was a real eureka moment. I didn't say anything to the guys but in my mind I already knew exactly what I was going to do.

By then I had already used eagles, not only on the Ramones' first album back cover, but also in my own art, when I took photographs

in 1973 of the 1972 'Eisenhower Dollar.' It celebrated the Apollo 11 mission with an image of an eagle landing on the moon in the center of the coin and with the words 'United States Of America—One Dollar' around it. This is exactly the same format I used later on the design of the Ramones logo. The photograph of my hand holding the coin was published in 1975 by the *New York Rocker*, a new tabloid gaining popularity among the music and art crowd in the Lower East Side. So the program was already in my head and in no time I decided I would make a collage and put all the ideas together. (This is before computers!)

I started to look for material. I didn't want to go straight to the presidential seal and take the eagle from there, so I looked till I found an eagle with the same look but a more organic feeling, because it was a painting. The names of the band members were all composed with Letraset press on type. The baseball came from a sports magazine. I picked Johnny's name to be on top of the circle because it was more American-sounding than the others. I replaced the arrows that represent the will and means to use force if necessary with a baseball bat because it too can be an instrument of power and a weapon, and also because of Johnny's passion for the sport. The idea was to keep it as all-American as possible which made everybody happy and proud."

WE'RE A HAPPY FAMILY—
ARTURO VEGA: THE 5TH RAMONE

01		
02	03	04
05		06

While the New York Dolls are rightly celebrated as the act that bridged the glam rock years with punk, the Hollywood Brats—largely unaware of such US developments, despite their name—served as the missing link in Britain, bringing a highly sexualized, devil-may-care attitude back to a moribund rock 'n' roll culture.

Bloated, witlessly self-satisfied, smugly complacent . . . but enough about me. Curiously though, these words also describe the general state of affairs in British art during the first half of the '70s.

Art you say, so what you say. Perhaps your conception of art is best articulated by Nazi propaganda motormouth Joey Goebbels, who opined, "When I hear the word art I reach for my Luger." It is easy to sympathize with the old grouch. The art world can indeed be a mincing swamp of narcissism, ego, and delusion. But let us not forget Art is important. It is what separates us from the beasts of the field, the slime in the petri dish, the orangutan or the Albanian. Art is society's rectal thermometer. It takes the temperature of a nation, of a culture. Sometimes making it wince while it does so. Art is the canary in our coal mine and, as such, it behooves us to give it a glance every now and again, make sure it is still on its perch, chirping away in its irritating fashion.

So let us now harken back to a time we like to call "the early '70s" when all Britain's canaries were feet up at the bottom of their cages. Because you see children, for Art, in all its forms, the early '70s were the pits, the doldrums, the knackered nadir, flatlined, no pulse, and worse the corpse had begun to stink. Oh there was lots going on, it's just that all of it made you want to do a Sylvia Plath, with an aperitif of bleach just to make sure.

Fashion: Mary Quant was a relic from the '60s, Mr. Fish was going broke, and Carnaby Street was jammed with Japanese and Yanks in plastic "bobby" helmets. England had degenerated into a nation of bank tellers and hippies. Trousers were no longer trousers, or strides, or drainpipes or jeans. No, they were 'loon pants.' Lapels were like twin ironing boards nailed onto the front of Checkerboard-Charlie jackets. The King's Road was full of provincials clomping around on platform soles. You'd swear a clubfoot convention was in town. Marks & Spencer got a name check in 'All the Young Dudes.' Fashion was shot.

Painting: Hockney decamped (well, hardly) to a swimming pool in Los Angeles. Britain's two best artists, Frankie Bacon and Lucian Freud,

skipped the early '70s and went to the pub. What's that tell you?

Film: What did we have? *A Clockwork Orange*. Great, what else? Nothing. *Confessions of a Window Cleaner*, that's what. Cheeky chappie up a ladder, script stuffed with double entendres, heaving bosoms and fade to black. Meanwhile, in the States, Coppola, Scorsese, and others, working on no to low budgets, were on fire.

Theater: Just as clapped out. The biggest hit in London's West End was *No Sex Please, We're British*, the cheeky chappie, etc., once again. And *The Mousetrap* was breaking all records for consecutive performances going back to Napoleonic times. Can you name one human being who has ever seen it? Of course you can't. For the world of theater it was time to look forward in anger.

The greatest British art form and export of the time was of course music, and Britain did unequivocally rule the airwaves. But from the heady heights of *Sgt. Pepper*, and Jimi, and Who, and Beggars Banquet, and on and on, to what depths had we plummeted? Hackneyed blues riffs cranked through Marshall stacks, concept albums, millionaires in manor houses preaching at us, drum kits that stretched for thirty feet featuring the obligatory and ridiculous gong, wheezy Old Grey Bob, and an endless procession of pop stars that made Bobby Vee seem edgy.

But somehow epitomizing the fat, the bloated, the Nero fiddling was the double or even triple album in the clumsy, overkill origami of the gatefold sleeve. Examples? Where to start? Roberta Flack killing us softly, not to mention relentlessly, with a cover that unfolded into, just what we always wanted, a cardboard piano. The vastly overrated *Exile on Main St.* a double album that barely deserved to be an EP with not one half-decent single in sight, but nonetheless a double gatefold with two cardboard inner sleeves and, just in case we can't get enough of this pulp and paper extravaganza, an insert of half a dozen confusing perforated postcards. Alice Cooper, the heir apparently to the two Screamings (Jay Hawkins and Lord Sutch), fresh out of Arizona with a regurgitated blues riff, sculpts "School's Out" and, natch, sticks it in a gatefold album. At least he had the class and good taste to put a pair of frilly white panties in each one. Even Rod was too far removed from "the mod" to help himself, and released *Never a Dull Moment* in a sleeve so pointlessly complicated the mewing mutants of Mensa couldn't figure out how to put the record back in after playing it. Here's a hint: via the spine.

And the music inside the gatefolds was as over-the-top as the packaging. It is difficult to believe now, but preening, self-adoring pretentiousness existed in music long before Sting. Witness the toe-curlingly lame concept of "Progressive Rock." Featuring hours of endless noodling, frenzied drum solos, Edvard Munch—inspired facial expressions, all capped with a denim halo and an unshakable belief in its own importance. The elitist toff rock of Genesis—I mean seriously, *The Lamb Lies Down on Broadway*? Yeah so what? Get it to a fast-food outlet. Doctors could confidently prescribe Emerson, Lake & Palmer or Yes and their ilk as a surefire snorefest for insomniacs. For all those posers who foisted the idiot-fest of prog rock on us, a particularly gruesome Pseuds' Corner of hell awaits and Brian Jones controls the thermostat.

And who can forget *Tubular Bells*, the album that gave Richard Branson the first million pounds not handed to him by his dad? Adored by wankers, narcoleptics, and that most myopic, navel-gazing, ovine quadrant of society, college students, it sold by the bucket load. And this was no sleight of hand, no shell game, no trick of the light. There was no false advertising here. "Tubular Bells" is what it was called and tubular bells is what you got. With a cover photo of something normally glimpsed only while unclogging the drain under your sink.

Speaking of hair-infested drain sludge, at the other end of the spectrum there was *Top of the Pops*, a TV show that had to be seen to be disbelieved. Week after week, things went from merely annoying to vomit-inducing to mass-murder inciting. The array of walking, wailing nonentities included Middle of the Road, the Sweet, Gary Glitter and (not to be out-ponced) Alvin Stardust, Mud, the New Seekers, Bay City Rollers, Showaddywaddy, David Cassidy, and an endless supply of fat, toothily grinning Osmonds. This last bunch was the worst, as bad as it could get, sweating and gyrating through choreography only a Mormon could love. A virtual Dalí painting featuring rows of teeth, chafing thighs, and Fat Elvis jumpsuits, they were everywhere, in all sizes and genders, a new Osmond every week. Did Mama Osmond spend her entire life with her feet up in the gynae's stirrups?

The early '70s were so boring that adjectives desert me. Bill Withers sat on a stool and asked us to lean on him. It was that boring. It took us a while but we were starting to figure it out. The emperor had no clues. The scene was ripe for a poke in the ennui. Politics were out. There is no mileage in satirizing something quite that bland. It's mocking the afflicted. Wilson, Callaghan,

ART IN THE DREADED EARLY '70S
BY ANDREW MATHESON

> **"The array of walking, wailing nonentities included Middle of the Road, the Sweet, Gary Glitter, and (not to be out-ponced) Alvin Stardust, Mud, the New Seekers, Bay City Rollers, Showaddywaddy, David Cassidy, and an endless supply of fat, toothily grinning Osmonds."**
>
> Andrew Matheson

Heath, et al., were too boring, and it would be years before the pillow-munching Jeremy Thorpe came along to brighten things up. So Her Majesty became the prime target. Photogenic, iconic, can't fight back, and guaranteed to cause umbrage with Disgruntled of Tunbridge Wells. It is no surprise that two bands emerged at this time named Queen.

Same thing with Nazi chic. On the main street the odd swastika armband, iron cross and Wehrmacht hat had the same attributes and effect as Liz Windsor with a safety pin through her schnoz. So the solution became forget the concepts, the suites, the fugues, and the bloody gongs. Plug in, turn up to pig-squealing decibels, and let 'er rip. What's the worst that could happen? Somebody check that canary.

01   01 02

_ Hollywood Brats, circa 1973. From left to right: Casino Steel, Andrew Matheson, Lou Sparks, ES Brady, and Wayne Manor. Keyboard player Casino Steel went on to form UK punk group the Boys, alongside Matt Dangerfield of UK proto punk legends, London SS.

02
_ *The Partridge Family*, a TV sitcom broadcast on the ABC network from 1970 to 1974, centering on the story of a widowed mother and her five children who embark on a musical career. The series was hugely popular in the US and subsequently around the world, launching the career of teenage heartthrob David Cassidy in the process.

Heart Of The City: UK Pub Rock

The pub rock scene in London from 1974 to 1976 provided a conducive environment for a more immediate form of rock music to prosper—away from the machinations of the music industry, which itself had moved on to more and more elaborate and spectacular approaches to rock show business. The resurgent rhythm & blues of Dr. Feelgood, Eddie & the Hot Rods, the Tyla Gang, and Ducks Deluxe provided a template for a simple but effective form of grassroots entertainment. Meanwhile, Kilburn & the High Roads and the 101'ers afforded apprenticeships to what were to become two of punk's great front men, and pub rock's network of venues provided a launchpad for the new punk generation. The Sex Pistols famously opened for Eddie & the Hot Rods at the Marquee (a gig that brought the group to the attention of the UK music press), and many of punk's first wave played the circuit regularly, including the Stranglers, the Damned, X-Ray Spex, 999, and the Only Ones.

01
Artist Dr. Feelgood
Title Down by the Jetty
Format LP, 12-inch
Label United Artists, UK, 1974
_ Debut album by key UK pub rock band Dr. Feelgood. The Canvey Island group's pared-down, no-nonsense approach to music won them critical acclaim and a loyal following, and the accompanying simple black-and-white portraiture on this album cover—shot near their hometown on the Thames estuary—emphasizes that approach. Design by A. D. Design Consultants Ltd.

02
Artist Dr. Feelgood
Title Stupidity
Format LP, 12-inch
Label United Artists, UK, 1976
_ The Feelgoods' third album was a live set that went to number one in the UK album chart upon its release—a highly unusual feat for a live recording. Design by Paul Henry.

03
Artist Kilburn & the High Roads
Title Handsome
Format LP, 12-inch
Label Dawn, UK, 1975
_ Debut album by pub rock stalwarts fronted by Ian Dury, later to find critical and commercial success with the Blockheads. Design by Elizabeth Rathmell.

04
Artist Eddie & the Hot Rods
Title Live at the Marquee
Format EP, 7-inch
Label Island, UK, 1976
_ Design by Michael Beal.

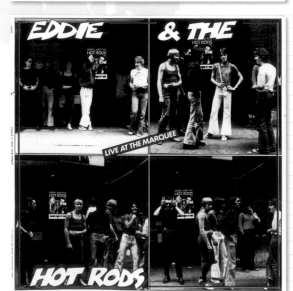

Artist Eddie & the Hot Rods
Title Teenage Depression
Format LP, 12-inch
Label Island, UK, 1976
_ Debut album by Essex pub rockers Eddie & the Hot Rods. The album cover utilizes a strong image appropriated from *True Detective* magazine, together with bold stencil typography—graphic styles that were to become central to the visual language of UK punk in ensuing years. Design by Michael Beal.

06

Artist The Count Bishops
Title Speedball
Format EP, 7-inch
Label Chiswick, UK, 1975
_ First release on the Chiswick label, including a frantic rendition of the rock 'n' roll classic "Route 66."

07

_ Poster for a gig by the Pirates at Derby College of Art, October 7, 1977. The group had been a successful, hard-hitting British rock 'n' roll act during the early 1960s, recording the hits "Please Don't Touch," "Shakin' All Over," and "Hungry For Love," but had split following the death of singer Johnny Kidd in 1966. They re-formed in 1976, now fronted by Mick Green, and found some success on the pub rock circuit with their own brand of supercharged R & B.

08

Artist Nick Lowe
Title So It Goes
Format Single, 7-inch
Label Stiff, UK, 1976
_ The first release on the Stiff Records label. The original Stiff identity was designed by in-house art director Chris Morton (who himself adopted a working pseudonym in keeping with the times, C More Tone). Design by Chris Morton.

09

Artist Tyla Gang
Title Styrofoam
Format Single, 7-inch
Label Stiff, UK, 1976
_ Some early Stiff releases featured plain white sleeves rubber-stamped with memorable and often self-mocking catchphrases—including in this case "artistic breakthrough! double 'b' side." Design by Chris Morton.

10

Artist Nick Lowe
Title Bowi
Format EP, 7-inch
Label Stiff, UK, 1977
_ A witty response by Lowe to David Bowie's *Low* album of the same year. Since Bowie was deemed to have used Lowe's name as an album title, omitting the last letter in the process, Lowe responded in kind. Design by Barney Bubbles. Photograph by Peter Gravelle.

11

Artist Various Artists
Title Submarine Tracks & Fool's Gold
Format LP, 12-inch
Label Chiswick, UK, 1977
_ Another key pub rock label, Chiswick Records was established by Roger Armstrong and Ted Carroll, drawing on their experience with their Rock On! record stall in Soho, London, popular with the early punk crowd. Design by Paul Wakefield/ Geoff Halpin.

01 02 03   07 08 09
04 05 06 | 10 11

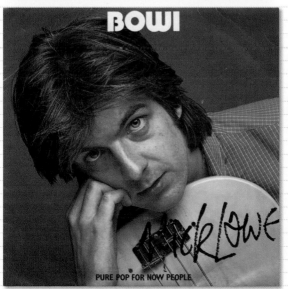

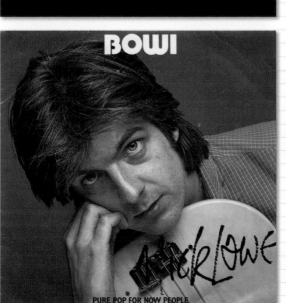

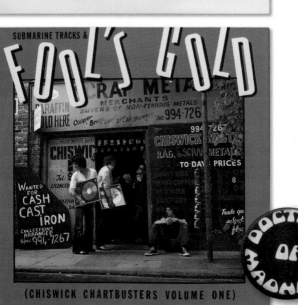

Though rarely recognized for its "punk" culture, France, via the interventions of Skydog Records owner Marc Zermati, can be argued to have given the entire punk movement liftoff. And he can trace that influence back even further. Right back, in fact, to Africa.

Marc Zermati's Skydog Records, based in Paris, issued its first record, Flamin' Groovies' *Grease* EP, in May 1973 (an original Skydog having been established in Amsterdam in 1972 with partner Peter Meulenbroek). He concurrently ran the "Open Market" stall in the city, which became a hub for the key characters in the later development of London punk. He subsequently partnered with Larry Debay to form Bizarre Records in Praed Street, London, while being the key distributor of US garage music by the Stooges, MC5, etc., across Europe. If the term proto-punk has any legitimacy, then the reason so many '76-'77 era bands were in thrall to Iggy and Asheton and the rest was primarily because of that first, tentative, independent record network. Or maybe not so tentative: *Metallic K.O.* by the Stooges alone shifted one hundred thousand copies.

Zermati also organized the first legendary French punk festival at Mont de Marsan in 1976 and was heavily involved in the release of "New Rose" (the first British punk single) and Motörhead's debut, among many others. Later the Skydog catalog became synonymous with the New York Dolls, and he would subsequently work with everyone from the Happy Mondays to Daft Punk:

Open was started in '72 as a head shop—we had all the underground music from around the world, comics, and bootleg records. Slowly we moved to another level by having bands rehearsing in our shop. Then we decided that we would be different. The punk scene back in '74 was French—all those guys from [Sex Pistols manager] Malcolm McLaren to [writers] Nick Kent and Jon Savage—they were coming to Paris. They knew something could happen. We were connected to what was happening in New York. For us, Iggy and the Stooges were really important—they were the revolution side of rock. We had a lot more of a political attitude in France than England. They did not know the political aspect of the situation.

We were political without even knowing. That's why Malcolm and all those guys came along—they wanted to check what was really happening. We were very few, but very active. We were active even in England—starting Bizarre in Praed Street in '74. So before anyone was distributing punk and rock stuff, I always say we were first. From '74 and '75 we started importing singles from America—Patti Smith and Television and all that, to distribute in England. Ted Carroll and Roger Armstrong had their Rock On! store and we pushed them to do their own label. So then there was Chiswick Records and Stiff and all those guys.

We took our idea of punk from the *Nuggets* [revered garage punk compilation] period in America, from Lenny Kaye. Back in '73 I met Lenny Kaye in New York and we realized we were on a similar wavelength. We started with garage punk and slowly the term became used everywhere. Malcolm wanted to call this movement the "nouvelle vague," from the French cinema tradition.

Most of the people in punk at the start came from the hippie movement. Guys like Malcolm and Bernie [Rhodes; Clash manager] had no clue—they weren't into a large spectrum of music. Malcolm was into rockabilly. He did not know anything about music. Bernie made the same mistake; they thought they were running boy bands, the Sex Pistols and the Clash. You can lose someone and it's OK. That's the worst piece of shit, people thinking they can change people like that. But they don't come from a music environment, they're just fashion guys. They were important because they were there, but not that important. They picked up on things. They came to Paris all the time because they were digging for something. The first time I met Malcolm was around '73, because the New York Dolls were in Paris, and they were an important band for us. And he destroyed them when he managed them! He had no clue! His did not respect the music side of the story. Jerry Nolan didn't like Malcolm at all because he destroyed everything for that band. When he sent the New York Dolls round America with Mao Tse-tung books on stage and the hammer and sickle . . .

Disaster! When Bernie had problems with the Clash, he would call me all the time. I liked them, they were my friends, but they were wrong. When Joe Strummer was in the 101'ers, he wanted to sign with Skydog. Ted and Roger went to a showcase and they wanted to start their label. I said I can't sign them because I was concentrating on Flamin' Groovies.

And then Malcolm started a press campaign saying I didn't want the Sex Pistols to play Mont de Marsan—total bullshit! But what can you do with a guy like Malcolm? The Damned were the only "real" punk band on there. But Nick Lowe and Jake Riviera [Damned manager and Stiff cofounder] could not understand when I was pushing this stuff—then when they saw the Damned on stage they started realizing. So we ended up producing and releasing the first Damned single, "New Rose," in England and France at the same time. I still have the studio invoice, for £70! And then I released the first Motörhead single, "White Line Fever."

I'm very different from most French people. I am "Pied-Noirs"—one of the French people who lived in Algeria when it was a French colony. I lived through the Algerian War. At the end of that war in 1962 we came to France and then I went to England. English kids were my friends: the mods and rockers. They could not believe a guy coming from North Africa could know so much about blues and rock. The French always expect the government to do everything for them. I was not born with that attitude. Never. I was like, OK, let's do something, don't wait for help from the government. It's a North African attitude. The music business in France has always been pushed by North African influences.

MARC ZERMATI— AGENT PROVOCATEUR

_ Benefit gig in aid of Zermati, London, 1979. Artists booked to appear covered the range of pub rock, proto-punk, and punk fields, demonstrating something of the overlap that the Skydog label signified, and the crossovers between the UK and French scenes. Designed by Loulou Picasso / Bazooka.

_ Marc Zermati with his old friend Joe Strummer prior to a concert by the Clash at the legendary club Le Palace in Paris, May 1981. Photograph by
• Catherine Faux.

02
Artist Iggy and the Stooges
Title Metallic K.O.
Format LP, 12-inch
Label Skydog, France, 1976
_ Designed by Michael Beal.

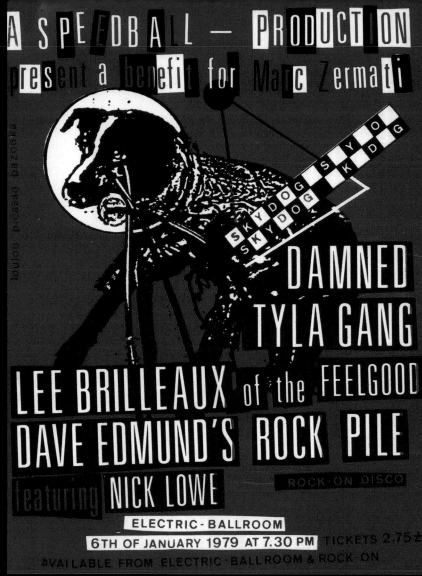

Even though punk's genesis was more complex and convoluted than some accounts maintain, by the advent of the UK's long, hot summer of 1976, the moment was ripe. The Sex Pistols, formed in 1975 from a group of London teenagers who hung around Malcolm McLaren's boutique on the King's Road, had already started gigging, in the process gathering interest from a number of tastemakers in the music press. Reviews were both supportive and critical, but seldom if ever neutral—a fact that captured the attention of those who had grown tired of the malaise in contemporary rock and pop.

Historical narratives are seldom neat, and overlaps between proto-punk survivors, adapters, adopters, and a new generation of innovators are markedly opaque. Many have laid claim to the "invention" of punk, but unique laboratory conditions were certainly more germane than any single contributor. That context—social, political, geographical, cultural, and economic—helped set in motion a chain reaction on both sides of the Atlantic.

This is not to deny the importance of the individuals involved in the Sex Pistols' camp—Malcolm McLaren's (often bizarre) management theatrics, Vivienne Westwood's acute fashion sense, Helen Wallington-Lloyd, Nils Stevenson, Jamie Reid's graphic design skills, and the individual talents of the group members. Reid took control of the group's visual identity in late 1976, drawing on his background in agitational art and design to create a new graphic style that reflected perfectly—and perhaps even helped to inform—the controversy that the group generated. By the time the Pistols earned their first television exposure, courtesy of a magazine program on Manchester's Granada Television in September 1976, the fuse was lit.

Other leading talents in the UK scene were already waiting in the wings. The Clash, the Damned, the Stranglers, 999, Chelsea, and the Vibrators led the way in London, while Buzzcocks, Slaughter & the Dogs, and the Drones quickly established Manchester as punk's second city. Designers working closely with these groups strived to create a new visual landscape that matched the "new wave" rhetoric of the early punk movement—a rejection of the past and a waymarking to the future. The impetus behind this new style, whether conscious or instinctive, was to escape convention. At the same time, parallels were being drawn and a collective sense of community and purpose was developing, as much as a defense mechanism as a sharing of ambition. Connections to US first-wavers were also strong—the Ramones made their first transatlantic trip to play the Roundhouse in London on Independence Day, 1976, inspiring or further refining many nascent UK punk bands' visions of the possible.

The publicity given to the punk phenomenon, particularly in the wake of the Sex Pistols' dismissal by two record companies who found them disagreeably troublesome, further incentivized scandal hunters. More importantly, a natural constituency formed among those who found resonance in much of what the Pistols said or were perceived to stand for. Some formed groups themselves—punk's "anyone can do it" rhetoric facilitated a call to arms and the sense of empowerment was tangible. UK punk's second-wave diaspora drew from cities, towns, and villages across the country—individuals who took their inspiration either from the news filtering out in the music press, or through first-hand exposure to touring punk bands. In the process, punk aesthetics, and musical and visual styles, morphed and changed as ideas were bent and reshaped through individual interpretation and local cultural perspectives.

Punk in the US was also changing radically, particularly on the West Coast, with vibrant punk communities established in Los Angeles and San Francisco. There were also stirrings in Middle America, the Pacific Northwest, Texas and elsewhere—proof that the punk ethos, though it remained impeccably resistant to a hard and fast definition, even if the music sometimes did not, was itinerant as well as restless.

The Ramones returned to Britain early in 1977 for a more extensive tour, this time with Talking Heads in tow, and released the era-defining "Sheena Is a Punk Rocker" to promote their visit. The single charted and

> **"Eater in 1976 was all about accidents, misunderstandings, chaos, and fun. Ripe for exploitation and destined to come to a messy and untimely end, we epitomized that initial punk impetus."**
>
> Dee Generate, Eater

> **"I was brought up on early funk, Motown, the Who, Hendrix, Free. Going right back to Buddy Holly. So listening to the Lurkers—complete and utter racket. But the one thing I liked was the freshness and the energy. I thought, this is all right, actually. I just got talking to them. [Guitarist] Pete Stride was there. I asked him, 'How are you getting on? How do you get gigs?' He went, 'Well, we could do with a manager, really.' I said, 'Can't you find one?' He turned round and pointed at me and said, 'Why don't you manage us?' I went, 'What? Oh, OK. I'll have a go, I'll ring round and get a few gigs.' That's how the collaboration with the Lurkers started, and also the beginning of Beggars Banquet Records."**
>
> Mike Stone, Beggars Banquet Records

kick-started the convention of US punk groups obtaining a better reception in the UK than they customarily did at home, at least until American media outlets were alerted to their overseas popularity. Two years before Blondie's new wave global bombshell *Plastic Letters*, the band made their first trip to Europe in May 1977 with Television opening; like the Ramones, they received a warm welcome in the UK while still being regarded as something of a cult underground band in the United States. Meanwhile, others were boarding flights in the opposite direction. A short US tour by the Damned in April 1977 was hugely formative in the development of the Los Angeles and San Francisco punk scenes.

The Sex Pistols finally made a transatlantic trip at the beginning of 1978, only to implode spectacularly when they reached San Francisco on January 14th. In the wake of their split, the individual group members followed alternative paths. Johnny Rotten reverted to his former self, John Lydon, and indulged his love of reggae and dub at the expense of Virgin Records, gradually assembling the cast of characters that would make up post-punk scene leaders Public Image Ltd. Paul Cook and Steve Jones continued to work with manager Malcolm McLaren, taking part in numerous scams for his ongoing movie *The Great Rock 'n' Roll Swindle*. Sid Vicious meanwhile slid further into drug addiction, until the chaos he seemed to thrive upon eventually overwhelmed him.

NEVER MIND THE BOLLOCKS

_ X-Ray Spex "Oh Bondage, Up Yours!" poster, based on the picture sleeve for the group's debut single on Virgin Records, October 1977. The central image of singer Poly Styrene was shot at the Roxy Club in London, and was color photocopied to increase its tonal depth. Design by Poly Styrene with hand-rendered typography by Sophia Horgan.

The Filth and the Fury

The visual and graphic identity of the Sex Pistols had a rich heritage, much of which was unapparent to their core audience at the time. Early flyers for the group designed by Helen Wallington-Lloyd employed "ransom note" typographic styles, whereby individual characters were cut from newspaper and magazine headlines and reassembled for dramatic, and threatening, visual effect. The technique mirrored earlier styles drawn from the radical art of the dadaists, surrealists, Lettrists, and Situationists, among others, though its use as a punk visual signifier was more of a graphic blunt tool than a lesson in art history. When Jamie Reid began designing officially for the group in the autumn of 1976, he drew upon his own background as an agent provocateur within the early 1970s radical underground, initially reusing material he had produced for the Suburban Press, a political print studio he originated in Croydon, South London, which was active between 1971 and 1975.

Once the Sex Pistols began attracting media attention, and notoriety, Reid was able to build on their reputation and to reflect on contemporary events as they occurred. The group signed to EMI in October 1976, releasing their debut single, "Anarchy in the UK," on November 19th. Initial designs for the record sleeve included a crude image of a monster adapted by Reid from his Suburban Press work, or plain black and red blocks to reflect the colors of the anarchist flag, but eventually the record was issued in a plain black card sleeve—the antithesis of the commercial pop picture cover. Following the group's notorious December 1st appearance on the *Today* program, a daily magazine show hosted by Bill Grundy for Thames Television, the Sex Pistols were fired by EMI, moving on to A&M and subsequently Virgin Records in the following six months of chaos. The resulting media backlash provided plenty of ammunition for Reid's playfully pointed graphic responses.

01
_ Sex Pistols "Pretty Vacant" poster. The poster appropriates the image of two buses from US West Coast Situationist group Point-Blank! who themselves produced publications stating "no copyrite, reproduce at will." Design by Jamie Reid.

02
_ Poster for a gig by the Sex Pistols at Queensway Hall, Dunstable, October 21, 1976.

07

Artist Sex Pistols
Title God Save the Queen
Format Single, 7-inch
Label Virgin, UK, 1977
_ Probably the most iconic example of punk art, the sleeve for the Sex Pistols' second single, "God Save the Queen," appropriated the official photographic portrait of the head of the royal family by Cecil Beaton, adding torn strips across the eyes and mouth and crudely rendered "ransom note" typography. Accompanying alternative posters used the same portrait, but with a safety pin added through the Queen's mouth and nose, or with swastikas covering her eyes. The track had originally been recorded for A&M Records, but the group was sacked by that label after just seven days, moving on to their third label, Virgin, for this defining moment in rock history. Design by Jamie Reid.

08

Artist Sex Pistols
Title Pretty Vacant
Format Single, 7-inch
Label Virgin, UK, 1977
_ Reid was only informed at the last minute that "Pretty Vacant" was to be the group's next single, and had only prepared the "boredom buses" image as a graphic for the reverse of the sleeve. On discovering a small, square picture frame in a local art shop near the Virgin offices on Portobello Road, London, Reid simply smashed the glass, added the group's name and song title from an earlier gig poster, and delivered the finished article to Virgin's art department for photographic reproduction. Design by Jamie Reid.

09

Artist Sex Pistols
Title Holidays in the Sun
Format Single, 7-inch
Label Virgin, UK, 1977
_ Reid appropriated a tourist brochure promoting holidays in Belgium for the cover of the Sex Pistols' fourth single, adapting the dialog in the cartoon strip to reflect the song's lyrics. Virgin Records faced legal action from the copyright owners of the original advertisement and were forced to withdraw the picture sleeve and revert to plain white record bags instead. Design by Jamie Reid.

10

_ Banner to promote the Never Mind the Bollocks album, 1977.

11

_ "Anarchy in the UK" poster, November 1976. The image was created from a torn 8- x 4-inch souvenir flag adorned with ransom note titles, binder clips, and safety pins. Design by Jamie Reid, photography by Ray Stevenson.

12

_ Poster for the Sex Pistols' projected gig at Derby King's Hall, UK, December 4, 1976. The gig was due to be the second date on the Anarchy in the UK tour, but following the backlash against the group after the Grundy incident three days earlier, many dates were canceled, including this one. The groups on the tour—the Sex Pistols, the Heartbreakers, the Damned, and the Clash—were asked to perform privately at the venue to local government officials before the planned concert, but refused to do so, and the gig was canceled.

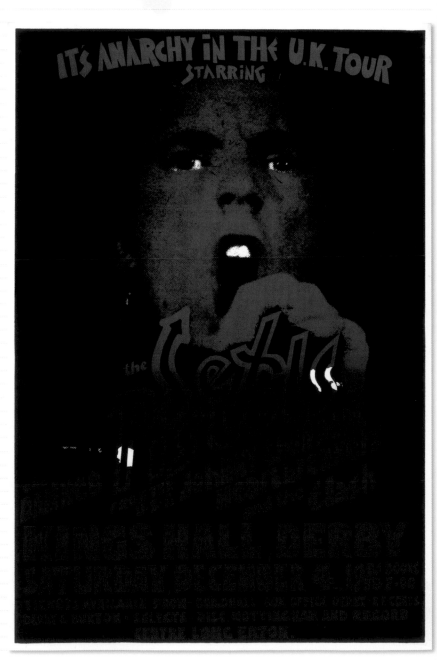

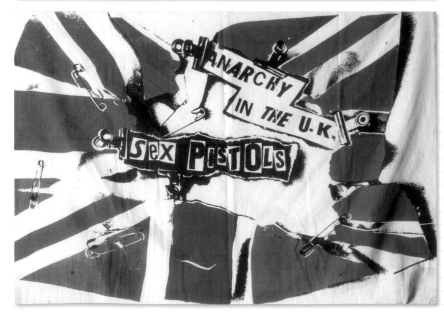

_ The album cover used
deliberately "loud"
fluorescent colors and a
provocative title which
led to further media
attention and a court
appearance on obscenity
charges for a record
shop owner in

Nottingham, UK, and
Virgin Records boss
Richard Branson. The
charges were successfully
defended by Virgin's
legal team, but the case
did little to calm the
controversy surrounding
the group. Design
by Jamie Reid.

_ Collage poster included
with the first edition of
Never Mind the Bollocks,
with individual
illustrations for
each song. Design
by Jamie Reid.

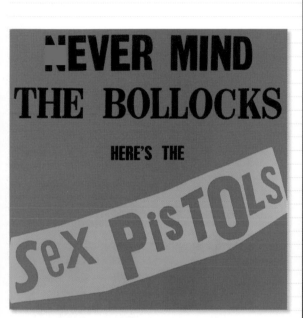

London's Burning

Following the Sex Pistols, there was no shortage of applicants vying for the mantle of spokesperson for a generation. Front-runners the Clash found a sympathetic music press keen to buy into their image of rock 'n' roll rebellion. Despite sharing an overlapping heritage with the Sex Pistols (manager Bernie Rhodes was an early collaborator with McLaren and Westwood), the Clash pursued their own agenda and accompanying distinctive musical style. Gathering critical and popular support as the biggest rivals to the Pistols' crown, their visual image often centered on the photogenic qualities of the group members themselves. After the Clash signed to CBS, meeting the opprobrium of their peers for "selling out," and the Pistols fell into disarray as live gigs were banned and the national media pounced, Sham 69's populist politics and street-level, soccer chant-style songs propelled the group into the public spotlight. But ultimately problems with right-wing skinheads at their gigs destroyed their chances of wider success.

Angels with Dirty Faces

Sham 69's early iconography was, perhaps predictably, about kids on the street. Their first single was released on Mark Perry (of *Sniffin' Glue*) and Miles Copeland's Step Forward Records. It featured a photograph from the Lewisham riots in south London between the National Front and anti-fascist demonstrators. It's interesting to note that the band's follow-up single for major label Polydor, "Borstal Breakout," featured the group in an action pose that could have been an extension of that same scene, again self-consciously positioning the band as "street" punks. Later sleeves were art-directed by Jo Mirowski at Polydor, who attempted to broaden their appeal. "The whole typography and cowboy imagery of [Sham 69's second album] *Adventures of the Hersham Boys*," he recalls of the gatefold sleeve, "was intended as a way of spitting back at everything that punk had become. It was a private protest from the art director, I'll rebel against them!"

Journalist Jive

Arguably the best place to read about UK punk as it happened, outside of the inky press and the fanzines, was in the pages of "halfway house" publication *ZigZag*. Originally started by Pete Frame in 1969, it attempted the feat of marrying fanzine enthusiasm to supposedly professional journalism and glossy covers. During the punk years, Kris Needs served as editor. "When I took over *ZigZag*," he recalls, "it was in the spirit of it being a magazine started by fans because they couldn't read about the music they liked anywhere else. And, quite simply, they wanted somewhere to ramble and enthuse as long as they wanted without being curtailed or interrupted. It was with this trust that I was handed the keys to *ZigZag* in mid-1977 by Pete Frame. I got my whole writing style and attitude to the music business from Frame. In other words, don't give a fuck about what the business thinks or decrees, just go on about the music you like." A steady diet of the Clash, the Slits, the Damned, and their ilk ensued.

01

_ Poster for the debut single by the Clash, "White Riot," March 1977, featuring a stark, high-contrast image of the group in posed "arrest" positions. Photography by Caroline Coon, design by Sebastian Conran.

02

Artist The Clash
Title S/T
Format LP, 12-inch
Label CBS, UK, 1977
_ Photography by Kate Simon, design by Sebastian Conran.

03

_ Cover of ZigZag magazine, no. 75, August 1977, featuring the Slits, an all-female group who opened for the Clash on their first UK tour, before going on to shape a definitive post-punk sound fusing reggae, dub, and punk.

04

_ Cover of ZigZag magazine, no. 76, September 1977, featuring the Clash. The group had recently played at the Bilzen Festival in Liège, Belgium, alongside the Damned and Elvis Costello—the headline here reflects a riot that took place during the group's set.

05

Artist Sham 69
Title I Don't Wanna
Format Single, 7-inch
Label Step Forward, UK, 1977
_ Design by Jill Furmanovsky.

06

Artist Sham 69
Title Borstal Breakout
Format Single, 7-inch
Label Polydor, UK, 1978
_ Design by Jill Mumford.

The Damned: Neat Neat Neat

The Damned formed from the remnants of several failed proto-punk projects, notably London SS, a nascent punk outfit that also spawned members of the Clash, the Boys, Chelsea, and Generation X. Opening for the Sex Pistols at the 100 Club, London, for their official debut in June 1976, the group quickly built a strong live reputation, fusing garage rock and glam with bludgeoning volume, chaotic energy, and vagabond charisma. Having signed to fledgling independent label Stiff Records in the summer of 1976, they became the first British punk band to record a single, "New Rose," in October the same year, and the first to release an album, *Damned Damned Damned* in February 1977. The group's first US tour in April 1977 took in CBGB, New York, Rat Club, Boston, the Starwood, Los Angeles, and Mabuhay Gardens, San Francisco. These West Coast gigs were credited as catalysts for the growth of the punk and hardcore scenes that were to take root in the region in subsequent years.

The Damned were arguably the most visually arresting of all the early punk groups—an act that record label Stiff capitalized on expertly. Stiff were past masters at using visuals as marketing aids. In addition to the "accidentally on purpose" inclusion of a picture of Eddie & the Hot Rods on the reverse of their debut album (to ensure instant collectability), they celebrated their two-year distribution deal with Island and the release of "Neat Neat Neat" by deleting all their previous single releases. They were certainly a label unhindered by sentiment. By the start of 1978 they'd dropped the Damned. "This is a record company," they stated to the press, "not a museum."

01
_ Poster for the debut single by the Damned, "New Rose," released in October 1976 on Stiff Records—officially the first single release by a UK punk rock group.

....

02
Artist The Damned
Title Damned Damned Damned
Format LP, 12-inch
Label Stiff, UK, 1977
_ Photography by Peter Gravelle, design by Barney Bubbles.

....

03
Artist The Damned
Title Neat Neat Neat
Format Single, 7-inch
Label Stiff, UK, 1977
_ As well as benefiting from working with Peter Gravelle on their debut album, Jake Riviera's Stiff connections also led the Damned to celebrated rock photographer Keith Morris (Nick Drake, T. Rex, etc.), who had previously collaborated with Riviera's charges Dr. Feelgood. Photography by Keith Morris, design by Barney Bubbles.

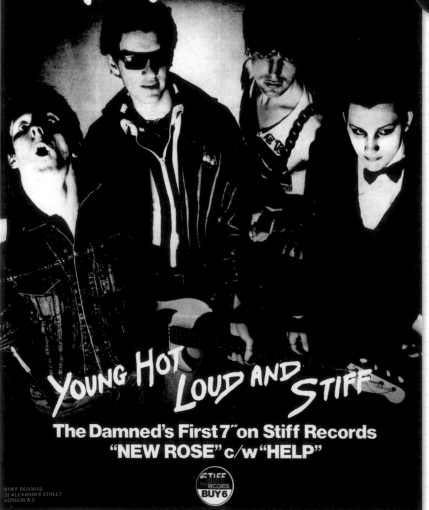

04

_ Poster for the Damned's first anniversary gigs at the Marquee, London, July 1977. The group would continue the tradition of anniversary gigs each year throughout the decade.

05

_ Screenprinted poster promoting a gig by the Damned and the Adverts, University of Lancaster, UK, June 27, 1977. Design by Angus.

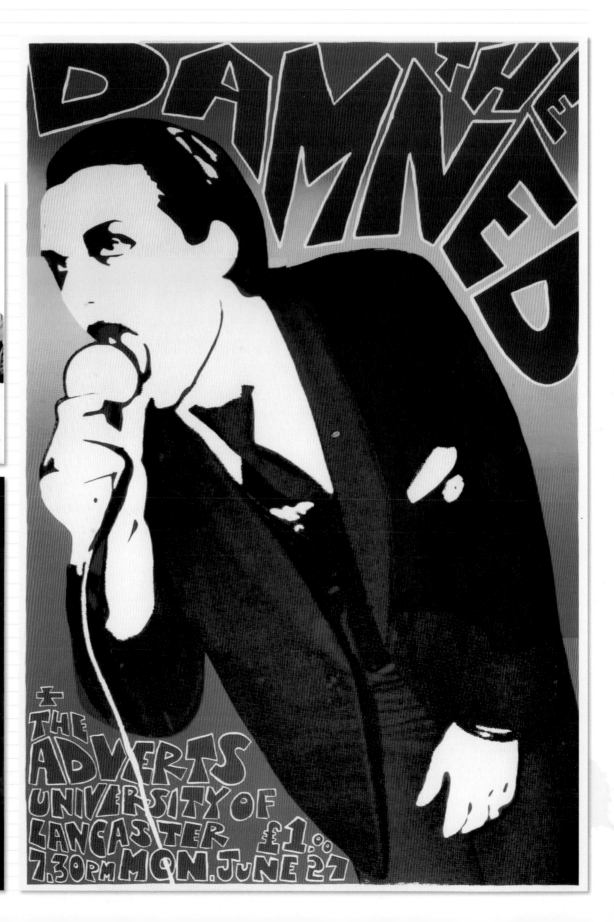

sleeve was a crucial aspect of the marketing
of punk and its consequent visual identity.
Few excelled at the process better than Peter
Gravelle, a London-based photographer who
later acquired a degree of fame through his
friendship with Sid Vicious. That his work
is not better known is at least partially
explained by his use of pseudonyms across
these projects, notably Peter Kodick, with
other variants including Hugh Heffer.

"I was a fashion and advertising photographer
in London. It came about through Judy Nylon.
She was a model who was going out with Brian
James from the Damned, and she was later half
of Snatch with Patti Palladin, who was my
first wife. Judy said, 'Oh, can you do some
photos?' So we did the pie-in-the-face shoot.
They didn't have any money so I said, 'OK, if
I can do what I want, I'll recover the money
from my other work.' We couldn't find proper
custard cakes. We used ketchup and shaving
foam and mustard, bought some flans and put
all that in there."

Jake Riviera at Stiff saw the results and
wanted them for the cover of *Damned Damned
Damned*. It was the first punk album.
They said, what do you want to work under?
Everyone's using pseudonyms. So I got Peter
Kodick from Kodak cameras. And then the work
started snowballing in, all these record
companies signing bands."

Thereafter he hooked up with Barney Bubbles,
with whom he'd collaborate on Nick Lowe's
"Bowi" and the debut albums by Alberto
Los Trios Paranoias and the Damned, to
form Exquisite Covers. The plan was to do
commercial album artwork—revamping old '70s
groups so that they looked a little more
contemporary in the punk age. "Things like
the Nice's *Greatest Hits*, or Humble Pie's
Greatest Hits. Not many people knew, but
that's how we made our money." He concurrently
worked for Ted Carroll and Roger Armstrong
at Chiswick, including the first Skrewdriver
album, Slaughter & the Dogs, Johnny Moped, and the
Count Bishops. "Roger or Ted said, 'We want
you to shoot this band called Skrewdriver.
We hardly got any money on this one, maybe
we could photograph them on the street?'
'No, tell them come down to my place, this
news place in Maida Vale.' I remember they
knocked on the door and there were these
four skinheads. What the fuck! I almost hid.
It was only years later I found out they
became a Nazi band."

He was also hired by Miles Copeland for his
various imprints, providing the artwork for
Chelsea's "Right To Work" and later the
Police's "Can't Stand Losing You" "suicide"
cover. "No health and safety in those days!"

"You'd always get, out of five, maybe one
good-looking kid, two that were average,
one that was a bit geeky, and one you'd have
to try to hide. It's quite a difficult job,
shooting bands! Especially 'cause most of
the punk bands were totally unused to being
in front of a camera."

Peter Gravelle

Most, however, were "band" shots. "You'd always
get, out of five, maybe one good-looking kid,
two that were average, one that was a bit
geeky, and one you'd have to try to hide.
It's quite a difficult job, shooting bands!
Especially 'cause most of the punk bands were
totally unused to being in front of a camera."
Other now familiar images either shot or
designed by Gravelle appeared on sleeves for
Generation X, Johnny Thunders, Snatch, Joe
Jackson, Penetration, John Cooper Clarke, and
the Boys. He also shot two of the definitive
LP jackets of 1978: the Only Ones' self-titled
debut and the Jam's *All Mod Cons*. "I had an
argument with the Jam. I got an apology from
Paul Weller, via the record company, because
of the way the other two behaved. We were
trying to shoot the record cover and they
were moaning about it being five o'clock and
getting home in time to watch *Coronation
Street*. It's your fucking record cover.
Don't you want to work until you get it
how you like it?"

"Punk bands had such bad reputations. Other
photographers wouldn't touch them originally.
Bands didn't traditionally have artistic
control, but with punk suddenly it was an
issue. Then you had things like Joy Division,
almost like greeting card companies. I came
from the old school whereby the band, for
their first single, they should always be
on the cover. So you know what they look
like. I also really liked 'destroying' the
images, making incisions in the negatives
for instance. I really thought that fitted
in with the times."

Gravelle eventually moved to New York when
the landlords at his old studio in Victoria,
London, upped the rent. "The music industry
there was completely different. No artistic
control at all. The record label told you
how they wanted it done." After Sid's death,
a disillusioned Gravelle left the music
industry to become a fashion photographer
based principally in Milan, shooting some of
the most famous models and designers of the
day for magazines including *Harper's Bazaar*
and *Vogue*. He also wrote extensively for
European editions of *Rolling Stone*. He
continues to work and exhibit in London,
though this time under his given name.

PETER GRAVELLE—THE KODICK YEARS

Bored Teenagers

Punk also opened up opportunities for those outside of the King's Road inner circle in London, drawing in like-minded individuals from farther afield. Tim Smith and Gaye Black, a young couple living in Bideford, Devon, heeded the punk call and relocated to London to form the Adverts, becoming TV Smith and Gaye Advert in the process, signing briefly to Stiff Records for their debut single "One Chord Wonders," and touring with the Damned. A typically self-effacing Stiff tour poster famously read: "The Adverts know one chord, the Damned know three. See all four at . . ."

Meanwhile, things were stirring in England's North West. Howard Trafford and Peter McNeish, two students attending Bolton Institute of Technology, were sufficiently inspired by an early report on the Sex Pistols in the *New Musical Express* to travel to London to make contact. They helped set up the Pistols' first Manchester gig at the Lesser Free Trade Hall in June 1976, changing their names to Howard Devoto and Pete Shelley and forming Buzzcocks as a planned opening act. In the end, they were unable to play, but did so after they organized a repeat Sex Pistols visit the following month. Releasing the first independent punk record, "Spiral Scratch," in January 1977, Buzzcocks were thereafter signed to major label United Artists, creating a string of hit singles over the ensuing two years. Manchester graphic design student Malcolm Garrett was brought in to work on the group's visual identity alongside manager Richard Boon, who had a background as a fine artist and a keen understanding of art history.

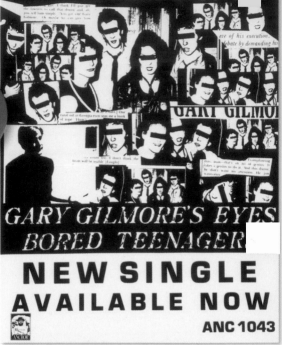

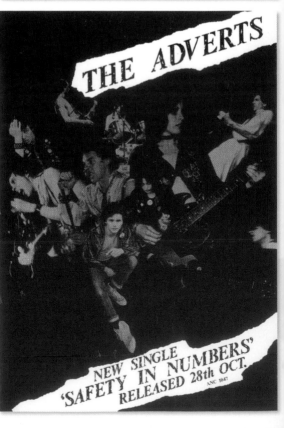

01

Artist The Adverts
Title One Chord Wonders
Format Single, 7-inch
Label Stiff, UK, 1977
_ Stiff switched a
projected group
photograph to the
reverse of the sleeve
and blew up this image
of bass player Gaye
Advert instead,
supposedly to capitalize
on her sex appeal.
The band responded
by leaving her image
completely off the
reverse of subsequent
single "Safety In
Numbers," substituting
a photograph of her
bass instead. Design
by Barney Bubbles.

02

_ Poster for the Adverts
"Gary Gilmore's Eyes,"
August 1977. It features
a monochrome version
of the sleeve collage
artwork by Nicholas
De Ville.

03

_ Poster promoting the
Adverts' third single,
"Safety in Numbers,"
released on the Anchor
label in October 1977.

04

_ Poster promoting
Buzzcocks' second single,
"Orgasm Addict," their
major label debut
released on United
Artists in October 1977.
The poster incorporates
the sleeve illustration
by Linder Sterling and
typography by Malcolm
Garrett. The grid was
reworked by the label's
design department with
neither the designer's
knowledge nor consent.
Malcolm Garrett: "The
first time I saw the
poster for the single
it was pasted up on the
street in Manchester.
It had been put together
by the United Artists
in-house design team,
and I was bitterly
disappointed. Not only
had they inverted the
image, they had added
some extra copy, 'new
single,' all in
lowercase, rather than
uppercase, and in an
effort to mimic my
typography turned it at
right angles but without
any real sensitivity
to the original design.
From that point on,
we insisted that all
Buzzcocks visual
material had to be
designed, and signed
off, by myself and
the group's manager
Richard Boon."

05

_ Poster for Buzzcocks'
debut album, *Another
Music in a Different
Kitchen*, released on
United Artists in March
1978, designed by Malcolm
Garrett. Initial copies
of the album came with
a specially designed
silver shopping bag
labeled "Product."

02

01 03 | 04 05

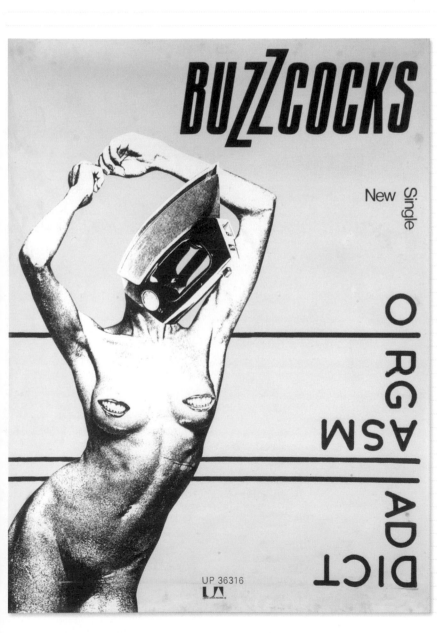

Pure Mania

Chelsea were among the original pioneers of the London punk scene, though their turbulent history and leader's erratic behavior led to them being largely written out of the narrative. The original lineup of the group was front man Gene October, guitarist William Broad (later Billy Idol), bassist Tony James, and drummer John Towe (who, along with James, had been a member of legendary pre-punks London SS). After a few gigs during 1976, Broad, James, and Towe left to form the highly successful, and photogenic, Generation X, while October persevered through a bewildering array of Chelsea lineups. The Vibrators had a stronger rock 'n' roll heritage than many of their peers, having come to public notice at a 1976 gig at the 100 Club when they acted as backing band for Chris Spedding, who produced the Sex Pistols' early demos. Signing to Mickie Most's RAK Records, the group backed Spedding on his novelty single "Pogo Dancing" and released their own debut, "We Vibrate," in November 1976. The Vibrators were subsequently picked up by Epic Records and achieved some chart success during 1977, together with media attention as much for the group's risqué name as for their music.

01
Artist Generation X
Title Your Generation
Format Single, 7-inch
Label Chrysalis, UK, 1977
_ Generation X's debut 45 "Your Generation" employed a striking Barney Bubbles graphic, inspired by Polish constructivist artist Henryk Berlewi. The original design, featuring a band photograph, was rejected as being too run of the mill by the band and manager Jonh Ingham. Bubbles merely flipped the 45 symbol he'd originally intended for the rear cover.

02
_ Photograph by Peter Gravelle of Generation X on the day that they signed to Chrysalis.

The floor reflection comes from spilled "complimentary" beer.

03
Artist Generation X
Title Ready Steady Go
Format Single, 7-inch
Label Chrysalis, UK, 1978

04
Artist The Vibrators
Title Baby Baby
Format Single, 7-inch
Label Epic, UK, 1977

05
Artist The Vibrators
Title London Girls (live)
Format Single, 7-inch
Label Epic, UK, 1977
_ The photograph used on "London Girls" self-consciously includes a road sign for the King's Road, the perceived hub of the London scene, as

if to authenticate the punk credentials of a group sometimes accused of jumping on the bandwagon. The girl on the cover was Carole Semaine, a girlfriend of singer Knox. The single's B-side, "Stiff Little Fingers," would be adopted by a notable second-generation Belfast punk band.

06
Artist The Vibrators
Title Pure Mania
Format LP, 12-inch
Label Epic, UK, 1977
_ The Vibrators' debut album was packaged by Eckford and Stimpson, a design team with a long industry association. "The cover was done by a proper graphics place which was used by Epic

Records I think," recalls Knox. "It was the graphics peoples' idea to use the 'V' as the front cover, but I think we already knew it was a strong image." Note the professionally typset imitation of "ransom-note" lettering at the bottom of the sleeve, and the use of a strong black and pink color palette across all three sleeves.

....

07

Artist Chelsea
Title Right to Work
Format Single, 7-inch
Label Step Forward, UK, 1977
_ Design by Peter Gravelle/Jill Furmanovsky.

Artist Chelsea
Title High Rise Living
Format Single, 7-inch
Label Step Forward, UK, 1977
_ Design by Sandra Tiffin.

09

Artist Chelsea
Title No Escape
Format Single, 7-inch
Label Step Forward, UK, 1980
_ Chelsea's Chris Bashford was working as an illustrator prior to joining the band as drummer. The sleeve for "No Escape" is an obvious tribute to M.C. Escher's *Relativity* lithograph, with one or two knowing references to the era added in the portrait gallery and elsewhere. Chris Bashford: "I can hardly

remember, but there's definitely a photograph of Steve Lewins, the bass player, and one of the portraits is of me. The couple on the sofa—if there's any significance there I've forgotten! But the person wandering upstairs with a knife in his hand, that's supposed to be Sid Vicious. I just used to whack them out for Step Forward. I did lots of single sleeves for Chelsea plus the album *Alternative Hits*. That one has a picture of me with a blindfold on, shooting up, with a cat on the sofa! Miles Copeland went apeshit. The Chelsea logo was actually from Mark Perry. That was just taken from how he wrote

down our name. Similarly the Step Forward logo is quite close to Chelsea's, and again it was taken from Mark's handwriting."

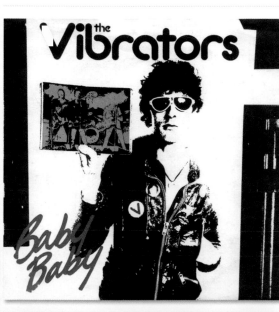

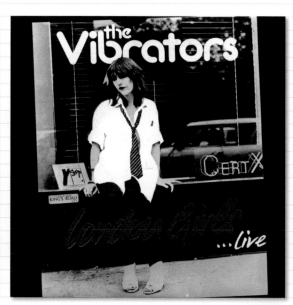

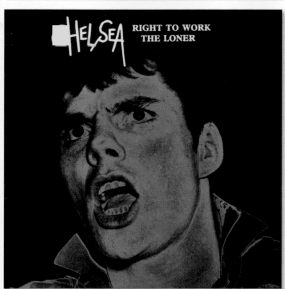

No More Heroes

The investment in punk by some proactive major labels allowed higher levels of production to underpin the punk aesthetic, sometimes to great effect. United Artists, a label with a strong back catalog in movie soundtracks and jazz music, merged with Liberty Records in 1969, with Liberty's former head of A & R Andrew Lauder transferring to UA and signing a range of influential acts including Hawkwind, the Groundhogs, and Dr. Feelgood. As punk gained a foothold, Lauder had the foresight to sign the Stranglers, 999, and Buzzcocks, all of whom benefited from the infrastructure of a major label. The Stranglers had been active on the pub rock scene since early 1975, and their menacing sound and forceful attitude found ready favor, despite some critical barbs about their age and musical accomplishment. Their early album sleeves, designed by Paul Henry, demonstrate a level of graphic sophistication at odds with contemporaneous punk outfits, but along with their polished sound (developed with the help of producer Martin Rushent) they helped propel the group to the top of the UK charts.

999, meanwhile, also had roots in the pub rock scene—singer/guitarist Nick Cash had been a member of Kilburn & the High Roads alongside Ian Dury, and lead guitarist Guy Days had been a session musician for the group. Recruiting bassist Jon Watson and drummer Pablo LaBritain, the group released their debut single, "I'm Alive," on their own label before signing to United Artists in the summer of 1977. The group's name was taken directly from Britain's emergency telephone number, and their graphic identity, developed by long-term collaborator George Snow, utilized the simple but effective device of a numbered ticket stub together with heavy use of high-contrast images, lurid colors, and strong photography. Though chart success was limited, the group enjoyed substantial attention in the US where they were able to tour far more heavily than many of their peers.

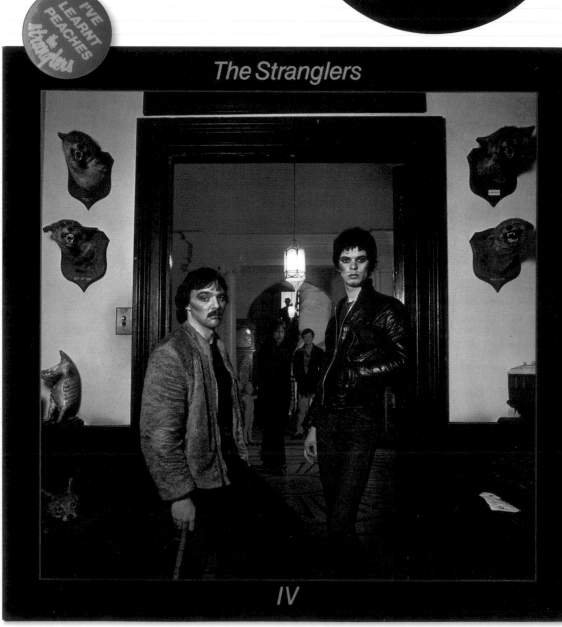

IV

01

_First used on the reverse of the group's debut album, *Rattus Norvegicus*, the iconic rat silhouette became symbolic with the Stranglers' visual identity.

02

Artist The Stranglers
Title Peaches
Format Single, 7-inch
Label United Artists, UK, 1977

03

Artist The Stranglers
Title No More Heroes
Format LP, 12-inch
Label United Artists, UK, 1977
_Design by Paul Henry.

04

Artist The Stranglers
Title Rattus Norvegicus
Format LP, 12-inch
Label United Artists, UK, 1977
_The debut album by the Stranglers, alternatively titled *The Stranglers IV*, was released in April 1977 and reached no. 4 in the UK album chart. Design by Paul Henry.

05

Artist 999
Title Emergency
Format Single, 7-inch
Label United Artists, UK, 1978
_999 sleeve designer George Snow, like Barney Bubbles, attended Twickenham College of Technology and joined the underground press (*Oz* and *International Times*) before designing record covers. He subsequently edited *Radical Illustration* and worked as a photojournalist in Northern Ireland for a variety of socialist publications, later becoming a video director (including work with the Art of Noise and Stranglers) and a multimedia artist. Design by George Snow.

06

Artist 999
Title Nasty Nasty
Format Single, 7-inch
Label United Artists, UK, 1977
_Design by George Snow.

07

Artist 999
Title I'm Alive
Format Single, 7-inch
Label LaBritain, UK, 1977
_Design by George Snow.

Whip in My Valise

Adam Ant (Stuart Goddard) studied graphic design at Hornsey College of Art, North London, and went on to pursue a career in music when punk served him with an appropriate opportunity. The Sex Pistols had opened for his first band, Bazooka Joe, at St. Martin's College, London, in November 1975, and Goddard was inspired to form his own punk outfit, initially called the B-Sides, later the Ants (or Antz). Key players in the early London punk scene, the group gained notoriety with their inclusion in the 1977 movie *Jubilee* by Derek Jarman, and through their manager, Jordan, who worked at McLaren and Westwood's SEX boutique on the King's Road.

Changing his name to Adam Ant, Goddard used his knowledge of art history and design to create striking photocopied flyers for the group's live gigs. Referencing Allen Jones's erotic furniture, vintage bondage illustrations, Richard Hamilton's pop art, futurism, Dada, and Eduardo Paolozzi's collages of ephemera (Goddard had been a student of Paolozzi's at Hornsey), these flyers set the group apart from their peers. Both graphical and lyrical flirtations with sexual and fascistic imagery would cause the Ants problems, particularly with suspicious Rock Against Racism organizers and the generally left-leaning music press. But the group built a large cult following across the UK capital, and by 1978 their explosive, often violent stage shows made them one of the biggest unsigned attractions in the punk underground, alongside similarly antagonistic peers (and post-punk pioneers) Siouxsie & the Banshees.

1
_ Adam & the Ants in live performance, autumn 1977. Photography by Ray Stevenson/Rex Features.

| | 01 | 02 |
| 03 | 04 | 05 | 06 |

2–6
_ Flyers promoting gigs by Adam & the Ants, 1977–1980. Design by Adam Ant.

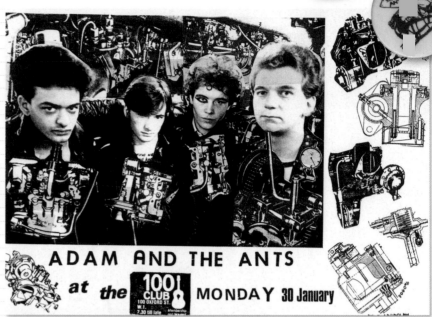

ADAM AND THE ANTS at the 100 CLUB 100 OXFORD ST. W.1. 7.30 till late MONDAY 30 January

ANTMUSIC
FOR SEX PEOPLE
MUSIC FOR A FUTURE AGE
DONT BE SQUARE BE THERE

DIRK WEARS WHITE SØX

JANUARY 1·1980 ELECTRIC LONDON

A TRIBUTE TO ANT FANS FROM

ADAM AND THE ANTS xxx

ADAM & THE ANTS

RETURN

AT THE

MUSIC MACHINE

The Roxy WC2

As punk's notoriety grew during the second half of 1976, the movement appeared to be in real danger of stalling due to widespread bans on punk gigs in and around central London. The "Grundy incident" brought the hostile gaze of the national media, and the Anarchy in the UK tour, featuring the Sex Pistols, the Clash, the Damned and the Heartbreakers, was widely disrupted, with many of the planned concerts canceled by local government. The knock-on-effect of all this negative publicity was that punk groups couldn't get to play anywhere, despite a huge demand for punk gigs from fans and interested bystanders.

Barry Jones was introduced to Andy Czezowski by his friend Chris Millar (aka Damned drummer Rat Scabies) in late 1976. Czezowski, one-time manager of the Damned and currently Chelsea, and his business partner Susan Carrington, saw an opportunity for a specialist punk venue in London. Jones pawned his Les Paul custom guitar to enable the trio to hire a rundown gay club in Covent Garden, Chaguaramas. Following a couple of smaller gigs in December 1976 to try out the venue, the Clash and the Heartbreakers headlined the official gala opening of the Roxy on January 1, 1977, and the club briefly became the center of the booming punk universe.

Jones used his art-school-honed skills to produce collage posters advertising shows at the venue. The use of a color photocopier, a very rare (and expensive) form of new technology at the time, allowed him to build dramatic, complex collages of comic strips, photographs, and hand-rendered colored text, giving the Roxy a futuristic and dynamic profile. The Roxy promoted gigs every week until a dispute over rents closed its doors in April 1977 (reopening briefly later and moving to a new locale). Two live albums were recorded at the club, one during each period of its short life, showcasing upcoming punk acts including Buzzcocks, the Adverts, X-Ray Spex, and Wire, together with lesser-known outfits such as the Bears, the Crabs, and the Red Lights.

> "I loved all the gigs at the Roxy. There was just such a great atmosphere and a real feeling that you were involved in something happening. I remember Jimmy [Pursey], with a broom, sweeping the place out to earn us enough money to go over the road for a Wimpy burger. [Journalist] Tony Parsons came backstage after the set, begging us to go out and play 'Hey Little Rich Boy' again. It was my introduction to a lifelong passion for dub music, my first joint, and a lot of sweat."
>
> Dave Parsons, Sham 69

01–05
_ Posters promoting gigs at the Roxy, 1977. "I didn't meet Johnny [Thunders] until they turned up for soundcheck at the Roxy. Lee, their manager, brought over the photos of all three American acts a few days earlier, and gave me complete freedom to 'mess with them.'" (Barry Jones) Design by Barry Jones.

06
_ Interior of the Roxy, 1977. Photography by Peter Gravellc.

07
Artist Various Artists
Title The Roxy London WC2 (Jan–Apr 77)
Format LP, 12-inch
Label EMI, UK, 1977
_ Design by K. R./ Barry Jones.

| 01 | 02 | | 03 | 04 | 05 |
| 06 | | | | | 07 |

The King's Road is written large—for many, the font size at odds with page constraints—in punk folklore. It served as a crucible for the intertwining of fashion and music, and the location from which Malcolm McLaren and Vivienne Westwood began to stalk the mainstream—employing either distilled Situationist strategies or opportunistically profiting from a peculiar kink in the historical narrative, depending on your preferred take on history.

Despite the "year zero" proclamations of the UK punk vanguard, the continuum of geography was important. The King's Road, which straddles the boroughs of Chelsea and Fulham in West London, was already a fixture on the countercultural map. During the late 1960s, the Granny Takes a Trip head shop was sited there—a magnet for rock stars and underground hipsters alike—and the road also had a strong association with the swinging sixties via Mary Quant and the miniskirt. Given the established bohemian credentials, 430 King's Road was a natural location for Malcolm McLaren and art school friend Patrick Casey to found their stall at the back of Trevor Myles's Paradise Garage boutique in 1971. On offer to discerning customers were vintage rock 'n' roll records and memorabilia as well as clothing.

Soon McLaren and Casey had the premises to themselves and they renamed it Let It Rock, catering for the teddy boy crowd, gradually introducing new designs by McLaren's schoolteacher girlfriend Vivienne Westwood. Some of the principal stock lines included drape jackets and "brothel creeper" shoes. By 1973, a name change to Too Fast to Live, Too Young to Die reflected an attempt to draw custom from rocker attire, but its most fateful makeover came a year later when it was renamed SEX.

"Punk is the most important thing that's happened in fashion over the past forty years. You can't say anything else. I was walking down the street in rubber negligees and high-heel stiletto shoes at a time when other people were wearing denim, flares, and platforms. You felt very heroic. I knew I looked good."

Vivienne Westwood

McLaren had just returned from his ill-fated efforts to manage the New York Dolls in the US, and SEX reflected his transformative experience. Having decorated its innards with

"Wearing bondage trousers in England in 1977 was almost more shocking than wearing nothing at all. To wear clothes from SEX and Seditionaries, outside of the small, protected London milieu, was to daily walk past the dumbfounded, the mocking, and the openly hostile . . . Just like the hero in the fairy story who finally triumphs by wearing his cloak of invisibility that liberates and transforms him, so punk was for me a transformative plumage. So in 1977, to become truly heroic, you had to be prepared to be visibly different from every other member of society, at every moment of every day. Even buying a loaf of bread becomes a trial then, an opportunity for some peculiar artistic triumph, a small but vital pledge of difference."

Linder Sterling

chicken wire and excerpts from Situationist texts and Valerie Solanas's SCUM Manifesto, the shop specialized in fetish wear and attracted the sort of clientele whose illicit sexual mores generally existed in inverse proportion to the respectability of their day jobs.

But there was another clientele attracted to the shop, and particularly its legendary jukebox—which hosted a carefully curated selection of garage and rock 'n' roll classics by the likes of Count Five, Vince Taylor, the Creation, and the Modern Lovers. The four original components of the Sex Pistols congregated therein (Steve Jones, a notorious thief, as much to shoplift as to browse, while Glen Matlock had a Saturday job behind the counter). This all led to the fateful and much storied John Lydon audition (at the behest of later Clash manager and McLaren collaborator Bernie Rhodes) singing along to Alice Cooper's "I'm Eighteen" on the jukebox.

Staff members included Jordan and Chrissie Hynde, while regular patrons numbered among them the Bromley Contingent, as subsequently named by journalist Caroline Coon, including Siouxsie Sioux, Soo Catwoman, Philip Salon, Billy Idol, and others. This small clique of suburbanites drawn to the excitement of London would become the Pistols' initial fan base—though rubber-clad rubberneckers at the subsequent carnage might be a more appropriate description.

While some of the garments were sourced from existing sex shop product lines, these were augmented by print designs including Jim French's homoerotic cowboys, schlongs out,

Alexander Trocchi's erotic text School for Wives, slogan-splattered T-shirts (including, of course, "Anarchy"), see-through jeans, and mock straitjackets. Meanwhile, punk fashion was hitting the headlines nationally and internationally, though it was spearheaded by haute couture interests as exemplified by designers such as Zandra Rhodes, rather than street-level modes of expression.

SEX became Seditionaries in December 1976, developing a range of expensive punk fashions that would be showcased by the Sex Pistols and their elite band of hangers-on. Further along the King's Road at number 151, John Krevine and Steph Raynor opened their own alternative boutique, Boy, in spring 1977 to exploit the rapidly expanding punk market.

"I used to manage Boy in the King's Road, hence my name DennisBoy. We were in direct competition with Malcolm McLaren but we ended up doing a deal with Malcolm and Vivienne to sell Seditionaries clothing when they decided to change their fashion industry into World's End."

DennisBoy

The King's Road itself was celebrated—and mocked in equal turns—by punk's cultural commentators, and became a landmark for visiting tourists and out-of-town provincial punks hoping to catch a little of the zeitgeist. 430 King's Road was eventually remodeled in 1980 as World's End; the Westwood brand was detoxified and eventually welcomed with open arms by prominent fashionistas. She herself became a dame, leaving long behind the days when "God Save the Queen" terrified chart compilers and a King's Road boutique commodified outrage.

"The first punk import from England wasn't the Sex Pistols, it was Zandra Rhodes, who received tons of publicity by selling ugly dresses with prefabricated rips and tears, held together with precious little gold safety pins and which sold for around $800 apiece. I actually went to Macy's to look at them, and saw 'PUNK' T-shirts displayed in their windows at ridiculous prices. I asked our lawyer, 'Hey! I thought we had a copyright on the word 'punk'? How can they do this to us?' And so began my long education about the intricacies of trademark and copyright law . . . "

John Holmstrom, PUNK magazine

SEX & THE KING'S ROAD

01

_The Sex Pistols, wearing Seditionaries clothing, photographed by Peter Gravelle prior to the press conference announcing the group's signing to A&M, March 10, 1977. Sid Vicious (left) had recently joined the group as replacement for original bassist Glen Matlock.

02

_SEX shop regulars and staff show their wares: unidentified customer, Alan Jones, Chrissie Hynde, Vivienne Westwood, Jordan, 1976. Photography by David Dagley.

03

_Jordan standing in front of the entrance to SEX shop, 1976. Photography by Sheila Rock.

04

_Vive Le Rock, SEX muslin shirt, based on an update of an earlier print created by McLaren for a concert by Little Richard at Wembley Stadium in 1972.

05

_Cambridge Rapist, SEX T-shirt based on a notorious contemporary news story about a masked serial rapist who terrorized women in Cambridge, UK, 1975.

| 01 | 02 |
| 03 | 04 | 05 |

Ain't Got a Clue

Punk was not only an attractive conduit for groups just starting out, but also those contemplating a bigger audience through a change in style. The freedoms promised by the "anyone can do it" manifesto were mirrored in the visual styles of accompanying record sleeves, posters, and flyers. Rules were there to be broken, or ignored, and alongside untutored rawness were attempts by professional designers to match the eclecticism of the amateurs and capture the zeitgeist; the overlaps between these seemingly distinct poles were not always easily identified.

Edwin Pouncey, aka *Sounds* cartoonist Savage Pencil, leader of the Art Attacks, drew the cover for the Lurkers' "Freak Show," the Fall's "Lie Dream of a Casino Soul," influential early independent compilation *Streets* (on which the Art Attacks appeared), and later covers for Big Black, Sonic Youth, and myriad others. "Savage Pencil was undoubtedly the main 'punk comix' name in the UK," notes comic expert Roger Sabin. "He developed a ratty style that launched an entire 'punk school,' and his 'Rock 'n' Roll Zoo' strips for *Sounds* were often hilarious takes on the music scene—depicting punk stars as animals doing none-too-bright things. The official line among punks about comics was that they were tainted by hippiedom and therefore naff. To be specific, the underground comics of the 1960s and '70s—by people like Robert Crumb—were seen as a part of the old counterculture (which they were) and therefore had no place once 'year zero' had been declared. As for mainstream comics, the previously cool superhero books were read by hippies, too, so they were no good, and anyway, weren't punks supposed to be bored with the USA? In reality, comics were everywhere. Zinesters especially used them to spice up the content of their lo-fi products, either drawn in a DIY spirit or cut and pasted from elsewhere. Sometimes the exchange was more knowing: *Sniffin' Glue* had a strip by Savage Pencil. Similarly, record sleeves often featured strips and cartoons, and folk like Sid Vicious and Dee Dee Ramone were more than happy to admit their comics habit. But the battle lines were real for some people. In the UK, there was a discussion in the comics zine *Kidz Stuff* about what form 'new wave' comics should take. The most passionate campaigner for a fresh approach was one Andy Dog, aka Andy Johnson (brother of Matt Johnson of The The), who saw the Pistols at the 100 Club, duly stuck a safety pin through his cheek, and was keen to explore a new direction in his own cartooning—which he eventually did with his *DOG Comix*. Pouncey was closer to the old underground than Dog's vision of a new wave cartoonist, and he was much in demand for record sleeves, flyers, and so on, just as the old undergrounders had been in their day."

01

Artist The Art Attacks
Title I Am a Dalek
Format Single, 7-inch
Label Albatross, UK, 1978
_ Design by Savage Pencil.

02

Artist Cyanide
Title S/T
Format LP, 12-inch
Label Pye, UK, 1978
_Design by Design Machine.

03

Artist The Drones
Title Temptations of a
White Collar Worker
Format EP, 7-inch
Label O.H.M.S., UK, 1977

04

_ Croydon Greyhound flyer
(later flyers exhorted
patrons "No Pogoing" in
order to "preserve the
structural integrity of
the ceiling").

05

Artist The Lurkers
Title Shadow
Format Single, 7-inch
Label Beggars Banquet,
UK, 1977
_ The group are depicted
on the sleeve in front
of the Red Cow, a
regular venue on the
London pub rock circuit.

06

Artist The Lurkers
Title Freak Show
Format Single, 7-inch
Label Beggars Banquet,
UK, 1977
_ Design by Savage Pencil.

07

_ Poster promoting the
first two singles by the
Lurkers, released by
Beggars Banquet, 1977.

08

Artist The Cortinas
Title Fascist Dictator
Format Single, 7-inch
Label Step Forward,
UK, 1977
_ The first release on
the Step Forward label.
Design by Jill
Furmanovsky.

09

Artist The Cortinas
Title Defiant Pose
Format Single, 7-inch
Label Step Forward,
UK, 1977
_ Design by Hipgnosis.

10

Artist Nipple Erectors
Title King of the Bop
Format Single, 7-inch
Label Soho, UK, 1978
_ The single features
singer Shane MacGowan,
later of the Pogues.
Design by Phil Smee.

| 01 | 02 | | 05 | 06 | 07 | 04 |
| 03 | | | 08 | 09 | 10 | |

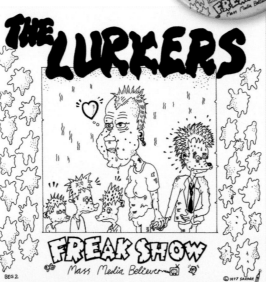

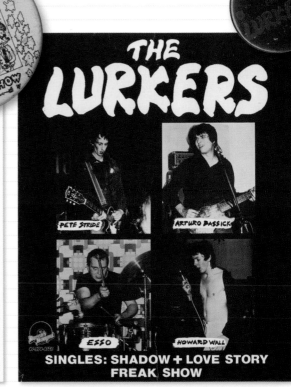

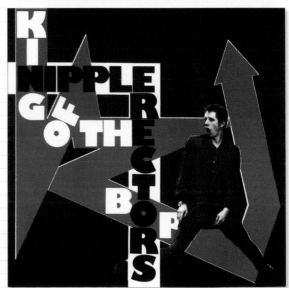

11

_ Poster promoting the single "How Much Longer" by Alternative TV, Deptford Fun City Records, 1977. The debut single release by the group fronted by Mark Perry of *Sniffin' Glue* fanzine offers some critical reflection on the future of the punk movement. Drawing some parallels with the Adverts' "Safety in Numbers" released a few weeks earlier, Perry asks: "How much longer will people wear Nazi armbands and dye their hair, safety pins, spray their clothes, talk about anarchy, fascism and boredom?" Though largely based on the cover of the single, the poster substitutes a documentary war photograph for the television image of the band.

12

_ Poster promoting the debut single by the UK Subs, "C.I.D.," on the City label, 1978.

13

_ Postcard insert from Pork Dukes' debut LP, *Pink Pork*, 1978.

14

Artist The Valves
Title Robot Love
Format Single, 7-inch
Label Zoom, UK, 1977

15

Artist The Radiators from Space
Title Television Screen
Format Single, 7-inch
Label Chiswick, UK, 1977
_ Design by Art on My Sleeve.

16

Artist Pork Dukes
Title Telephone Masturbator
Format Single, 7-inch
Label Wood, UK, 1978
_ Design by Simou Gooley.

17

Artist London
Title No Time
Format EP, 7-inch
Label MCA, UK, 1977

18

Artist The Depressions
Title S/T
Format LP, 12-inch
Label Barn, UK, 1978
_ Polydor art director Jo Mirowski supervised three albums by Sham 69. The Depressions were signed to boutique label Barn by former Animals bassist Chas Chandler, one-time manager of Jimi Hendrix and at that time Slade. The connection came after Mirowski had art-directed Slade's *Whatever Happened To*, the album on which the Wolverhampton glam rockers had attempted to accommodate the new mood of punk. "Because there was no title for the Depressions album," Mirowski recalls, "we just thought we'd do a moody shot." The Brighton band were an example of a group gravitating from pub rock roots; on taking the decision to turn punk they all dyed their hair blonde and adopted hysterical pseudonyms, including "Crowbar," "Hammer," and "Rico the Knife." Ozzy "Crowbar" Garvey took the image makeover one step further, possibly unwisely, by sporting an eye patch.

19

Artist Slaughter & the Dogs
Title Do It Dog Style
Format LP, 12-inch
Label Decca, UK, 1978
_ McGarry's credits would also extend to sleeve designs for Joy Division, Jilted John, and John Cooper Clarke. He later became a two-term president of the National Cartoonists Society. Design by Steve McGarry.

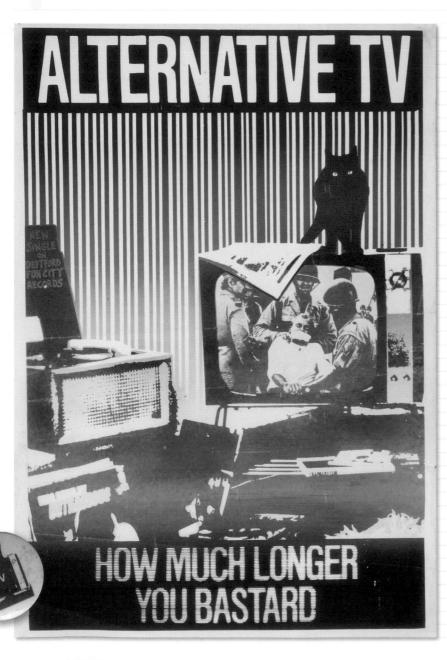

Do It Dog Style

13

14 15 16

11 12 | 17 18 19

"I was good friends with Rob Gretton [Joy Division manager] from school and from following [soccer team Manchester] City, and he volunteered to be Slaughter's fan club manager. He asked me to design a logo for the band and I came up with the Alsatian's head and block lettering. Rob had badges made up from the design. When the band became involved with Tosh Ryan, they asked me to design a poster—so I came up with the Slaughter & the Dogs Will Tear You Apart design, again using the dog's head logo.

Shortly after, Tosh formed Rabid Records to release the debut Slaughter single and they came to me and asked me to design the sleeve, using a photo they already had. In those days, before computers and desktop publishing, you either had type sent out to a typesetting house or you used sheets of rubdown transfer lettering from Letraset. All the type on the sleeve, with the exception of the bloody hand-lettering on the front of the sleeve, was Letraset, using whatever fonts I had to hand. The lettering on the front of the sleeve was a hybrid of Letraset and the blood streaks were drawn on. I was trying to get a sort of punk-gothic feel, which I think I achieved.

I went on to design the *Do It Dog Style* album sleeve when the band signed to Decca, and there's where I came up with another version of the blood lettering that was purely hand drawn, and the rabid terrier. Both those dogs' heads and the bloody lettering designs are still used heavily by the band and fans thirty-five years later, so I must have done OK! It's amazing how often you see those images turn up on promo material, painted on jackets, and, incredibly to me, in tattoos! People contact me on Facebook to share photos of their Slaughter tatts!"—Steve McGarry

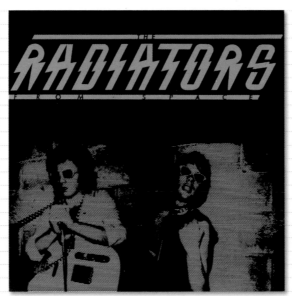

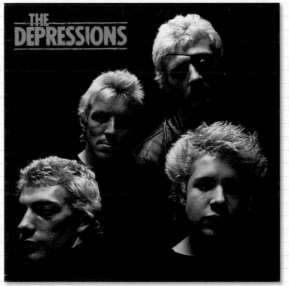

Punk in the Faraway Towns

Punk gigs, and even regular punk venues, sprang up across the UK during 1977 as promoters began to service audiences. Visual styles were varied, though a spontaneous amateurism held sway where more sophisticated tools were unavailable, with a reliance on simple, lo-tech reproduction methods and often hand-rendered and collaged type, with imagery very much keeping stride with the do-it-yourself fanzine boom. In some ways, more sophisticated visual strategies could be counterproductive, with perceived collaboration with commerce raising the specter of "selling out." Amateurism and authenticity went hand in hand, and a suitably rough and ready aesthetic was necessary to articulate the "underground" nature of the event.

01
_ Poster promoting a gig by the Depressions and the Killjoys (featuring Kevin Rowland, later of Dexys Midnight Runners), Derby College of Art, UK, January 27, 1978.

02
_ Hand-rendered poster for a series of punk gigs at Brannigans, Leeds, UK, January 1978.

03
_ Poster for a gig featuring the Fall, the Users, Dolly Mixture, the Transmitters, and the Sinix, Cambridge Corn Exchange, UK, May 26, 1978.

04
_ The Vacants, 8-track cartridge, 1977. If this 8-track cartridge was an unusual artifact, the Vacants were an unusual band. In fact, they were formed by RCA staff (and future Pretenders drummer Martin Chambers) who had been asked by an "exploitation" company if they could release an everyman punk record for the international market. The initial request included specific covers of the Sex Pistols, the Clash, the Stranglers, and the Jam, but that was refused in favor of material by the Seeds and Standells, with which the band were more comfortable. The album was issued with completely different sleeves in Germany, Australia, Italy, France, and Spain, but never Britain. The 8-track cartridge comes from Canada.

_ Hand-rendered poster for a series of punk gigs at the Zip Club, Hull, UK, autumn 1979, including Destroy All Monsters from Detroit. Note the final appearance of Hull punk band the Void, whose guitarist, Sebastian Horsley, would later become a celebrated bohemian artist and author of the memoir *Dandy in the Underworld*.

_ Poster for a gig by Sham 69 at Derby College of Art, UK, November 12, 1977. Colleges around the country promoted gigs by up-and-coming punk groups, and often posters were designed in-house by student design teams—with a resulting tendency not to follow the style guidelines or art direction of the record label or group identity.

07
Artist Blitzkrieg Bop
Title Let's Go
Format Single, 7-inch
Label Lightning, UK, 1977

08
Artist The Jerks
Title Get Your Woofing
Dog off Me
Format Single, 7-inch
Label Underground,
UK, 1977

09
Artist Headache
Title Can't Stand Still
Format Single, 7-inch
Label Lout, UK, 1977

10
Artist Subway Sect
Title Nobody's Scared
Format Single, 7-inch
Label Braik, UK, 1978
_ A group managed by
Clash manager Bernie
Rhodes, Subway Sect
was fronted by the
charismatic Vic Godard.
The group rehearsed

11
Artist The Snivelling
Shits
Title Terminal Stupid
Format Single, 7-inch
Label Ghetto Rockers,
UK, 1977
_ Group fronted by
Sounds and ZigZag
journalist Giovanni

using the Clash's
equipment at their base
in Camden, London, and
were earmarked to follow
on their heels.

Dadomo. The cover
photograph by Brian
Randle shows a female
fan at a Stranglers gig
in Manchester, UK,
originally published
in a punk shock exposé
story in the Sunday
Mirror newspaper,
June 1977.

12
Artist Neon Hearts
Title Regulations
Format Single, 7-inch
Label Neon Heart, UK, 1977

_ Released in 8-inch
square format, designed
to stand out on record
racks in shops and
personal collections.

13
_ Generic poster
designed to promote gigs
by the Suburban Studs,
along with their debut
single, "Questions," July
1977. Specific dates and
venues could be written
into the blank space at
the bottom of the poster.

14
Artist Suburban Studs
Title Questions
Format Single, 7-inch
Label Pogo, UK, 1977
_ The first issue of
this single featured
a saxophone, courtesy
of group member Steve
Harrington, but the band
decided that saxophones
weren't "punk" enough
and rerecorded the
tracks without it.
Harrington left to
front his own group,
Neon Hearts.

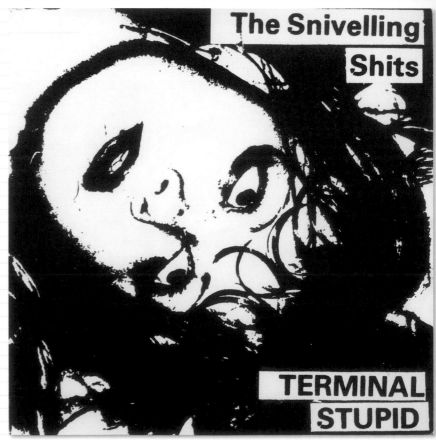

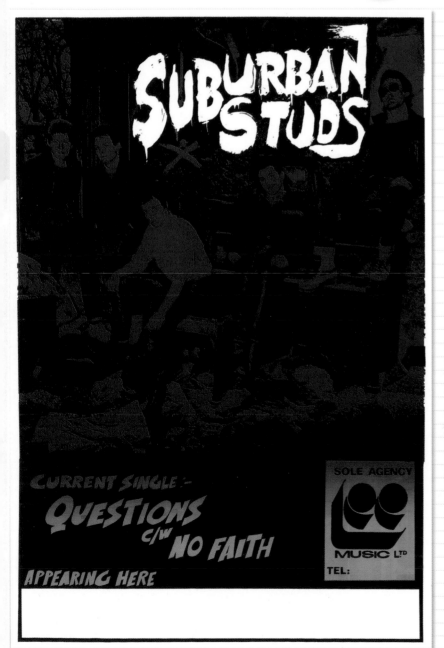

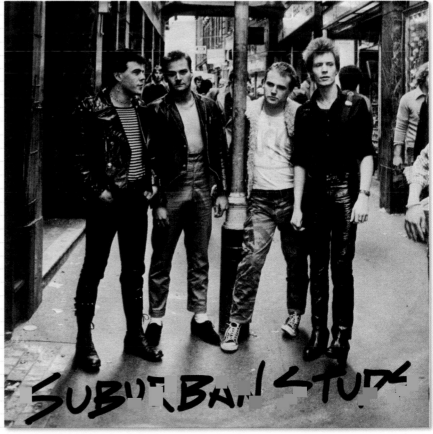

Destroy All Music: The US West Coast

The early Californian punk scene, ignited by interest in the Pistols and particularly the Damned, carried the punk energetic to new creative heights. The Germs, led by Darby Crash, were Los Angeles's most obvious successors to the Sex Pistols, their status as exemplars of the "live fast die young" ethos indelibly cemented via their singer's overdose at the age of twenty-two. But others such as X, the Bags, and the Weirdos also thrived, all of whom would appear on LA's Dangerhouse imprint—for many the greatest American punk label of any era, despite its truncated life span. Possibly the most revolutionary of all the LA first-wave bands, the Screamers, never even cut a record.

San Francisco's early movers were Crime and the Nuns, shortly followed by the Avengers; the latter two bands opened for the Pistols at their final show at the Winterland Ballroom. The city's hub was the Mabuhay Gardens, or Fab Mab, run by benevolent dictator Dirk Dirksen, just as Brendan Mullen's Masque had provided a home for the Hollywood punk set.

Jennifer Egan is the author of the Pulitzer-winning novel *A Visit from the Goon Squad*, part of which is set in San Francisco's punk moment and references both the Mabuhay Gardens, which she frequently visited, and the fortunes of fictional punk band the Flaming Dildos.

"I wasn't a punk, and while I knew a couple of bona fide punks . . . Still, the Mab was a weekend destination for some of us; it was a scene, and we felt exhilarated just being near it, even though we weren't *of* it. Sometimes we 'punked out' a little before going; in my case that meant teasing and spraying my hair and wearing a lot of black eye makeup and really red lipstick. I doubt I fooled anyone. My point of view is that of an outsider, of course, but to me the Mab seemed to do more than provide a venue; it became a kind of center of gravity for the punk scene in San Francisco that may have helped that scene to coalesce. There were other clubs, of course, but the Mab always felt like the primal, dominant club—to such a degree that in later years it became fashionable to reject it."—Jennifer Egan

01
Artist The Rotters
Title Sit on My Face
Stevie Nix
Format Single, 7-inch
Label Rotten, USA, 1979
_ Design by Ron Spencer.

02
Artist The Nuns
Title S/T
Format LP, 12-inch
Label Bomp!, USA, 1980
_ Like many of their peers, the Nuns had little record company support to testify to their impact. Their debut album was issued after the band had folded a year previously, and even then proved contentious when singer Jennifer Miro walked out on the sessions. Design by Diane Zincavage and H. Bosch, photography by Ogilvy.

03
Artist The Weirdos
Title Destroy All Music
Format EP, 7-inch
Label Bomp!, USA, 1977

04
Flyer for the Nuns at the Mabuhay Gardens, San Francisco, August 3, 1978.

05
_ Blank gig poster for the Screamers, Los Angeles, 1977. The Screamers were one of the most popular and distinctive first-generation LA punk bands, although they never released a record. Design by Gary Panter.

06
_ Flyer promoting a gig by the Weirdos at Whiskey a Go Go, Los Angeles, June 20, 1977.

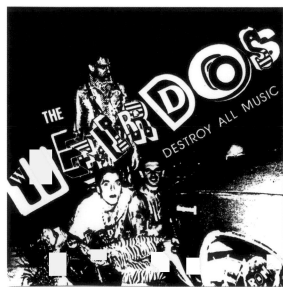

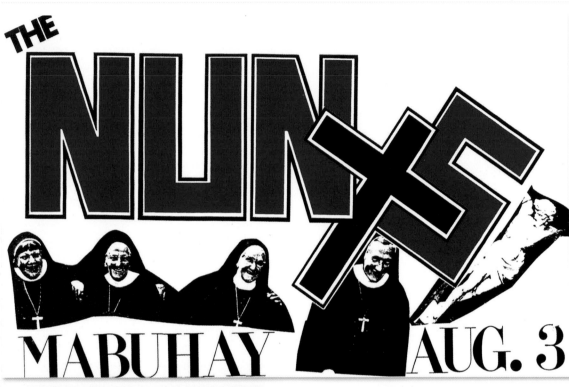

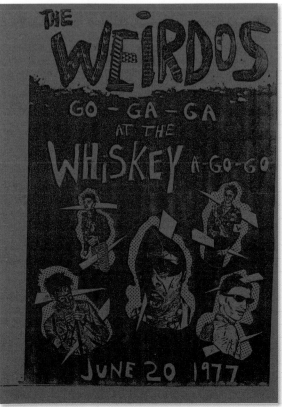

Kill the Hippies: Dangerhouse Records

Of the few recordings that do exist capturing the first-wave American punk scene, Geza X produced or engineered many of them, including the Germs, the Bags, the Deadbeats (he was a member of both the latter bands), the Avengers, and later early recordings by both Black Flag and Dead Kennedys.

"I think Dangerhouse Records were absolutely perfect as far as getting a feel of the flavor of the first wave of Southern California or Hollywood punk if you want to call it that," Geza recalls. "It really sounds like the bands. We didn't have enough money and I didn't know enough about recording to overproduce anything. I was lucky to be asked to do it. I fell into the right situation. I had a little bit of recording experience and I started spreading the word at the Masque that I was a producing—I didn't even know what a producer was, to tell the truth. I had done some engineering and I knew what that was, but I wanted to be a producer. Darby Crash of all people came up to me one day at the Masque and said, 'You're a producer, produce us! Produce the Germs!' I was like, OK, fine. He said *Slash* [magazine] was going to pay for it. I was like, 'Wow, that's so cool,' because at that time *Slash* was our mouthpiece. I was going up and down the coast—I was going to San Francisco and mixing bands at Mabuhay Gardens and other places. I knew the clubs pretty well and I could handle any mixing console within reason. I ended up doing a lot of live stuff. And that's also how people got to know me and when they saw the records word just got around. The whole punk contingent was relatively small. They were all into the same records—the 45s that came from England or New York or LA. I didn't have the opportunity to *really* produce records in any kind of legitimate way back then. I thought maybe the whole scene would explode, but my basic urge was just to document it. So anybody who wanted to work with me got to, back then. And I knew that some of these things would just never get recorded unless I was around. I was the one with the tape recorder and the ability to sort of make something sound right. I was well enough known on the circuit, so I had the opportunity. I was very, very passionate about what I was doing. I was always trying to make a little money, and I didn't make a living, but I made survival and extra pocket money through these records. They'd take me up there, they'd give me a couple of hundred bucks, I'd hang out for a couple of days and sleep on their floor. I was just part of the scene and like the house sound guy for everybody."

01

Artist Various Artists

Title Yes L.A.

Format LP, 12-inch

Label Dangerhouse, USA, 1978

_ Clear vinyl, single-sided album, titles printed on blank side.

02

Artist X

Title Adult Books

Format Single, 7-inch

Label Dangerhouse, USA, 1978

_ Design by Jules Bates.

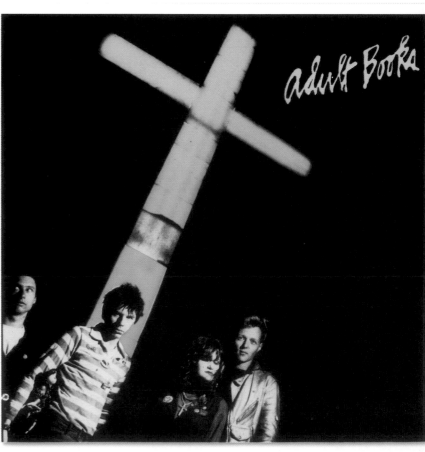

03 04 05
01 02 | 06 07 08

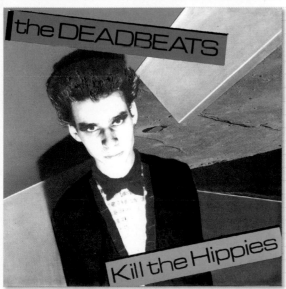

The Great Rock 'n' Roll Swindle

At the culmination of their disastrous US tour in 1978, the Sex Pistols split after a final show at the Winterland Ballroom in San Francisco on January 14th. Plans for a Sex Pistols movie had been germinating for some time under the working title *Who Killed Bambi?*, largely at the behest of Pistols manager Malcolm McLaren and originally with veteran US sexploitation moviemaker Russ Meyer as director. That movie project ground to a halt during 1977, but was resurrected a year later with new director Julien Temple under the title *The Great Rock 'n' Roll Swindle*. McLaren decided to press ahead fully with the project as the group imploded.

Sid Vicious was by this time struggling with drug addiction, and McLaren's decision to bring in guest vocalists to front the group,

including notorious train robber Ronnie Biggs, exiled in Brazil, distanced him further from departing vocalist Johnny Rotten (who had reverted to his birth name John Lydon and was soon to found Public Image Ltd). However, *The Great Rock 'n' Roll Swindle* did lead to the production of some genuinely exciting graphic material by Jamie Reid, who was at this point disenchanted with the whole industry and keen to see how far he could go in publicly registering his disapproval. Following the death of his girlfriend, Nancy Spungen, in suspicious circumstances in October 1978, Vicious was arrested and charged with murder. He died of a drug overdose three months later while on remand, during which time the movie was still being made—a situation that was not without its own possibilities for further exploitation.

01
_ Poster promoting the Sex Pistols single "The Great Rock 'n' Roll Swindle," released by Virgin Records, October 1979. The poster and single cover featured a striking image of a Sex Pistols credit card; American Express took legal action, citing the similarity to their own card design, and the record cover was withdrawn.

02
_ Jamie Reid "Vicious Burger" poster. The concept stemmed from a sick joke following the death of Sid Vicious in February 1979 while

awaiting trial for the murder of his girlfriend, Nancy Spungen. A number of fictitious Sex Pistols "products" were invented as props for the movie—in this case, burgers made from the corpse of the dead bassist.

03
Artist Sex Pistols
Title C'mon Everybody
Format Single, 7-inch
Label Virgin, UK, 1979
_ Design by Jamie Reid.

Artist Sex Pistols
Title Something Else
Format Single, 7-inch
Label Virgin, UK, 1979
_ Featuring a still from an animated section of the movie. Design by Jamie Reid.

05
Artist Sex Pistols
Title Silly Thing
Format Single, 7-inch
Label Virgin, UK, 1979
_ More ironic Sex Pistols product from the cinema kiosk featured in the movie. Other products including Anarkee-ora, Piss Lemonade, a Rotten Bar, and Sid Vicious Action Man were used as movie props and included on the cover of an interview outtakes album, *Some Product: Carri On Sex Pistols*, in August 1979. Design by Jamie Reid.

06
_ Fake album cover for album by "Los Pistoleros del Sexo," used during the "Cambridge Rapist Hotel" sequence in *The Great Rock 'n' Roll Swindle*. Reid simply took the cover from an existing album and added his own title as a witty addition to the props for the movie.

Jamie Reid's graphics, promoting friend Malcolm McLaren's charges the Sex Pistols, and incorporating blackmail lettering, cut 'n' paste, détournement, and the abstracted or inverted slogan, have become the visual signature for much of punk. His corruption of Cecil Beaton's portrait of Queen Elizabeth II, with a safety pin through the sovereign's nose, has been called "the single most iconic image of the punk era." The cover of the Pistols' debut album *Never Mind the Bollocks* prompted a court case that was as historic as it was farcical. Whereas now it is an indelibly familiar image, it's worth recalling that in the years with postwar austerity and a cap-doffing class structure still very much in place, "God Save the Queen" was a genuinely shocking assault on Britain's status quo. Reid will readily admit that his punk-era work, and that image in particular, has overshadowed his prolific work elsewhere. But he hasn't quite escaped its gravitational pull.

As with the music of punk—so too the art. Just as the myth of "year zero" has exploded with the recognition that most key, early participants had a prehistory in pub rock or other musical fields, Reid's graphic designs grew from an extensive apprenticeship in countercultural mischief-making. At the community printing/anarchist organization Suburban Press, based in his native Croydon, South London, he developed not just his mastery of design, screenprinting and rapid response to prop, but also sharpened a political philosophy rooted in social activism. That, in turn, was informed by his involvement in student politics, staging sit-ins at Croydon Art College alongside McLaren, inspired by the Paris student riots of May '68. That has led to his work being broadly associated with the Situationists, a characterization he accepts and nuances. For a start, he points out, there were important influences at work beyond Lettrism, Guy Debord and the Situationist International. "There's a whole esoteric to the northern European and Danish Situationists," he recalls. "The psychogeography coming out of Dadaism is very interesting as well. It was being prepared to have a critique that was as against communism as it was capitalism, which is the same fucking scenario in many ways."

It was in 1975 that Reid received a telegram from McLaren asking him to return from the Isle of Lewis, where he had been living off the grid, to collaborate on a new project that would turn out to be the Sex Pistols. "There was so much spontaneity," Reid recalls. "Me and Malcolm knew each other really well and we just got on and did what we did. It was an attitude. In many ways, I find the Suburban

Press stuff far more resonant now than I do the Pistols. But the thing I did appreciate from the Pistols thing was the attitude."

One of the often overlooked aspects of the supposed "iconic" imagery of the Pistols was how piercingly funny, as well as piercingly subversive, it was. "The thing that's very glossed over is the fact that it was done with a great sense of humor. It's funny for me, because yes, the Pistols were part of it, but I'm more proud of things I've done in music with other people, like the stuff with Afro Celt Sound System, which is a whole different ball game, or Dead Kennedys, or Transvision Vamp, or the Almighty. Some of the artwork I did for them I'm probably more proud of than the stuff I did for the Pistols, but because the Pistols were what they were, that's what gets hung around your neck."

Some of the best of Reid's work accompanied the post-Lydon version of the Pistols, the one that's routinely dismissed despite its mass-market penetration, where their descent into self-parody could not obscure how hilarious the entire music and graphics package had become. "*Flogging a Dead Horse* [the title of the 1980 compilation issued by Virgin after the band had dissolved] and all that? There was a great element of taking the piss with all that. No disrespect to the band itself, but I do think Malcolm was right when he said they should have packed it in and disappeared after "God Save the Queen." In an ideal world, that would have been brilliant! It was downhill from there in many ways."

In fact, the post-Lydon work, as well as being intensely self-mocking, was perceptive about the processes underway in the myth industry. Reid saw that coming "to some extent." But he exploited it brilliantly. "The whole thing of the 'Rotten Bar,' [promotional poster for another cash-in album, 1979's *Some Product*, and also a prop made for *The Great Rock 'n' Roll Swindle*] turning it all into product. All that humor was meant to be—everything should have a sense of humor."

Alongside "God Save the Queen," Reid's most enduring punk-era image is the cover of *Never Mind the Bollocks*, which launched an obscenity case under the UK Indecent Advertisements Act of 1889. It went to court before Richard Branson's lawyer argued successfully that "bollocks" was a legitimate Anglo-Saxon characterization of the priesthood. And again, it's something that comes back to haunt Reid. "I get sick of the people who come up with *Never Mind the Bollocks* sleeves saying, 'Can you sign this?' As I say, it's time to move on. Things are moving on at such speed, we won't recognize this planet in five years' time."

His resistance to being pigeonholed as a punk graphic artist has caveats, however. An exception is where he can see the connection with other musics and cultures. "A great example of that—I was living in Paris in the early '80s—is the whole Algerian Raï thing, Cheb Khaled and all that. They were really influenced by punk, but they didn't want to sound like punk bands. They did it in a way that was totally immersed in Algerian culture, but with a great radical tip to it. Things like that are happening everywhere. I did some work with a Finnish movie director, Aki Kaurismäki who was inspired by punk, making his own movies in Helsinki. I find that more interesting, all those offshoots."

Some aspects related to the afterglow of his association with the Pistols are more rewarding, however—especially those where the process of moving from outsider to cherished, if reluctant, scion of the British establishment can be observed, and give further cause for merriment. "I was up in Edinburgh a couple of months back, because the National Galleries are touring this exhibition of portraits of the Queen [*The Queen: Art and Image*]. Inevitably the "God Save the Queen" poster is in there, so I went up. I got a great reaction. A lot of radical, really interesting artists were giving me a really bad time—'Don't you think it's a bit hypocritical, this being in the National Gallery?' Such a laugh."

Indeed, Reid's work is now regularly exhibited in the UK's museums and galleries, including the Victoria and Albert Museum, whose Jamie Reid collection includes the aforementioned "Rotten Bar." "It always makes me a bit sad, that. When I was squatting in Brixton and I was desperate for money, you know the big Pistols' mural I did? That was actually the wall of the gallery underneath the railway in Brixton, and they took it away. People were actually giving us cigarettes and food and drinks. I needed to sell some work. And Robert Fraser brokered the deal with the National Gallery—he's the one in that famous photo in handcuffs with Mick Jagger. They've got a lot of the work. I like the V&A, as museums go."

So, Situationist, anarchist, or someone who belongs in the broader tradition of British satire? "Half the thing with me and the Suburban Press and the Situationist thing—you'd get all these diatribes and pamphlets, and you almost needed a degree to read them. It was trying to create visuals that said those ideas, which I loved, very simply. And with a whole battering of humor to them as well."

01

_ Dog food can label designed by Reid as promotion for the debut single by Bow Wow Wow, the group put together by Malcolm McLaren following the demise of the Sex Pistols. "C30, C60, C90, Go!" was released by EMI Records in 1980 as the world's first cassette single, celebrating the upsurge in home taping on inexpensive cassette recorders—a fact that led to EMI's refusal to promote the group. The song's deliberately provocative lyrics included the direct call to arms "C30, C60, C90, Go! Off the radio I get a constant flow, Hit it, pause it, record it and play, Turn it, rewind, and rub it away".

02

_ "Out of the dross and into the age of piracy." Collage for the proposed book *Chaos in Cancerland*, designed by Reid around 1981 and initially intended for use by Bow Wow Wow. The reference to piracy refers to campaigns by record companies to prohibit the home taping and sharing of music. The book was later re-titled *Up They Rise* and was eventually published by Faber & Faber in 1987.

03

_ "Peace is Tough" poster using a détourned picture of famous Hollywood movie star John Wayne. The image was originally designed as the jacket for Greil Marcus's book of writings on punk,

In the Fascist Bathroom. The addition of lipstick to Wayne's photograph is a reference to Marcus's earlier book, *Lipstick Traces*.

04

_ Poster designed by Reid to promote the debut single by Dead Kennedys, "California Über Alles." Though the imagery mixes *Triumph of the Will* with a reminder of Altamont thuggery, Reid actualy used a photograph from the Reading Festival.

05

_ Poster questioning the marketing of a punk "uniform" comprising a leather jacket, army jeans, and bovver boots.

03

FISH 'N' HIPS

NEW WAVE & POST-PUNK

The nouvelle vague has in various forms been applied to both pre-punk performers and by proxy to an array of subsequent musical trends, starting with the New Romantics and continuing through such genre cul-de-sacs as the New Wave of the New Wave. It is an apposite and alluring prefix for marketeers to imbue a product with contemporary zeal, especially in industries that display an unhealthy preoccupation with being "now." Within the punk context, however, it has served a multitude of purposes. New wave provided a blanket generic with which to bracket what were, in terms of both New York and London traditions, diverse streams of music whose aesthetic kinship could be musical, sartorial, or presentational. (Or, in some cases, none of the above—though they could still apparently be included for not fitting in with their peers in a particularly interesting way.) For the industry, it was indeed a marketing category and, in some cases, a process of self-definition for artists who were not prepared to fence-sit.

Contemporaneously, things were much less clear. To some audiences, Elvis Costello's "(I Don't Want To Go To) Chelsea" was a legitimate punk artifact; so too were the wares of Ian Dury & the Blockheads (profanity always helps) or the Boomtown Rats, despite the funny smell. Retrospectively we can see the join of course, and accept that the broader-brush definition of new wave is perhaps more appropriate, but it was not ever thus. And we can also note the manner in which punk's critical stock has risen over time. It was common at one point to posit that Costello and Dury were substantive artists who had "escaped punk's ghetto" and gained a measure of credibility in the process—whereas now the new wave genre has lost both gravitational pull and a degree of critical respectability.

A similar battle for "authenticity" played out in the visual representations of new wave material. While early punk displayed a remarkably broad range of graphic and stylistic approaches, the simple process of financial investment, increasing maturity and public awareness of the genre, higher production values, mass production, and the adoption of industry standard marketing and advertising techniques cast a sheen over the rough edges left on display in more low-key artists and labels. In short, the shift to a mass market meant the adoption of mass-market aesthetics. After all, a production run of perhaps a few hundred records or posters could just about be handled by hard work and largely hands-on creative efforts, but a run of several thousand copies required the machinery of mass manufacturing.

In-house graphic design and production teams at the major labels used industry standard techniques, materials, and processes. Content was less of a driving force and marketing, styling, and visual identities were often handled by professionals outside of the bands and their immediate circle of contacts. Standard packaging and graphic representation (with a bit of a twist to indicate modernity) abounded. This isn't to say that the music, and its visual presentation, was not valid or interesting: the combination of punk's vital energy and untethered experimentalism with the greater artistic freedom (and investment) brought about by increasing commercial success ensured that genuinely new musical and visual practices could take root.

Such license to produce visual material with greater budgets and higher production values allowed key designers such as Barney Bubbles and Chris Morton at Stiff Records and Malcolm Garrett's Arbitary Images (and various subsequent pseudonyms) to play with style and form—while labels such as Chrysalis, Gem, and Virgin picked up on the design and marketing power of the independents. These and others similarly replicated the independent labels' opportunism in tapping into the new collectors' market set in motion by the popularity of the new wave. Colored vinyl, shaped discs, limited editions, collectible sets, alternative formats, free gifts—all became crucial weapons in the battle for the buyer's heart, mind, and wallet.

This Is Not a Love Song

While punk was gathering pace—or dying an early death, depending on your critical position—and new wave was hitting the charts and pumping some life into a previously moribund music industry, music critics and journalists struggled to find an alternative term for another strand of the story. These groups operated beyond what was by now seen as "traditional" punk (how brief that flame had burned in the UK—within eighteen months of the summer of '76, many critics were banging the last nail in punk's coffin), but were still too new, too left-field, too edgy, or simply too uncommercial to sit comfortably under the new wave umbrella. "Post-punk" groups drew upon the creative spirit of the early years together with the eclecticism of the DIY punk scene, while reaching out to other genres and styles for creative influence.

Funk, jazz, reggae, dub, and even the previously off-limits blues and disco genres were raided and fused with punk attitude and style—or perhaps simply reinterpreted with a combination of naïveté and musical ineptitude

to result in something new and unusual that was struggling for an identity, and a name. The catchall post-punk term, then, was an attempt to draw a line around regional punk interpretations, hybrid aesthetic experiments, increasingly successful DIY artists, and the difficult to define avant-garde. It also cast a critical shadow of "authenticity" over that elite set, segregating them from the muddy past of punk's old guard and the contemporary commercial mainstream of the new wave.

British designers such as Malcolm Garrett (Buzzcocks, Magazine, the Members, the Yachts, 999) and Peter Saville (Factory Records, Joy Division, New Order) were at the forefront of a new post-punk visual aesthetic that reflected the stylistic changes of the music. Saville helped shape a visual identity for Factory Records that was both modern and classically cool at the same time, forging a crossover visual style that impacted on fashion, magazine, branding, and identity design throughout the 1980s.

Post-punk styles also tapped into the spirit and experimentalism of the DIY and independent scene, and a new graphic minimalism was embraced by groups such as Public Image Ltd, Wire, XTC, and Gang of Four, and by labels including Factory, Malicious Damage, and Radar Records. Designers helping to shape a new graphic language included Bob Last (Fast Product), Mike Coles (Killing Joke and Malicious Damage), Vaughan Oliver (4AD), and Alex McDowell and Neville Brody at Rocking Russian.

> **"One group that was hugely influential, not just on myself but on the wider punk and post-punk aesthetic in general, was Throbbing Gristle. They operated in parallel to the Sex Pistols, and there are many crossovers and comparisons to be drawn between them. Their first album, *Second Annual Report*, was released in 1978 on their own label, Industrial Records. With limited budget they couldn't afford to print a cover, so stuck a simple small sticker on the blank white card sleeve from the pressing plant, throwing the whole idea of a "punk" graphic image, and of the album cover itself, up in the air. Throbbing Gristle group member and designer Peter Christopherson was working with the well-known sleeve design company Hipgnosis, so he was well versed in the language of the music industry. He had some really powerful ideas about exploring hidden subversion, and the way that seemingly innocuous images could be much, much darker on closer inspection!"**

Malcolm Garrett, Assorted Images design studio

REVOLT INTO STYLE

01

Artist The Rezillos
Title Top Of The Pops
Format Single, Cassette
Label Sire, UK, 1981

02

_ Portrait of the Jam by
Peter Gravelle for the
All Mod Cons album cover,
released by Polydor in
October 1978.

03

_ Poster promoting the
compilation album *New
Wave*, released by Vertigo
Records in 1977. The
album featured a
disparate range of
artists patched together
from the Sire Records
catalog, including a few
from the hopelessly late-
to-the-party Mercury/
Vertigo roster who still
weren't really punk *or*
"new wave." Photography
by Peter Gravelle,
design by Sue Dubois
and Dennis Walden.

04

_ John Lydon and
Jeannette Lee of Public
Image Ltd. Photography
by Peter Gravelle.

05

_ Poster for the Heatwave
Festival, Toronto, Canada,
August 23, 1980. The
Clash were originally
booked to appear, but
canceled prior to the
actual event.

01
02 03
04 05

Be Stiff

Stiff Records was originally established by Dave Robinson and Andrew Jakeman (who adopted the pseudonym Jake Riviera), with a loan from Dr. Feelgood frontman Lee Brilleaux in 1976, to tap into the pub rock and nascent punk market. The label adopted a witty and ironic series of references to the music industry and its own location within it; Stiff catchphrases included the classic, "if it ain't Stiff, it ain't worth a fuck." Following major success with early signings Nick Lowe, the Damned, and Elvis Costello, the label found itself at the heart of the UK new wave. Innovative and humorous marketing scams, frequently including limited-edition colored vinyl, free gifts, and promotional items, found strong support among audiences and

critics. In-house designers Chris Morton and Barney Bubbles employed similarly audacious design strategies for the graphic identity of the label. Bubbles's detailed typographic games reached right down to the center labels, catalog numbers, and credits on Stiff record releases—strategies he also employed on his work for Radar Records, a new label set up by Andrew Lauder. Radar took over contracts for several Stiff artists including Lowe and Costello when their manager, Riviera, left Stiff in 1978 and took them with him.

Andy Murray, Stiff Records, on the Be Stiff tour: "They'd done the first Stiff tour, Live Stiffs, which finished at the Lyceum. Then Jake Riviera left for Radar, and you're into

the second generation of Stiff, which was just Dave Robinson running it. I had to book the trains through British Rail, have the meetings, and also present it to the trade press. And then I did all the regional press. Every morning I'd get up at seven and get on a train, get off at the station wherever the tour was going by, go round the town, speak to the retailers, go back to the station, lead them off the train, make sure they'd go to the soundcheck—they'd still have a bus to go to the soundcheck and gig. I'd whip up a bit of interest, talk to local dealers, give them some free records, go to bed, get up the next day, do it all over again. I'd see the artists occasionally, and they'd say, 'Why are you here?' I'd go, 'Yeah, I'm here every day.'"

01
_ Live Stiffs tour poster, October 1977. Stiff released a promotional LP for the tour containing cover versions of Devo's "Be Stiff," performed by each of the artists: Lene Lovich, Mickey Jupp, Wreckless Eric, Jona Lewie, and Rachel Sweet (with hilarious, additional lyrics by Devo's fellow Akron-ites). For the tour itself, Lovich was backed by Fingerprintz and Sweet by the Undertones. Photography Chris Gabrin, design by Chris Morton.

02
_ Poster announcing the Be Stiff tour, 1978. In keeping with their outlandish marketing scams, Stiff decided to send the whole tour party from venue to venue by train. The poster emulates UK train travel posters of the 1950s. Photography by Chris Gabrin.

03
_ Be Stiff Route 78 tour program. Following the UK leg of the tour by train, the party traveled to the US. The tour program plays on the iconography of America's Route 66, together with conventions taken from US road signage.

04
Artist Wreckless Eric
Title Whole Wide World
Format Single, 7-inch
Label Stiff, UK, 1977
_ Design by Barney Bubbles.

05
Artist Wreckless Eric
Title Reconnez Cherie
Format Single, 7-inch
Label Stiff, UK, 1978
_ Design by Barney Bubbles.

06
Artist Nick Lowe
Title I Love the Sound Of Breaking Glass
Format Single, 7-inch
Label Radar, UK, 1978

03
04
01 02 | 05 06

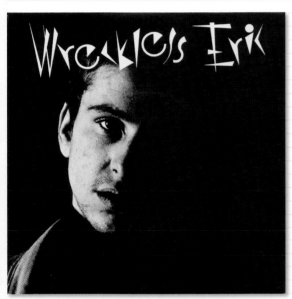

This Year's Model

Early competitors as Stiff's biggest draw, Elvis Costello and Ian Dury were both heavily promoted through a variety of gimmicks and publicity stunts. On the first national Live Stiffs outing, all groups on the itinerary were scheduled to take turns headlining each night, but as the tour continued it became something of a showdown between Costello and Dury. Both artists were defined as much by their idiosyncrasies and un-rock-star-like attitudes as by their musical merit: Costello's horn-rimmed Buddy Holly spectacles and Dury's street urchin wardrobe provided a rich visual resource for Barney Bubbles's playful graphic approach. Early commercial and critical success for both artists saw Stiff invest heavily in promoting for their follow-up records and tours, pushing the marketing envelope with a variety of tactics. When Costello left for Radar Records in 1978, Bubbles continued to work with him as well as Dury, who remained the premier attraction at Stiff. When Dury enlisted an official backing band, the Blockheads, Bubbles created an iconic typographic logo for the group, apparently drawing inspiration from the graphic identity of the Left Book Club, a political publishing house that operated in the UK between 1936–48.

"When it came to the record label, we found between Jake [Riviera] and I we had pretty much all the talents to make it work, from the advertising through to the physical production of the vinyl. We had a lot of music that was organically produced by the bands themselves, we had Nick Lowe to do it in the studio, and Jake and I were, I think, quite talented promotion men. And we put it in picture bags because we were keen on artwork—we had Barney Bubbles, probably one of the great UK graphic artists. So we had great art."

Dave Robinson, Stiff Records

01
_ Stiff Records promotional poster for Elvis Costello, October 1977. Design by Barney Bubbles, photography by Chris Gabrin.

02
_ Elvis Costello *Get Happy!!* promotional poster, February 1980. Design by Barney Bubbles.

03
_ Foldout inside cover for Elvis Costello's *Armed Forces* album, January 1979. Designed by Barney Bubbles in collaboration with Bazooka, French illustrators and frequent collaborators of Skydog's Marc Zermati.

04/05
_ The Blockheads logo, first used on Dury's "What A Waste" single in April 1978, and the logo of the Left Book Club. Design by Barney Bubbles.

06
Artist Ian Dury & the Blockheads Title Do It Yourself Format LP, 12-inch Label Stiff, UK, 1979
_ The second album by Ian Dury & the Blockheads, *Do It Yourself* was issued in over thirty sleeve variations, each based on a different Crown Wallpaper design. Design by Barney Bubbles.

07
_ *Do It Yourself* promotional poster, May 1979. Design by Barney Bubbles.

08
_ Promotional poster for Ian Dury's debut album, *New Boots and Panties!!*, September 1977. Design by Barney Bubbles, photography by Chris Gabrin.

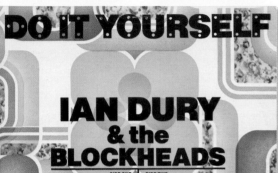

The Modern World: The Rise of UK New Wave

While wrangling continued over definitions of terms, some artists thrust into the limelight through punk's initial explosion—but lacking punk "credibility"—got on with the task of developing things their own way. Chief among those were the Jam, from Woking, Surrey, in the UK, whose back-to-basics reappraisal of 1960s rhythm & blues set the scene for the upcoming mod revival. The Clash may have mocked their suits, but the Jam's visual identity was soon mirrored by others under the new wave umbrella. Many early punk record sleeves had tended to avoid picturing the group at all, but labels and designers working within the new wave understood the value of representing the performer, and visual recognition in the eyes of their audience. Meanwhile, what would retrospectively be termed "pop punk" was achieving substantial commercial success across the UK, with groups such as the Undertones, Skids and the Rezillos making inroads into the charts.

The Jam: Carnaby Street

The Jam were famously parodied for their attire in "(White Man) In Hammersmith Palais" by the Clash: "In your Burton suits, you think it's funny, turning rebellion into money." Yet those same suits also provided a ready sartorial distinction with the distressed (but heavily designed) look modeled by the Clash. The Jam's visual stamp encompassed Paul Weller's fixation with Carnaby Street and the mod era, retained despite his initial enthusiasm for the possibilities of punk. Their wardrobe also announced a class distinction: Burton suits occupied an elevated space in style-conscious working-class circles at the time.

"Looking at some of those old photographs," says drummer Rick Buckler, "the trousers were like tights, they were very snug. And the suits just used to be wringing wet after a gig. They could walk out of the venue on their own. But that's how we felt more comfortable."

"I did a number of punk and new wave bands whilst art director at Polydor and then with my own studio," recalls Bill Smith. "The Jam were the first punk band to be signed to Polydor by Chris Parry, although they were really on the cusp of new wave. I wanted to get punk elements into the first sleeve for *In the City*, such as the graffiti logo and the feeling of a train station toilet with them 'crashed out' against the wall, and as if they left their mark on the back cover. I wanted to get a black-and-white feel to give it a news story look, with that strong graphic approach. Paul's influences were early mod bands like Small Faces and the Who and the Englishness of the Kinks. I tried to bring this into their sleeves with the first two or three covers. The arrows on Paul's jumper are a take on a Townshend look in a postmodern setting. All the sleeves were reinforcements of their image and outlook."

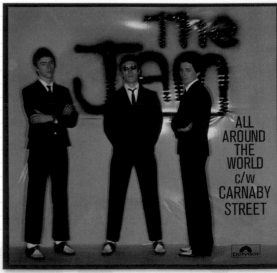

01

Artist The Jam
Title This Is the Modern World
Format Single, 7-inch
Label Polydor, UK, 1977
_ Photography by Martyn Goddard, design by Bill Smith.

02

Artist The Jam
Title In the City
Format Single, 7-inch
Label Polydor, UK, 1977
_ Photography by Martyn Goddard, design by Bill Smith.

03

Artist The Jam
Title All Around the World
Format Single, 7-inch
Label Polydor, UK, 1977
_ Design by Bill Smith.

04

Artist The Police
Title Fall Out
Format Single, 7-inch
Label Illegal, UK, 1977
_ Before they dyed their hair . . . the debut of the Illegal label, set up by drummer Stewart Copeland's brother, Miles (IL-001).

05

Artist Pretenders
Title S/T
Format LP, 12-inch
Label Real, UK, 1979
_ Photography by Chalkie Davies.

06

Artist Joe Jackson
Title I'm the Man
Format LP, 7-inch box set
Label A&M, UK, 1979
_ An unusual marketing gimmick, this box set featured all the tracks from Jackson's *I'm the Man* album on five separate 7-inch singles, with sleeves that can be placed next to each other to form a large image of the cover portrait.

07

Artist Lene Lovich
Title Stateless
Format LP, 12-inch
Label Stiff, UK, 1978
_ Photography by Brian Griffin, design by Barney Bubbles.

08

_ Squeeze "Cool for Cats" promotional poster, March 1979.

01	02		04	05
	03	|	06	07	08

09

Artist The Boomtown Rats
Title Looking After No. 1
Format Single, 7-inch
Label Ensign, UK, 1977

10

Artist Tom Robinson Band
Title 2-4-6-8 Motorway
Format Single, 7-inch
Label EMI, UK, 1977
_ TRB's logo was designed by Roger Huddle of Rock Against Racism in early 1978: "The first time Tom did work with RAR was when we did a benefit gig for Icebreaker, a gay switchboard in Islington. On the gig poster I used a clenched fist I had found on a publication from the Black Panthers in the US. I loved the graphic line and simplicity of this traditional icon for struggle. I worked in the printshop of the SWP [Socialist Workers' Party] in Bethnal Green, and Tom would come in now and again when we were working on RAR's Temporary Hoarding newssheet. He was in a real state about getting some graphics for the first release by the band. I took the fist image and, using a copper stencil, I drew the Tom Robinson Band name in a circle around the fist." The image was widely appropriated in contemporaneous graffiti, perhaps unsurprisingly since the original LP version of Power in The Darkness came with a cardboard stencil of the logo and the possibly disingenuous legend, "This stencil is not meant for spraying on public property."

11

Artist Penetration
Title Moving Targets
Format LP, 12-inch
Label Virgin, UK, 1978
_ Design by Russell Mills/Robert Mason.

12

Artist The Rezillos
Title Top of the Pops
Format Single, 7-inch
Label Sire, UK, 1978

13

Artist The Undertones
Title Here Comes the Summer
Format Single, 7-inch
Label Sire, UK, 1979
_ The Undertones' fourth single included an Irish picture postcard.

14

Artist The Rods
Title Do Anything You Wanna Do
Format Single, 7-inch
Label Island, UK, 1977

15

_ Rezillos "picture cards," insert with the group's debut Can't Stand the Rezillos album, July 1978.

16

Artist Skids
Title Days in Europa
Format LP, 12-inch
Label Virgin, UK, 1979
_ The controversial "Teutonic" cover image for this album caused it to be withdrawn and reissued with completely new artwork. Illustration by Mick Brownfield, sleeve design by Pearce Marchbank.

17

Artist Skids
Title Charade
Format Single, 7-inch
Label Virgin, UK, 1979
_ "Charade" featured a poker scene painted by artist Jill Mumford, who would work with the band throughout their career and also collaborate with the Banshees, XTC, Mark Stewart, and others. "It was my idea to use that image of Steve McQueen from Cincinatti Kid," she recalls. "I used to work closely with Richard [Jobson]. It was purpose-painted by me for the song—I still have that picture."

18

_ Skids Scared To Dance poster, based on an illustration by Russell Mills.

				15
09	10	11		16
12	13	14		17	18

-YING SAUCER ATT

BLAH BLAH BLAH BLAH BLAH

NO

SKIDS

SCARED TO DANCE

SKIDS: Days in Europa

SKIDS CHARADE

Etymological payback's a bitch. We know that the word "punk" was used extensively by Shakespeare, and had been bandied about to indicate prison "receivers" before Misters Rotten or McLaren got their grubby hands on it. We might be equally conversant with how the term "new wave" resonates through the French avant-garde and European film traditions. Yet the two terms embrace, depart, and interchange throughout the story, and can only be reconciled within both historical and geographical contexts.

Conventional wisdom holds that new wave was a marketing aggregate which helped the music industry pacify its enfant terrible, punk. This was all supposed to have happened, neatly enough, in 1977, and clear dividing lines ensued, readily observable in graphical and musical content. The truth is far more elusive. We know, for example, that Malcolm McLaren had intended to use the term new wave for his movement but was dissuaded from doing so by wiser counsel. We also know that the term punk was applied to a generation of New York musicians from much earlier in the piece. These ranged from Blondie, for many the definitive new wave band, to Television, led by a man who took his name from a French symbolist poet. Both groups bore little musical or presentational comparison to the nascent London set. We can begin with accepting therefore that the transatlantic constructs of what "punk" was were radically divergent from the outset. And the same is true of new wave.

"Please don't use the term new wave," Damian O'Neill of the Undertones once stated to an author who had mistakenly applied the phrase. "We were punk." The group still claimed brotherhood with that tradition when they were peddling the Northern Irish city of Derry's take on Motown. But that rather illustrates the inadequacies of the category in terms of musical description. For artists like the Undertones, new wave was a brand to be suspicious of, lacking in authenticity and complicit with major label conceits.

(It is interesting to note, for example, that "new wave" was not a term that generally lent itself adjectivally to DIY or independent releases.)

Punk, in shorthand, represented an "attitude." That attitude, however, could present a threat to the parent company image if it wasn't handled correctly and the wilder elements of the new artistic progenies brought to heel. EMI and A&M both had their fingers burned by the Sex Pistols before the summer of 1977, and other major labels were taking note: while the new movement was gaining a huge amount of media and public attention (always a good thing in an industry obsessed with reinventing itself on a regular basis), the grubbier elements and negative associations of the product needed to be kept at arm's length from the brand image of the corporation. A sense of edginess and danger had been a staple element in the marketing mission of rock 'n' roll since its inception—but now there was a feeling that some parental control was necessary to ensure the security and future of the family.

Other artists self-elected the term new wave to distance themselves from some of punk's more disagreeable aspects, notably gobbing. For the more career-minded bands, punk's short shelf life and the lack of avenues for advancement that the genre was perceived to offer within the music industry—where doors were quickly being closed by nervous executives desperate for a return to the safe confines of AOR (Album-Oriented Rock) and easier listening—made new wave a preferable choice.

The greatest schism was in the US, where the battle lines became more entrenched. A fascinating example here came courtesy of the Knack, a featherweight pop-rock band whose "new wave" affectations backed by huge industry spending led to chart-topping albums and the irksome "My Sharona." In the eyes of detractors, they represented a betrayal of the punk spirit and a neutering of its message—particularly when creative and

adventurous punk scenes were emerging in several cities across the US. San Francisco conceptual artist Hugh Brown, who had designed the Clash's second album cover (itself a record that prompted a rich dialogue about punk authenticity) headed a campaign that inverted Capitol's "Get the Knack" slogan. His "Knuke the Knack Sack" incorporated pins and photographs, alongside T-shirts bearing the Knuke the Knack legend, that would be worn by members of Squeeze, Patti Smith Group, and others.

Another San Francisco resident, Jello Biafra, took the premise one step further. Asked to attend the *BAM* Awards in March 1980, as a token punk band to prove the magazine's hip credentials, Dead Kennedys took to the stage in white shirts emblazoned with a prominent "S." Expected to play their "hit" "California Über Alles," they abruptly halted, Biafra's stage oratory crystallizing the punk community's objections to its mealy mouthed cousin, new wave. They then proceeded to play a pastiche of "My Sharona" with the words changed to "My Payola" and unveiled skinny black ties (a fashion garment synonymous with the Knack, and new wave generally). When unfurled, these conjoined with the "S" on their shirts to form a dollar sign.

Punk and new wave may have ended up with a messy divorce, but for some years it was a shared journey, with many artists flitting between or sharing affiliations with both. Like its hipper cousin post-punk, new wave has been retrofitted to suit a neat and precise historical framework, placing it even more firmly within the corporate stereotype that it initially set out to oppose.

NEW WAVE VS PUNK: ALL MOD CONS

01

Artist Blondie
Title Parallel Lines
Format LP, 12-inch
Label Chrysalis, UK, 1978
_ Design by Ramey
Communications.

....

02

Artist The Knack
Title Get the Knack
Format LP, 12-inch
Label Capitol, USA, 1979

....

03

_ Patti Smith Group
drummer Jay Dee
Daughtery wearing a
Knuke the Knack T-shirt,
1979. Photography by
Hugh Brown.

04

Artist The Photos
Title S/T
Format LP, 12-inch
Label CBS, UK, 1980
_ Much to the band's
chagrin, the Photos
were marketed by CBS
as the UK's answer to
Blondie, as this cover
illustrates. As Satan's
Rats, they had released
three widely celebrated
punk singles before the
addition of Wendy Wu
on vocals. Though the
production on the main
LP was pure commercial
new wave, the band's
unvarnished eight-song
demo was included as a

bonus LP, *The Blackmail
Tapes*. The album was
later engulfed in
controversy over
chart-fixing due to the
promotional "camera"
given away to reps.
Design by Keith Breeden/
Malcolm Garrett.

....

05

_ Dead Kennedys in
suitable award ceremony
attire, March 1980.

01 02 03
04 05

Parallel Lines: International New Wave

The success of punk and new wave in the UK was mirrored in the United States—though the larger and more conservative US music industry proved harder to break. During 1977, new wave received little radio airplay, and the charts remained dominated by arena rock and disco. However, overseas success for some homegrown acts proved hard to ignore: early proponents of the New York CBGB scene received warm welcomes on European tours, and their stars began to rise at home partly as a result. Blondie and Talking Heads led the field, and as their music matured and crossed over with more "acceptable" genres, the record companies began to sit up and take notice. Though still a little too left-field for mass commercial acceptance, these groups helped create the foundation for a new wave marketplace.

The Cars began a steady journey toward global superstardom with their self-titled debut album in May 1978, but it was Los Angeles group the Knack and producer Mike Chapman who seemed to hit the right formula for the US market with their debut album and single

"My Sharona," topping the Billboard charts in the summer of 1978. After two albums developing their sound but lacking crossover appeal, Blondie married their pop sheen to disco beats—again with Mike Chapman at the helm—to create the radio-friendly breakthrough album *Parallel Lines* in September 1978.

These new wave pop crossovers were not the only developments arising from the punk milieu; they were soon followed by the extraordinary, and unexpected, rise of Devo, a seriously weird outfit from Akron, Ohio. Formulating their highly theatrical stage shows and experimental electronic sound since 1973, the group gained a positive UK reception in the wake of punk, with early records on their own Booji Boy imprint co-released with Stiff Records. Devo subsequently signed to Virgin in the UK and Warner Bros. in the US, but it wasn't until the video for the 1980 single "Whip It" found regular circulation on the newly created MTV television channel that they finally achieved a commercial breakthrough.

01
Artist The Knack
Title My Sharona
Format Single, 7-inch
Label Capitol, Italy, 1979
_ Italian issue of the Knack's global powerpop hit.

02
Artist Nina Hagen Band
Title African Reggae
Format Single, 7-inch
Label CBS, Netherlands, 1979

03
Artist Blondie
Title Picture This
Format Single, 7-inch
Label Chrysalis, UK, 1978

04
Artist Devo
Title Jocko Homo
Format Single, 7-inch
Label Stiff, UK, 1978

05
Artist Devo
Title Satisfaction
Format Single, 7-inch
Label Stiff, UK, 1978

06
Artist Devo
Title Be Stiff
Format Single, 7-inch
Label Stiff, UK, 1978

07
Artist Talking Heads
Title Psycho Killer
Format EP, 12-inch
Label Sire, UK, 1977
_ Design by David Byrne.

08
Artist Talking Heads
Title Pulled Up
Format Single, 7-inch
Label Sire, UK, 1978
_ Design by David Byrne.

09
Artist Talking Heads
Title Take Me to the
River
Format EP, double 7-inch
Label Sire, UK, 1978
_Design by David Byrne.

10
_ Poster promoting debut album by Blondie, on Private Stock Records, USA, 1977. So much of the attention the group received was centered on singer Debbie Harry —a situation hardly contradicted by their record label's marketing campaigns—that the 1978 tour carried the slogan, "Blondie is a group!" Photography by Shig Ikeda.

11
_ *Talking Heads:* 77 album poster, October 1977. The typographic simplicity of the album cover is repeated on the poster, though with a series of playful variations of cropping and framing to give the overall design a dynamic impact. The angular layout also dramatizes the choice of italicized type on the original cover. Designed by David Byrne and Jerry Harrison, photography by Mick Rock.

BLONDIE
IS A
GROUP!

BLONDIE
NEW ALBUM NOW AVAILABLE ON RECORD & TAPE
also NEW SINGLE "IN THE FLESH"/"X OFFENDER"

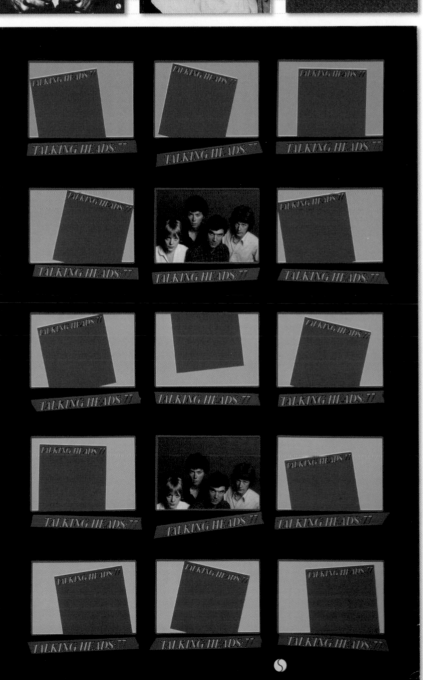

Once punk and new wave music had become broadly accepted and could be marketed by the major labels, chart entries became far more familiar during 1978 and 1979. The major labels were quick to recognize the business potential for a punk collector's market, following the success of independents such as Stiff who had started to produce "alternative" versions and formats of their new releases. Stiff saw the possibilities for limited-edition colored vinyl releases, picture sleeves, and alternative formats such as 10-inch albums and oddly shaped discs—reflected in good sales in the first few weeks following a release date and hence vital chart returns. They were soon followed by other independents such as Small Wonder, Chiswick, and Beggars Banquet. Virgin also offered limited-edition colored vinyl versions of singles by the likes of X-Ray Spex, the Members, and Skids, while US-based major label A&M tapped into the trend with releases by the Dickies, the Tubes, Squeeze, and the Police.

The natural conclusion of this marketing initiative saw the second pressing of the Lurkers' debut "Free Admission Single," issued in red, white, and blue vinyl versions. The fourth single by Generation X, "King Rocker," featured four different sleeves, each featuring an individual member of the band, and corresponding colored vinyls. The sleeve for the second single by Skids, "Sweet Suburbia," even included a sticker declaring, "This white vinyl single has a WEIRD GIMMICK. You'll like it!" The UK Subs managed to achieve a surprising run of single and album chart successes from 1979 to 1981, and their early singles and albums adopted a range of brightly colored vinyls. It was a tactic that helped propel the group into the charts in the first week of each release, as fans rushed to secure the first edition before it reverted to standard issue black—though there were cases where sales were actually insufficient to merit further pressings, leading to the conundrum whereby the "standard" issue became ultimately more collectible.

Notably, some colored vinyl releases did reflect a deeper intent. The green vinyl edition of the Undertones' "Jimmy Jimmy" integrated the disc itself with the transparent, silk-screened sleeve, and

"For 'The Sound Of The Suburbs', I took inspiration from the lyrics, which are about the tedium of ordinary homelife, and created a die-cut on the front of a television screen, through which distorted images of suburbia could be seen, printed on the sleeve inner. The single itself was pressed on totally clear vinyl—with no label, just the song titles etched into the vinyl—so the image could be seen through the record, thus metaphorically offering a snapshot of the suburban world behind it. In this way it wasn't simply using coloured vinyl just as a gimmick, it played a more serious role in the commentary."

— Malcolm Garrett, Assorted Images design studio

at least there was a conceptual relationship between the color of the vinyl and the song lyric on X-Ray Spex's "The Day the World Turned Day-Glo." Malcolm Garrett's sleeve design for the Members' "The Sound of the Suburbs" even integrated the color of the disc with the sleeve design and concept of the song, though such considerations were unusual.

Although the marketing strategies based on limited editions and colored vinyl proved initially very successful, the inherent conflict with what could be seen as punk ideology did lead to criticism from both punk bands and audiences. Stiff Little Fingers even insisted on a clause in their contract with Chrysalis Records that all releases by the group would be on black vinyl and standard 7-inch and 12-inch formats. The trend for colored vinyl was also savagely parodied in both song lyrics and interviews. Brighton, UK, new wave group the Piranhas recorded the track "Coloured Music," which questioned the purpose of colored vinyl as being anything other than superficial decoration: "Colour is cool, hanging on your wall / Records are really neat / And every lump of wax is an artefact / Music is obsolete."

Sometimes, too, the quality of colored vinyl was questionable. Penetration fell foul of their record label Virgin when they complained that the luminous vinyl of

their debut album rendered the actual disc unplayable. The label had seen the opportunity for a collector's edition of the album that glowed in the dark after exposure to light for three seconds—though the visually impressive gimmick had a drastic effect on the actual sound quality of the recording. The relationship between group and label soured resoundingly when guitarist Neale Floyd wrote an open letter to the "Fair Deal" column in British music paper *Sounds* soon after the album's release in 1978, beginning, "Dear anyone who bought our shitty luminous disc."

Eventually there was a backlash against such blatant marketing techniques. The shift in the late 1970s and early 1980s to a more ideological, austere, and politicized punk, especially within the Anarcho Punk subgenre, saw a decline in the market for alternative formats and colored vinyl releases and a return to basic, black vinyl—often housed within a simple black-and-white folded sleeve. This can be seen as not only reflecting low-cost production techniques on the part of independent labels, but the employment of deliberate visual codes with which to denote austerity and a "back-to-basics" approach. Crass had already adopted a policy of plain black clothing and white stage lighting as a marked shift away from colorful punk stereotypes early in their career, and the reflection of this approach within their sleeve graphics was almost inevitable—as was the adoption of similar graphic styles by a range of Anarcho Punk groups heavily influenced by Crass themselves.

Contemporaneously, others within the punk community, following the rise and fall of the compact disc, have increasingly returned to the limited-edition colored vinyl format, though now any impetus to do so is largely drawn from aesthetic rather than commercial considerations. Color is, after all, still cool.

"They'd like to buy the O-Level single, or 'Read About Seymour,' but they're not pressed in red, so they buy the Lurkers instead!"

— The Television Personalities, "Part Time Punks"

COLORED VINYL & THE HARD SELL

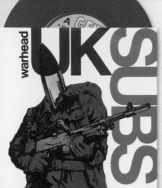

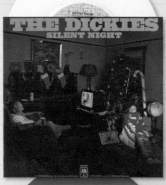

All the Young Punks

With major labels now seeing the potential for worthwhile returns on their investments, higher production levels began to blur any distinction between punk and new wave. Meanwhile, newer groups were adapting punk styles to formulate what would become key aspects of its evolution over the following decade. One of the most important, and often maligned, releases of the era was the second album by the Clash, *Give 'Em Enough Rope*. Producer Sandy Pearlman attempted to apply a more sophisticated polish than had been the case with the rough edges of the group's debut, in order to reach an American audience.

The cover of *Give 'Em Enough Rope* was developed by US artist Hugh Brown: "I had a show called 'Chinese Tourist Art' in a San Francisco gallery, Postcard Palace. Sandy Pearlman brought Joe and Mick to the show. They saw the piece that was to become the cover. They liked it and wanted to use it. I thought they were joking. While in Los Angeles I got an urgent call from CBS's art department, asking where the cover was. That's when I realized they weren't joking. I flew back to San Francisco, got the picture out of the show, did some faux Chinese writing (not the horrible shit CBS put on the second version) and took it to the airport to send it. I also gave them the picture from the same Chinese magazine where I got the horseman and used that for the back cover. Gene Greif worked in the art department at CBS. He got my artwork, took the shadow out from under the horse, the red hammer and sickles in the vulture's feathers, and put blocky type across the top. Even though CBS asked me to rush the cover to them, the Clash hadn't finished recording the album yet. That's why the tracklisting is wrong. Several months later the record's about to come out and Sandy Pearlman calls me to tell me that my name's not on it and they took off the Chinese type. He didn't tell me that Gene Greif put his name on it. The second version has 'cover concept by Hugh Brown.'"

01
Artist The Ruts
Title The Crack
Format LP, 12-inch
Label Virgin, UK, 1979
_ A cast of thousands including punk celebrities such as Jimmy Pursey, as well as John Peel and astronomer Patrick Moore. Design by John Howard.

02
Artist Angelic Upstarts
Title I'm an Upstart
Format Single, 7-inch
Label Warner Bros., UK, 1979

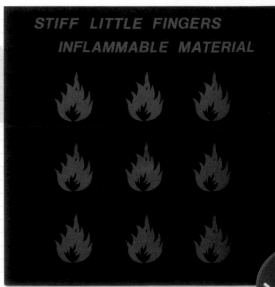

03

Artist Stiff Little
Fingers
Title Gotta Gettaway
Format Single, 7-inch
Label Rough Trade,
UK, 1979
_ Design by Janette
Beckman.

04

Artist UK Subs
Title Another Kind
of Blues
Format LP, 12-inch
Label Gem, UK, 1979
_ Design by Hothouse.

05

Artist Cockney Rejects
Title Flares 'n' Slippers
Format Single, 7-inch
Label Small Wonder,
UK, 1979
_ The cover photograph
features the group in
the studio with Jimmy
Pursey of Sham 69 and
Garry Bushell, *Sounds*
magazine journalist and
champion of the emerging
Oi! movement.

06

Artist Stiff Little
Fingers
Title Inflammable
Material
Format LP, 12-inch
Label Rough Trade,
UK, 1979
_ Hugely successful debut
album by Stiff Little
Fingers, from Belfast.
Though it owes a
definite musical
allegiance to the Clash,
the hard-hitting and
passionate lyrics
applying punk attitude
to the group's local
political situation set
a standard for others to
follow, despite arousing
suspicion from their
Northern Irish peers.

07

Artist The Damned
Title I Just Can't Be
Happy Today
Format Single, 7-inch
Label Chiswick, UK, 1979
_ Design by Phil Smee.

08

Artist Rich Kids
Title Ghosts of Princes
in Towers
Format LP, 12-inch
Label EMI, UK, 1978
_ Design by Rocking
Russian.

09

Artist The Clash
Title Give 'Em Enough Rope
Format LP, 12-inch
Label CBS, UK, 1978
_ Design by Hugh Brown.

01	02	03		07	
04	05	06	|	08	09

OVERLEAF

_ Poster image of Clash
ephemera collection, 1981.

I Found That Essence Rare: Post-Punk

One of the early ambitions of punk had been to reject the standardization and "boredom" of rock clichés, but within two years of punk's original "year zero," it appeared to some that punk had created a few stereotypes of its own. Post-punk symbolized an attempt to re-embrace the nonconformism and experimentalism of the original movement without the boundaries of "appropriate" musicianship or mainstream commercial ambition. Not that it was either unmusical or uncommercial—overlaps with other musical genres, the DIY punk underground, and the popular new wave abounded. Punk's old guard themselves were taking note, or as in the case of John Lydon, né Rotten, leading the way. Graphically, too, this was a time of creative ingenuity, as designers sought to parallel the new mood through radical imagery and typographic experimentation.

01
Artist The Fall
Title Totally Wired
Format Single, 7-inch
Label Rough Trade, UK, 1980

02
Artist Throbbing Gristle
Title United
Format Single, 7-inch
Label Industrial, UK, 1978
_ Design by Peter Christopherson.

03
Artist Throbbing Gristle
Title 20 Jazz Funk Greats
Format LP, 12-inch
Label Industrial, UK, 1979
_ Design by Peter Christopherson.

04
Artist The Fall
Title Lie Dream of a Casino Soul
Format Single, 7-inch
Label Kamera, UK, 1981
_ Design by Savage Pencil.

05
Artist Siouxsie and the Banshees
Title Hong Kong Garden
Format Single, 7-inch
Label Polydor, UK, 1978
_ Jill Mumford art-directed both "Hong Kong Garden" and the Banshees' debut album, *The Scream*. "Siouxsie brought the image in for 'Hong Kong Garden,'" she recalls. The Banshees had legendarily stringent artistic control over their output. "The band had very strict control on everything," she confirms. "Siouxsie was a complete control freak to work for. I rang her mum in Bromley once because I needed to talk to her and she went ballistic! We fell out big time over this."

06
Artist Siouxsie and the Banshees
Title Mittageisen
Format Single, 7-inch
Label Polydor, Germany, 1979
_ The cover appropriates a photomontage by John Heartfield from *AIZ* magazine, 1935.

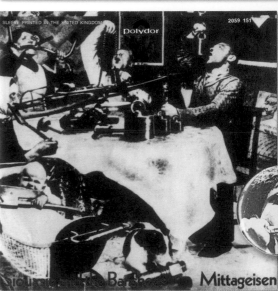

07
Artist Various Artists
Title A Factory Sample
Format Double Single,
7-inch
Label Factory, UK, 1978
_ The first release on
Manchester's Factory
Records, featuring
Joy Division, Cabaret
Voltaire, Durutti Column,
and John Dowie. Numbered
FAC 2 in the label's
celebrated cataloging
system (FAC 1 being a
Saville poster). Design
by Peter Saville.

08
Artist The Pop Group
Title Y
Format LP, 12-inch
Label Radar, UK, 1979
_ Photography by Don
McCullin/*The Sunday Times*.
Design by Malcolm
Garrett and Rich Beale.

09
Artist Magazine
Title Shot by Both Sides
Format Single, 7-inch
Label Virgin, UK, 1978
_ Design by Malcolm
Garrett.

10
_ Promotional poster for
the debut album by the
Slits, *Cut*, released by
Island Records in
September 1979. With
strong photography by
Pennie Smith, the three
main members of the
group, Ari Upp, Viv
Albertine, and Tessa
Pollitt are shown
covered in mud and
wearing just loincloths.
The same image was used
for the album cover,
gaining much publicity
in the process.

11
_ Factory Records
promotional poster FACT
10 + 4, June 1979. Design
by Peter Saville.

FAC-2

A FACTORY SAMPLE

FACT 10 + 4 —FACTORY RECORDS

JUNE '79

FACT 10 —UNKNOWN PLEASURES
The first album by Joy Division.

FAC 5 —ALL NIGHT PARTY
Single by A Certain Ratio.

FAC 6 —ELECTRICITY
Single by Orchestral Manoeuvres in the Dark.

JULY '79

FAC 11 —ENGLISH BLACK BOYS
Single by X-O-Dus.

FAC 12 —TIME GOES BY SO SLOW
Single by The Distractions.

12
Artist Killing Joke
Title Wardance
Format Single, 7-inch
Label Malicious Damage,
UK, 1980
_ Design by Mike Coles.

13
Artist Killing Joke
Title Nervous System
Format EP, 10-inch
Label Malicious Damage,
UK, 1979
_ Design by Mike Coles.

14
Artist Killing Joke
Title Follow the Leaders
Format Single, 7-inch
Label Malicious Damage,
UK, 1981
_ Design by Mike Coles.

15
_ _Killing Joke_ album
poster, designed by
Mike Coles, 1980.

16
_ Killing Joke poster,
designed by Mike Coles,
1981, featuring a
photograph of
German abbot Albanus
Schachleiter at the
Nazi Party Convention
in Nuremburg,
September 1934.

17
Artist Public Image Ltd
Title Metal Box
Format LP, 12-inch
Label Virgin, UK, 1979
_ Lydon's Public Image
Ltd (or PiL), were visual
as well as musical
innovators. Their second
album was released in
a circular metal tin
containing three 12-inch
discs. There had been
prior discussions about
issuing it in a sardine
can. According to
guitarist Keith Levene,
"Just to make sixty
thousand of them cost
the band £33,000 and
Virgin £33,000." Their
debut single, meanwhile,
came in a specially
designed "tabloid"
newspaper. It was
filled with cryptic
stories, including one
mocking Virgin boss
Richard Branson.

18
Artist Public Image Ltd
Title Public Image
Format Single, 7-inch
Label Virgin, UK, 1978
_ Foldout "newspaper"
poster cover for single.

19
Artist Public Image Ltd
Title Death Disco
Format Single, 7-inch
Label Virgin, UK, 1979

20
_ Public Image Ltd debut
album poster, 1978. The
album cover concept by
Terry Jones and Dennis
Morris, reflected in the
poster design, was to
present a completely new
corporate image for the
new group, in the style
of high-end fashion
magazines.

12	13		17	
	14		18	
15		16	19	20

PUBLIC
IMAGE

PUBLIC IMAGE THE ALBUM FROM THE BAND PUBLIC IMAGE LTD (PIL)

OUT NOW ON
VIRGIN
RECORDS
V2114

DEATH
DISCO

21
Artist XTC
Title Go 2
Format LP, 12-inch
Label Virgin, UK, 1978
_ The cover of XTC's
second album, released
in October 1978, features
a short essay reflecting
on the purpose of the
album cover itself.
Designed by Hipgnosis—
who had previously
created iconic sleeves
for Pink Floyd, Led
Zeppelin, 10CC, and Bad
Company—the text is a
classic example of
postmodern wit: "This
is a RECORD COVER. This
writing is the DESIGN
upon the record cover.
The DESIGN is to help
SELL the record. We hope
to draw your attention to
it and encourage you to
pick it up. When you
have done that maybe
you'll be persuaded to
listen to the music—in
this case XTC's Go 2
album. Then we want
you to BUY it."

22
Artist Gang of Four
Title Entertainment!
Format LP, 12-inch
Label EMI, UK, 1979
_ Design by Jon King &
Andy Gill/Cream.

23
Artist Wire
Title Dot Dash
Format Single, 7-inch
Label Harvest, UK, 1978

24
Artist Wire
Title I Am the Fly
Format Single, 7-inch
Label Harvest, UK, 1978

25
Artist The Mekons
Title The Quality of
Mercy Is Not Strnen
Format LP, 12-inch
Label Virgin, UK, 1979
_ Design by Mekons/
Cooke Key.

| 21 | 22 |
| 23 | 24 | 25 |

This is a RECORD COVER. This writing is the DESIGN upon the record cover. The DESIGN is to help SELL the record. We hope to draw your attention to it and encourage you to pick it up. When you have done that maybe you'll be persuaded to listen to the music – in this case XTC's Go 2 album. Then we want you to BUY it. The idea being that the more of you that buy this record the more money Virgin Records, the manager Ian Reid and XTC themselves will make. To the aforementioned this is known as PLEASURE. A good cover DESIGN is one that attracts more buyers and gives more pleasure. This writing is trying to pull you in much like an eye-catching picture. It is designed to get you to READ IT. This is called luring the VICTIM, and you are the VICTIM. But if you have a free mind you should STOP READING NOW! because all we are attempting to do is to get you to read on. Yet this is a DOUBLE BIND because if you indeed stop you'll be doing what we tell you, and if you read on you'll be doing what we've wanted all along. And the more you read on the more you're falling for this simple device of telling you exactly how a good commercial design works. They're TRICKS and this is the worst TRICK of all since it's describing the TRICK whilst trying to TRICK you, and if you've read this far then you're TRICKED but you wouldn't have known this unless you'd read this far. At least we're telling you directly instead of seducing you with a beautiful or haunting visual that may never tell you. We're letting you know that you ought to buy this record because in essence it's a PRODUCT and PRODUCTS are to be consumed and you are a consumer and this is a good PRODUCT. We could have written the band's name in special lettering so that it stood out and you'd see it before you'd read any of this writing and possibly have bought it anyway. What we are really suggesting is that you are FOOLISH to buy or not buy an album merely as a consequence of the design on its cover. This is a con because if you agree then you'll probably like this writing – which is the cover design – and hence the album inside. But we've just warned you against that. The con is a con. A good cover design could be considered as one that gets you to buy the record, but that never actually happens to YOU because YOU know it's just a design for the cover. And this is the RECORD COVER.

GANG OF FOUR
entertainment!

The Indian smiles, he thinks that the cowboy is his friend. The cowboy smiles, he is glad the Indian is fooled. Now he can exploit him.

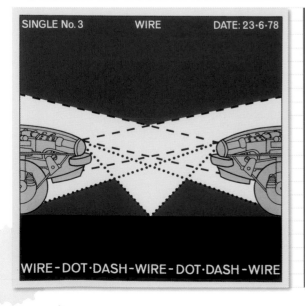

SINGLE No. 3   WIRE   DATE: 23·6·78

WIRE·DOT·DASH·WIRE·DOT·DASH·WIRE

21   W I R E

I A M T H E F L Y

the quality of mercy is not strnen

The MEKONS

Big Time (You Ain't No Friend of Mine)
Northern Ireland proved hugely receptive
to punk, with Stiff Little Fingers and the
Undertones its most renowned exports.
The spirit of the region was best represented
by Terri Hooley's Belfast label, Good
Vibrations. Hooley issued the Undertones'
immortal *Teenage Kicks* EP alongside several
highly accomplished pop-punk records from
the province, notably Rudi's "Big Time,"
Belfast's first punk anthem.

"As far as I remember, most of Terri's Good
Vibes sleeves were designed by his hippie
throwback pals who were at, or had been to,
the Art College here in Belfast. As with
everything else with 'Big Time' we were all
literally making it up as we went along.
We never thought about sleeves, or their
design, until the record was due back from
the pressing plant. Some of Terri's pals
had taken live pictures of us at one of
the gigs we played to raise the money
to pay for the pressing and recording
costs. They'd then used some of these to
put together a rough ad for the single
in some of the local zines—and this
initial design was basically us flying
over Belfast in a Rolls-Royce sprayed
with the sort of slogans we had painted
on our boiler suits. I thought it looked
OK, but it was kinda dark colored, hard
to make out from a distance and frankly
not that striking. We decided we needed a
different sleeve design. I remember all
of us looking through old mags and flyers
Terri had in his shop and at home, lots of
bad psychedelic trippy stuff. I'm pretty
positive we turned down the design that
was later used on the Victim 45 (it looked
like King Billy with a gas mask on which we
thought was a bit crass). But we all loved
the Boris Karloff 'Mummy' design. We all
loved old horror films, but it also had
the bright red lipstick, which we thought
was very New York Dolls-ish (probably more
Andy Warhol in hindsight). It was also VERY
striking and completely different from
anything we'd ever seen on any other punk
sleeves—either nationally or locally.

As the print workshop upstairs from Terri's
did the printing and could only print on
plain paper (for whatever reason) Terri
came up with the idea of folding A3 paper
into sleeves. They were a pain to fold and
none of us really thought they were as good
as proper glossy record company sleeves—
but, in hindsight, they certainly helped
establish a visual identity which helped
put Good Vibes on the map as a label."

Brian Young, Rudi

01
Artist Rudi
Title Big Time
Format Single, 7-inch
Label Good Vibrations,
Northern Ireland, 1978
_ Design by Terri Hooley.

02
Artist Victim
Title Strange Thing by
Night
Format Single, 7-inch
Label Good Vibrations,
Northern Ireland, 1978
_ Design by Terri Hooley.

03
Artist XDreamysts
Title Right Way Home
Format Single, 7-inch
Label Good Vibrations,
Northern Ireland, 1978
_ Design by Terri Hooley.

04
Artist Various Artists
Title Battle of the Bands
Format EP, Double 7-inch
Label Good Vibrations,
Northern Ireland, 1979
_ Design by Terri Hooley.

05
Artist Outcasts
Title Justa Nother
Teenage Rebel
Format Single, 7-inch
Label Good Vibrations,
Northern Ireland, 1978
_ Design by Terri Hooley.

06
Artist Protex
Title Don't Ring Me Up
Format Single, 7-inch
Label Good Vibrations,
Northern Ireland, 1978
_ Design by Terri Hooley.

01   02
03   04   05   06

Graphic designer Malcolm Garrett created the visual identity for successful Manchester punk group Buzzcocks, operating under a range of pseudonyms derived from "Arbi-trary Im-ages," a creative name adopted for the credits on his first professional commission, the cover for the single "Orgasm Addict." He went on to work extensively for new wave and post-punk groups Magazine, Nachts, Red Crayola, and others, becoming a hugely influential force in British graphic design over the following decade through his Assorted Images studio:

Orgasm Addict

I had originally been commissioned to design the "Orgasm Addict" sleeve, which, after some discussion between the band and manager Richard Boon, was based around a collage chosen from a number of options by Linder Sterling. The original montage was full-color, but as the record company stipulated that the sleeve design could be in two colors only, the solution for reproducing it needed to be found. At that time, single picture covers weren't common, and therefore not considered particularly important, and of course record companies were always reluctant to spend too much on production.

I needed to reduce the size of the montage to produce a visual for the sleeve, so I photocopied it—remember photocopiers were quite new and generally unavailable technology at this time. Happily this also gave the image a higher contrast, so that it could be better printed in a dark color (I chose dark blue, with a contrasting color, yellow, for the background). I was pleased with the way that the image gained from the photocopying process—it took on a more even tone and felt less disjointed than the original, blending the various elements together quite well. I think it brought it to life in a more dramatic way. Crucially, to me at least, I arranged the sleeve with the image upside-down, and with typography that could be read from any angle.

What Do I Get?

If you search any of the Buzzcocks singles, they don't have an A-side and a B-side, they are labelled as side A and side 1. For the "What Do I Get?/Oh Shit" single sleeve, I was playing with a wraparound grid that could show two images, but with each folding around to display on both sides effectively denoting neither front nor back. I mocked up a visual to show how it would work—I decided to skew it slightly at an angle for a stronger visual effect, and put it together with two different tones of green paper merely as an example. We then decided that the flat colors worked well in themselves, and we didn't actually need to

include images. I also ran the song titles around both sides of the sleeve, so it should have said "Shit" and "What" on one side, and "Oh" and "Do I Get?" on the other, but the record label disapproved of that so we removed the "Oh Shit" title completely. Following on from this, the group adopted stage clothing incorporating diagonal flat colors, and that way of extending the visual identity into other areas.

I was also very keen to include technical information, such as catalog numbers and the text that is normally consigned to the small print on the back of a record cover. I always worked with that material to include it as a feature of the design. At the pressing plant, the record isn't actually known by the artist or title, but simply by the catalog number, and I was very interested in this element as a driver of the design. There was a movement at the time in interior design, Hi-Tech, that advocated bringing industrial design elements into domestic environments. Plus, I was interested in the ways that the graphic language of corporations could be adapted to make them "pop." I felt that this approach reflected the group's lyrics, which were on the one hand quite "domestic," but also bittersweet, slightly dehumanized (there is no "he" or "she" in a Buzzcocks lyric), and somewhat aggressive all at the same time.

The songs by Buzzcocks were often unashamedly "pop" songs, but with an edge—different from mainstream pop music but also fitting into punk in their own individual way. My design work attempted to reflect those themes, using appealing graphics that were also discordant and angular. I also tried to establish a vision of how things would develop over time—if you look at the three albums, you'll notice that the group are depicted in a square, a circle, and a triangle—very much a tribute to the Bauhaus. This attempt to anticipate the future, laying hooks to revisit later with each new sleeve, is one that I adopted again with other bands.

Magazine

Much of the original visual identity for Magazine was driven by Howard Devoto. He frequently had very strong ideas about the images that he wanted to use on record covers, and had often chosen an image before the sleeve was discussed. Before working on *The Correct Use of Soap*, the idea was originally to release a series of singles, rather than an album. The concept was to make them look like packaging for old 78 rpm records, with brown card sleeves and shiny labels. The record company, Virgin, initially resisted saying that the covers needed to be

printed on standard stock white card, but I realized that to achieve the desired effect we could simply turn it over and print on the uncoated reverse. The cover for each was the same, with a die-cut hole simple typography in silver, but each label was to have a different colored label.

Nevertheless Virgin insisted on developing an album from the material, so we applied the same technique. I worked out that we could screenprint in two colors for the same cost as a litho full-color cover, again on the reverse of the board. As it was white on the inside, and I was keen to press the album on white vinyl, so that everything coming out from within this brown exterior was pure white, and quite soap-like. That idea was rejected by Howard as being too "gimmicky," which was a real shame, I think. I was very lucky that we had a supportive production team at Virgin, including Charlie Dimon, and Simon Valley. If he was enthused, Charlie would help to push through some ideas that were a bit more unusual than standard cover design—it was him that developed the Public Image Ltd *Metal Box* album as three 12-inch discs in a metal canister.

Assorted Images

I've always had an empathy for people behind the scene who help to make things happen. I have an appreciation for the obscure influences that contribute to the success of others. Initially I didn't want to put my own name on the covers, but at the same time I wanted to hint at an identity for the creator of the work. For "Orgasm Addict," my first sleeve, I added the cryptic epithet "Arbi-trary Im-ages" at the edges of the back of the sleeve, as a playful mark which in time might identify the author. I continued to play a similar game for several years, adding the same kind of cryptic mark, though each time changing the first word to another beginning with the letter A, often with some reference to the circumstances surrounding the release in the choice of word.

In the days before the Internet, Richard Boon would often need to post Buzzcocks information or lyrics to me when I was working on design material for them. He picked up on the same game, and sent me a package knowingly addressed to "Assorted Images." I liked the inclusive way that this title worked, summing up the entire collection of credits, and when in 1983 I formalized the design company with Kasper de Graaf, as up to that point it was me acting as a freelance, we naturally called it Assorted Images.

MALCOLM GARRETT

01

Artist Magazine
Title A Song from under the Floorboards
Format Single, 7-inch
Label Virgin, UK, 1980

02

Artist Magazine
Title Thank You (Falettinme Be Mice Elf Agin)
Format Single, 7-inch
Label Virgin, UK, 1980

03

Artist Magazine
Title Upside Down
Format Single, 7-inch
Label Virgin, UK, 1980

04

Artist Magazine
Title Sweetheart Contract
Format Single, 7-inch
Label Virgin, UK, 1980

05

_ Poster for Buzzcocks single "What Do I Get?," January 1978. Drawing on the simple geometric angles of the single sleeve designed by Malcolm Garrett, the poster creates an intriguing puzzle for the viewer to solve.

06

Artist Magazine
Title The Correct Use of Soap
Format LP, 12-inch
Label Virgin, UK, 1980

07

Artist Buzzcocks
Title Another Music in a Different Kitchen
Format LP, 12-inch
Label United Artists, UK, 1978

08

Artist Buzzcocks
Title Love Bites
Format LP, 12-inch
Label United Artists, UK, 1978

09

Artist Buzzcocks
Title A Different Kind of Tension
Format LP, 12-inch
Label United Artists, UK, 1979

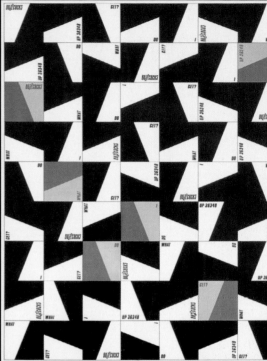

"It was easy, it was cheap, go and do it!"

When Danny Wigley, singer with the Desperate Bicycles, shouted that simple phrase in the dying coda of the group's debut single ("Smokescreen" backed with "Handlebars," April 1977), it wasn't empty punk rhetoric. Early press reports on the punk phenomenon had made much of the technical incompetence of the musicians concerned, and indeed certain punks had come to wear their lack of musical sophistication as a badge of honor. "Anyone can do it" became something of a punk credo, although in practice many of the more successful punks paid no more than lip service to the idea of helping their peers along.

In December 1976, Tony Moon added a simple diagram to the first issue of his new punk fanzine, *Sideburns*. The crude drawing, entitled "Playin' in the band," showed three schematic guitar chord positions with the captions, "This is a chord. This is a second. This is a third. Now form a band." This sense that the world was opening up to potential punk performers proved liberating, but while possessing the skills (or at least the chutzpah) to get up on stage in front of a crowd was one thing, the ability to make and flog one's own record was quite another.

Though Buzzcocks' *Spiral Scratch* became symbolic of the potential for do-it-yourself record manufacture, it was others like the Desperate Bicycles who saw making records as a way to empower others to do the same. In fact their first records were *about* making records: their manifesto, "it was easy, it was cheap, go and do it!" became the chorus of their second single, "The Medium Was Tedium," with the additional qualification, "so if you can understand, go and join a band!"

Many were eager to do just that, and to share their experience in practical as well as philosophical ways. Inspired by the Desperate Bicycles, Leeds group Scritti Politti relocated to London in September 1978 and released their debut *Skank Bloc Bologna* EP two months later on their own St. Pancras label. The folded sleeve included a detailed list of recording and pressing costs, together with addresses and contacts for accessing each service—in other words, a template for others to follow to create their own record: "*Recording: Space Studios @ 19 Victoria Street, Cambridge. £98.00 for 14 hours, master tape included. Mastering: Pye London Studios @ 17 Great Cumberland Place, London W1 – IBC (George) Sound Recording Studios @ 35 Portland Place, London W1. £40.00 for cutting of lacquer from master tape. Pressing: PYE Records (Sales) Ltd.*

@ Western Road, Mitcham, Surrey. £369.36 for 2,500 copies at 13p, £27.00 for processing (electro plating of lacquer). Labels: E.G. Rubber Stamps, 28 Bridge Street, Hitchin, Herts. £8.00 for rubber stamp on white labels (labels included in cost of pressing.)"

A similar approach was adopted by the Television Personalities for the second pressing of their *Where's Bill Grundy Now?* EP, including a note about the frustrating convention of the punk picture sleeve, "sleeves 2,000, £110 by Delga, Kent. We didn't want to, but what else do we do?" It is not well remembered that in 1977 photocopies cost substantially more than offset printing. Band members duly raced to find employment at copy shops so that they could run off sleeves and flyers after hours, but the first year or two of self-released punk 45s featured a merry pissing contest of bands vying to prove who could make their records more cheaply than anyone else.

If DIY punk started out with a very singular premise, the freeze-framing of a particular group at a particular time with no expectations of the future à la *Spiral Scratch*, it quickly became evident that there existed both a curious media and a significant market for such enterprises. When you've had your fifteen minutes of fame and released your own do-it-yourself manifesto to the wider world, then what next? For many, achieving the status of "recorded artist" was enough in itself—Buzzcocks were not the only punk outfit for whom their debut record release coincided with the partial (or sometimes complete) splintering of the group. Others, like the Undertones, whose Good Vibrations debut "Teenage Kicks" was, like *Spiral Scratch*, envisaged as a one-shot memento, found that interest in follow-up material drove further releases. Certainly a receptive audience, now able to source those records via either mail order or a burgeoning independent retail network, was not only in place, but growing.

Meanwhile, hundreds of DIY bands (though no one called them that at the time) tumbled into the fray en masse. An alternative infrastructure developed. Once you'd joined the dots provided by the Bicycles or Scritti, you could trek down to London to hawk as many copies as you could to Rough Trade or Small Wonder Records, then attempt to ingratiate yourself with John Peel at the BBC, who would play almost anything once. *ZigZag* magazine's *Small Labels Catalogue* listed over eight hundred labels in its 1980 edition, which meant a rough tripling of the number that existed two years previously. The floodgates

had opened for punk's do-it-yourself revolution, and a market was established to support an eclectic and diverse range of experimental new sounds and new styles.

By 1980, hundreds of bands had embraced the increasingly attainable ideal of controlling their own means of production. Their DIY "labels" had no interest in roster-building or a coherent artistic vision. These were often throwaway, capture-the-moment artifacts recorded in bedrooms—their artwork drafted and assembled there once the pressing plant had returned the product, with no eye to longevity or legacy. And often, but not always, presentational differences were at least as self-evident as the aural experience.

> **"If the tsunami of 1979–81 DIY records showcased a wildly variable range of musical competence, it's interesting that their graphics were similarly uneven (if uniformly low-budget). You see handwritten scrawls cheek by jowl with painstakingly earnest sixth-form art class draft work—and there is no telling from either whether the band will actually be able to play their instruments. Just as a generation of teenagers fumbling with hand-me-down instruments had been inspired to record themselves by hearing Swell Maps or the Raincoats on vinyl or John Peel, there was a brand new realm of possibility for art college backbenchers as well. Prior to the DIY era, the chance to do a record sleeve was a holy grail for any young graphic designer or artist. The proliferation of punk bands gave many folks fresh opportunities to work for established labels (Linder, Phil Smee) and the indie-friendly climate created an extra inducement to Phil and others to leapfrog past the traditional dreary apprenticeships and freelance trench work into starting their own labels. But DIY records offered *anyone* the chance to decorate their own release, or those of their friends. A simultaneous phenomenon might be summarized thus: 'This is a photocopy shop. Get a job there. Now print your sleeves after hours.' The readily assimilated subtext was that just as you did not have to be a musician to start a band, you did not need any artistic chops at all to put a sleeve on your record. So, often, you had some great music in frightfully inept sleeves, but on the other, you also saw records with compelling graphics . . . that contained the most tedious, imitative music imaginable. And many, many mixtures in between."**

Chuck Warner, proprietor of hyped2death.com and the Messthetics reissue series

AN IDEAL FOR LIVING

01

_ Cover bag, *Adventures in Reality* fanzine, Coventry, 1981. Issue E came packaged in a hand-screenprinted brown paper bag. Design by Alan Rider.

02

Artist The Desperate Bicycles
Title The Medium Was Tedium
Format Single, 7-inch
Label Refill, UK, 1977
_ Reverse of single sleeve, giving details of costs and methods of production.

03

Artist Scritti Politti
Title Skank Bloc Bologna
Format EP, 7-inch
Label St. Pancras Records, UK, 1978

04

_ Play'in in the Band, illustration from *Sideburns* fanzine, no. 1, January 1977, by Tony Moon.

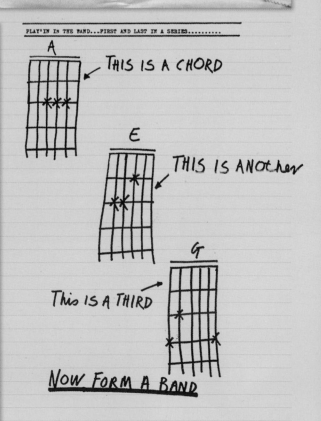

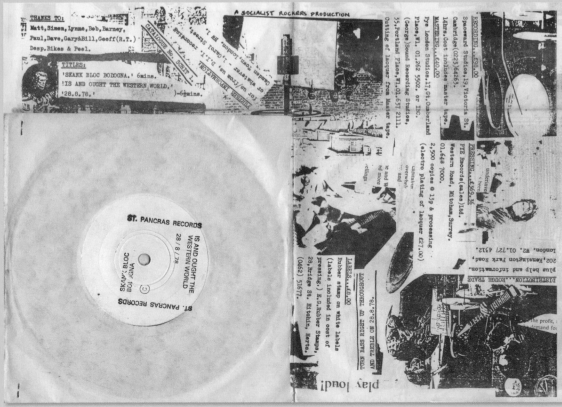

The DIY Pioneers

01
Artist The Desperate Bicycles
Title Smokescreen
Format Single, 7-inch
Label Refill, UK, 1977
_ Debut single. Both tracks pressed on each side of the record, as the group couldn't afford to cut two separate masters.

02
Artist The Desperate Bicycles
Title Occupied Territory
Format Single, 7-inch
Label Refill, UK, 1978

03
Artist The Desperate Bicycles
Title The Medium Was Tedium
Format Single, 7-inch
Label Refill, UK, 1977
_ As with the first single, both tracks were pressed on each side of the record.

04
Artist The Desperate Bicycles
Title New Cross, New Cross
Format EP, 7-inch
Label Refill, UK, 1978

05
Artist Buzzcocks
Title Spiral Scratch
Format EP, 7-inch
Label New Hormones, UK, 1977
_ Design by Richard Boon.

06
Artist Swell Maps
Title Read about Seymour
Format Single, 7-inch
Label Rather, UK, 1977

07
Artist Spizzenergi
Title Soldier Soldier
Format Single, 7-inch
Label Rough Trade, UK, 1979
_ Design by Spizz.

08
Artist Spizzoil
Title 6,000 Crazy
Format Single, 7-inch
Label Rough Trade, UK, 1978
_ Design by Spizz.

09
Artist Spizzoil
Title Cold City
Format EP, 7-inch
Label Rough Trade, UK, 1978
_ Design by Spizz.

01			
02	03	05	06
	04	07 08	09

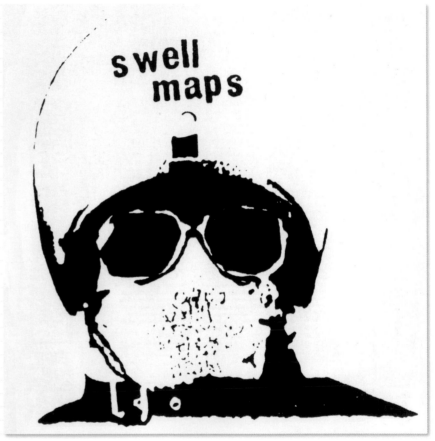

Part-time Punks

The new punk spirit of independence could be communicated through words, or simply through actions. While the Desperate Bicycles were lyrically exhorting others to do it themselves and follow their example, Buzzcocks were simply blazing a trail for others to follow without the need for introspection. Sometimes, the handmade and lo-tech rationale spoke for itself. At other times, as with the second issue of the Television Personalities' *Where's Bill Grundy Now?* EP, instructions were set out in far more explicit terms, providing followers with a clear route map and a "how-to" guide to the recording and production process.

01
Artist The Banned
Title Little Girl
Format Single, 7-inch
Label Can't Eat, UK, 1977

02
_ Spray-painted stencil poster for a gig by Dolly Mixture at Portsmouth Polytechnic, UK, February 13, 1982.

03
Artist Scritti Politti
Title Peel Sessions EP
Format EP, 7-inch
Label St. Pancras, UK, 1978

04
Artist O Level
Title East Sheen
Format EP, 7-inch
Label Psycho, UK, 1978
_ Design by Nik Aleg/ Rodent.

05
Artist O Level
Title We Love Malcolm
Format EP, 7-inch
Label Kings Road, UK, 1978
_ The lineup included Ed Ball and Dan Treacy of the Television Personalities and the Bennett brothers from fellow DIYers, Reacta.

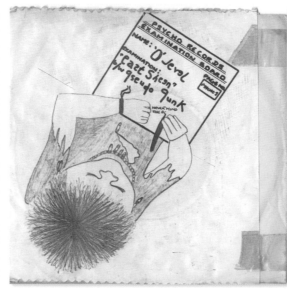

_Hand-rendered poster for a gig by the Table at the Fleet Centre, London, October 17, 1980.

07
Artist Fifty Fantastics
Title God's Got Religion
Format Single, 7-inch
Label Dining Out, UK, 1980
_ Another DIY innovation. Dining Out took unsold blank-label 45s by the Steppes (aka the Disco Zombies), "Beat Drill" b/w "God's Got Religion," and with the aid of a rubber stamp made the B-side the A-side, and decreed a new group name, Fifty Fantastics

(which may or may not have preceded Steve Pyke's artwork for the all-new sleeve), then sold them all over again—as a new release— to Rough Trade et al. Design by Steve Pyke.

08
Artist Television Personalities
Title 14th Floor
Format Single, 7-inch
Label Teen '78, UK, 1978

09/10
Artist Television Personalities
Title Where's Bill Grundy Now?
Format EP, 7-inch

Label Kings Road, UK, 1979, re-pressed (as TV Personalities) Rough Trade, UK, 1979
_ The Television Personalities' defining moment, featuring "Part Time Punks." After several sleeve designs for their own, blank-labeled King's Road pressing ("headless man" variants came first; the Shane MacGowan "punk" sleeve featured here came fourth), the TVPs signed to Rough Trade, who re-printed the best-known sleeve with the band's name abbreviated to TV Personalities.

11
Artist TV Personalities
Title Where's Bill Grundy Now?
Format EP, 7-inch
Label Rough Trade, UK, 1979
_ DIY advice showing details and expenses of recording and production appeared on the sleeve's reverse, as did the TVPs' alter egos—named for UK TV celebrities Nicholas Parsons, Hughie Green, Russell Harty, and Bruce Forsyth. "Parsons" and "Harty" are represented by photos of George Harrison and Ringo Starr.

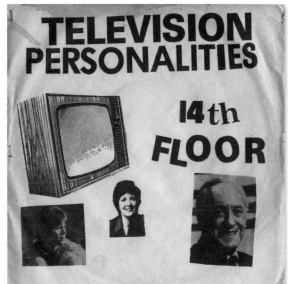

Fast Product

Providing a do-it-yourself template needn't be a reason to dumb down content. Some DIY producers played clever games with their audiences, inviting them in as equal participants in the "experience." Fast Product, established by former Rezillos' roadie Bob Last, demonstrated a particularly sophisticated grasp of what would later be called "postmodern" graphic design. Fast attempted to show that all aspects of the record business, from musicianship to design to distribution, could be taken out of the hands of the major labels, and the label's early catchphrases, "difficult fun" and "mutant pop," betrayed both a keen intellectual vision and a knowing humor.

Fast Product was the "perfect" independent label in that it unearthed several key artists, displayed an equally impeccable instinct for design and presentation, and then ceased to be at the exact high point of its success, thereby preserving its mystique. "Fast was started as a brand," says Last. "It was a bit of a provocation to call it that in 1976. I just hadn't decided what we were going to do with it! I was a fan of

movies and interested in the visual side of things. But I was waiting for the right thing, a means of communication. Then my partner, Hilary, bought me a copy of *Spiral Scratch*. That's it, this is what we're going to do . . . We were always deadly serious and also making jokes at the same time. The Mekons' '32 Weeks' was like that. Part of the whole point was to keep people unsure, to tread that line—it was up to you if you wanted to take it seriously, and if you did you'd find things in there, and if you wanted to take it as a joke, you could. Part of that joke was you had to be in the know to get it. There was a whole visual thing I was always interested in, coming from graphics and architecture, using the opportunity of that aesthetic. I was familiar with people like John Heartfield, who did the propaganda posters just before the Second World War. I've always been interested in skills, and have respect for skills, but I'm not interested in cultural products that are defined by those skills. I'm only interested in skill in the service of something interesting. I suppose the Mekons were the absolute extreme example of that."

01/02
Artist The Mekons
Title Never Been in
a Riot
Format Single, 7-inch
Label Fast Product,
UK, 1978
_ Design by Bob Last.

....

03
Artist 2-3
Title All Time Low
Format Single, 7-inch
Label Fast Product,
UK, 1978
_ Design by Bob Last.

04/05
Artist Gang of Four
Title Damaged Goods
Format Single, 7-inch
Label Fast Product,
UK, 1978
_ On being sent a letter
and enclosed photograph,

with instructions from the group on how to design the record cover, Last simply added both elements directly to the reverse of the sleeve. Design by Bob Last.

....

06
Artist . . . and the
Native Hipsters
Title There Goes
Concorde Again
Format Single, 7-inch
Label Heater Volume,
UK, 1980
_ The full-color cover is simply a 14- x 7-inch cutoff from a billboard advertising poster stickered with the band's name: all sleeves were different and individually made.

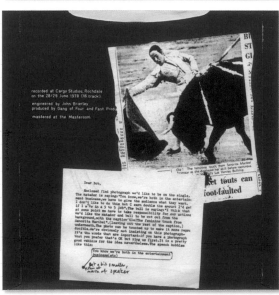

Artist The Raincoats
Title Fairytale in
the Supermarket
Format Single, 7-inch
Label Rough Trade,
UK, 1979

08

Artist Girls at our Best
Title Nowhere Fast
Format Single, 7-inch
Label Record Records,
UK, 1980

09

_ Screenprinted poster
for the Girls at Our
Best album, *Pleasure*,
October 1981.

Messthetics

If the recording and production elements of creating a record were no longer to be seen as a barrier, then what about the concept of "musicianship" and the values implicit to that craft? The framework of traditional rock 'n' roll instrumentation was brought into question by the likes of Mark Perry's ATV side project The Door & the Window, utilizing household appliances and cheap synthesizers to deconstruct the music itself. Relatively new cassette tape technology also allowed for cheap recording and duplication. Punk had clawed back control of the live and recorded music scene from "professional" agencies, and this home recording boom was in some ways an attempt to emulate in sound what the fanzines had done for written media.

01
Artist The Door & the Window
Title Subculture
Format EP, 7-inch
Label NB, UK, 1979

02
Artist The Door & the Window
Title Production Line
Format EP, 7-inch
Label NB, UK, 1979

03
Artist The Walking Floors
Title No Next Time
Format EP, 7-inch
Label My Death Telephone, UK, 1981

04
Artist The Manchester Mekon
Title Not Forgetting
Format Single, 7-inch
Label Newmarket, UK, 1979
_ All covers individually hand-printed.

05
Artist Record Players
Title Double C Side
Format EP, 7-inch
Label Wreckord, UK, 1978

06
Artist Armed Force
Title Popstar
Format Single, 7-inch
Label Armed Force, UK, 1979

07
Artist Atoms
Title Max Bygraves Killed My Mother
Format Single, 7-inch
Label Rinka, UK, 1979
_ All covers silkscreen-printed by hand, together with labels and inserts. "I got a bloke in Swansea who owned a restaurant to loan me £500. And I paid him back. I pressed two thousand. I printed all the inserts and cover myself, hand-printed everything. Did two thousand of them and sold them all through Rough Trade. It was brilliant. When I heard it played on

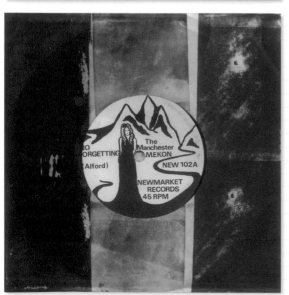

John Peel, I remember us being in a squat off the Harrow Road, it was one of the greatest moments of my life. John Peel played it three times. And twice, he segued at the end Max Bygraves's 'You're A Pink Toothbrush.'"
(Keith Allen, who worked briefly for Bygraves)

The fanzine is the definitive article of punk literature, the preferred mode of communication, and the forum for the exchange of ideas within its disparate communities. While punk fanzine history traditionally begins with the 1976 arrival of Mark Perry's *Sniffin' Glue*, the proud, impassioned, and colorful tradition of the irregular press in the English language stretches back to the dawn of printing.

A fanzine could be planned and executed in a few hours after school. Or during. Even if they weren't xeroxed on the sly for free, costs were minimal compared to a DIY 45, and, besides, the whole point of the enterprise was circulation, not sales. The fanzine press was about getting the word out. It was missionary and evangelical in spirit—little different from the broadsides of four hundred years earlier, with a comparable range of outraged protest, fresh lyrics, lurid misadventure, and heartfelt advocacy of causes (bands!) near and dear. There were certainly more recent carryovers as well—from the underground press of the '60s and magazines such as *International Times*—but *Sniffin' Glue* and its ilk definitively recalibrated the format.

Another contrast with punk's progress on vinyl was the fanzines' astonishing success at landing their author/editor/designers paying gigs with the music weeklies. While the major labels and major indies seemingly snatched up an entire generation of punk bands, it was a long wait between Buzzcocks and the next band to make the leap from a DIY 45 to the pop charts and UK TV show *Top of the Pops*. But Jon Savage, Paul Morley, Simon Reynolds, and Mark Perry all parlayed fanzine résumés into marquee freelance and even staff positions.

Photocopy technology drove much of the visual style of the punk fanzine, along with the lo-tech staples of home production: typewriters, Berol felt-tips, John Bull rubber stamp letter kits, scissors, and the Sunday paper. Painfully expensive Letraset rub-off type demonstrated that one was particularly serious. All these elements were equally part of the armory of DIY record sleeves, flyers, and pin producers.

US fanzines enjoyed first-mover status, of course, just as the Ramones had over the Pistols. Fanzine culture was sparse but well entrenched, due both to the vastly smaller market for professional rock writing in the US and its corollary, the dearth of national coverage for underground/unsigned local artists. *Gulcher* emerged from the fertile Bloomington, Indiana, art-rock and radio scene in 1974–75, but more often American efforts began as collector zines—most notably Greg Shaw's garage rock bible *Bomp!* and *Trouser Press* (née *The Rock Marketplace*). The first issue of *PUNK* hit the streets in January 1976, authored by John Holmstrom, Ged Dunn, and Legs McNeil, and did much to shape the idea of the movement that would come to be synonymous with its title (indeed, their championing of the Ramones was instrumental in the band's signing to Sire). The prose was crisp, gossipy, and occasionally vicious, and Holmstrom's cartoon drawings were a delight. Holmstrom was no ingenue, however, having already worked for *Mad* magazine and designed posters for the Fillmore East. *PUNK* was deliberately arty in its conception, and self-consciously an artifact in its execution. Its large, unfolded tabloid format, better paper, and high-quality printing were things that "ordinary" zines could only aspire to. *PUNK's* writing standards were also—if not uniformly higher—far more professional, operating in earnest discipleship of Lester Bangs, R. Meltzer, et al.

British zines (the "fan" prefix was increasingly dropped as such an act of supplication ran contrary to punk values) mushroomed alongside independent record releases. The best examples included *Ripped & Torn*, *Jamming!*, *Panache* and *Chainsaw* (whose issues were typed up on a typewriter lacking the letter "n," which was laboriously filled in by hand and fooled many into believing it was a deliberate design feature). Many were distributed by Joly MacFie's Better Badges enterprise.

Image as Virus

The links between the '60s counterculture and punk-era graphic insurgency were explicit in former Pink Fairies roadie Joly MacFie's Better Badges enterprise. It was run from the former premises of the *International Times*, for whom MacFie had served as music editor. BB became the market leader in the new button badge explosion, with designs incorporating snatched revolutionary rhetoric, band logos, or simple, shiny, plastic-redux picture sleeves. By 1978, he was publishing a weekly Top Ten of his team's most popular creations in *NME*.

As well as issuing cassettes, Better Badges subsequently found itself at the forefront of the fanzine revolution after MacFie purchased print equipment in 1979. Whereas with pins BB would donate two hundred free copies to bands for newly adopted designs, fanzine editors essentially had their print runs serviced at cost. The grunt work was shared by a plethora of struggling musicians, including, at various times, members of the Pink Fairies, Luscious Jackson, the Electric Chairs, Metal Urbain, Pigbag, Zounds, and Neneh Cherry. MacFie would go on to co-found *i-D* magazine before moving to the US.

"The underground press had been mostly killed off by inflation in the early '70s, but former writers had ensconced themselves in the (formerly stodgy) weekly music press, and set the tone for '76. Greg Shaw [*Bomp!*] showed up in London in early '77. He visited Better Badges, and I let on to him a key esoteric secret, the Buzzcocks' use of *Futura Bold Italic*. Subsequently he totally went over the top for it. I was a facilitator. I don't remember ever turning anything down [as Rough Trade sometimes did on political grounds]. I liked them all. *Ded Yampy*, a one-off from Coventry, was one of my favorites. I liked the weirder creative stuff, and the things we did for bands like the Raincoats and Young Marble Giants booklets."

Joly MacFie, Better Badges

Subsequently the impact of Crass's anarchist worldview reshaped the discourse again, and resulted in another glut of self-starter publications. In many ways the likes of *Toxic Grafitty* and *Kill Your Pet Puppy* helped define a British zine aesthetic thenceforth, combining articles covering local issues and political causes as well as music.

In the US *Slash* (later a record label) and the highly literate *Search & Destroy* flourished alongside the galvanized music scene of the West Coast, in Los Angeles and San Francisco respectively. The wonderfully resilient *Big Takeover* chronicled punk in New York after beginning life as a tribute to local band the Stimulators. (Other New York forebears, the aforementioned *Trouser Press* and *New York Rocker*, despite self-evident professional leanings, were also part of the mix.) LA's *Flipside* was a less reverent entrant thereafter, though the most influential of all fanzines came from San Francisco. *Maximumrocknroll*, established by Tim Yohannan in 1982 and still published monthly, begat the template for thousands of similar enterprises. Favoring acres of content to production values, its cheaply printed pages were filled with scene reports from around the world, record reviews, opinionated columnists, and band interviews, all under the umbrella of a puritanical editorial stance that MRR defended against all threats. Any number of personal and political offenses might lead to a band being shunned (however popular they might have been in the previous issue!), but the surest way of incurring instant nonperson status was for a band to sign with a major label.

XEROX CULTURE

An Independent Future

The success of early independent punk singles led to the establishment of a number of labels once it was apparent that their initial outlay could be recouped sufficiently to fund subsequent releases. While some early labels had centered on an individual group and were chiefly a vehicle for them to reach an audience, others were established by entrepreneurs and nonmusicians with an ear for new talent or an eye for the potential of this new era. Among the most notable in the UK was Rough Trade, based around a small independent record shop in West London. The subsequently famous Rough Trade imprint, founded on Geoff Travis's astute A & R instincts, was an afterthought, however; the fundamental importance of the project was in servicing the proliferation of other small labels springing up across the country. This led directly to the establishment of distribution networks, notably the self-mockingly titled Cartel, overcoming the last great obstacle facing a generation of home producers.

01
Artist The Fakes
Title Production
Format Single, 7-inch
Label Deep Cuts, UK, 1979

02
Artist The Shapes
Title Wot's for Lunch Mum
Format EP, 7-inch
Label Sofa, UK, 1979

03
Artist Wasteland
Title Want Not
Format EP, 7-inch
Label Ellie Jay, UK, 1979

04
Artist The Nightingales
Title Urban Ospreys
Format Single, 7-inch
Label Cherry Red,
UK, 1983

05
Artist Mike Malignant
& the Parasites/
Pink Flamingos
Title These Things
Are Sent to Try Us
Format EP, 7-inch
Label Para-mingo,
UK, 1979

06
Artist Swell Maps
Title Let's Build a Car
Format Single, 7-inch
Label Rough Trade,
UK, 1979

07
Artist Prag Vec
Title Existential
Format EP, 7-inch
Label Spec, UK, 1978

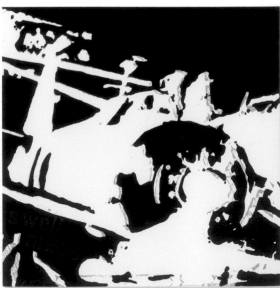

It was intended, however,
as a one-time event; it
was only when the single
attracted international
attention that Miller,
aka the Normal, was
persuaded to release
the work of others.
Design by Daniel Miller.

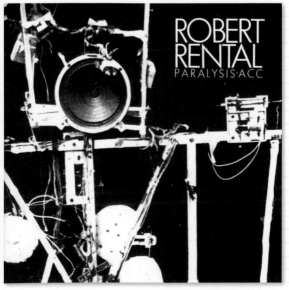

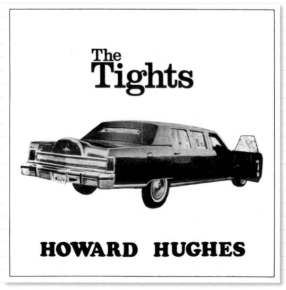

Punk's shock wave radiated well beyond music and fashion . . . in particular, into mass media, art, and commerce. But if its most visible effect was social empowerment—enabling an instant cult of belonging—its more enduring legacy has been the empowerment of individual voices and visions. Stiff Records, Chiswick, Radar, and other early independent labels had proved wildly successful at promoting and selling punk records despite their disdain for music industry conventions. Even so, they quickly came to depend on the majors to sponsor their manufacturing and distribution, and ceded more and more of their creative autonomy as a trade-off.

In January 1977, however, Manchester's Buzzcocks (who had already opened for the Sex Pistols and the Clash) became the first UK punks to release an independent record through their own auspices. *Spiral Scratch* proved that with a few friends throwing student grants or parental indulgences into the pot, a group could achieve vinyl immortality despite low finances, minimal graphics, and a lack of professional grooming. The participants were more surprised than anyone when it sold in quantity; they pressed one thousand copies at first, but the EP earned rave reviews from *Melody Maker*'s Caroline Coon and the new crop of fanzines (and more puzzled enthusiasm via *New Musical Express* and *Sounds*). With the critical patronage of John Peel, it quickly sold out, allowing the group to press another fifteen thousand copies of the now "rare" original, many either dispatched through mail order or sold at gigs. The 1979 reissue with the words "featuring Howard Devoto" spent six weeks in the pop charts.

Inevitably some independent labels were more successful than others. Chiswick was the most prominent front-runner, having established itself as a niche outlet for the sort of off-the-beaten-track records Ted Carroll and Roger Armstrong would sell from their Rock On! stalls. Stiff were also of an earlier musical generation and were more truly in the tradition of A & R-driven breakout indies such as Virgin, Island, Elektra, and Asylum, although their marketing gimmicks were a welcome alternative to the mainstream punk perennials of packaged outrage and horror.

"That whole idea of making money and being successful just never entered the equation, perhaps naively. It just wasn't part of it. It was more about having fun, and creating an opportunity, and creating a structure, which was hard, hard work, to allow these musicians and artists to realize their dreams—that was the all-important thing. It wasn't even really about Rough Trade. It wasn't about us."

Geoff Travis, Rough Trade founder

But thereafter the likes of Rough Trade, Small Wonder, Beggars Banquet (and its subsidiary, Ivo Watts-Russell's 4AD) began to establish themselves as distinctive entities. Some, like 4AD, Daniel Miller's Mute, Bob Last's Fast Product, and Tony Wilson's Factory, were essentially auteur labels, with A & R policies that allowed individuals to build catalogs based around their own tastes. Others such as Cherry Red were more pragmatic (though they underwent their own period of auteur stewardship under Mike Alway), or were simply commercially opportunistic businesses operating under a flag of convenience. While the former boutique labels increasingly veered away from a punk "sound," often markedly so, each was grateful for the punk moment in terms of the possibilities it offered.

In the US, things were altogether different. The country's vast geography meant that small labels had to build local profiles, mirroring the way its music media operated. The UK had at least three weekly "inkies"—*New Musical Express*, *Sounds* and *Melody Maker*—to trumpet the latest ingenues. The US had no equivalent, nor did the few national fanzines have anything like similar distribution. Labels that wanted to "go national" had limited options: established "import" wholesalers like Jem picked up the occasional American title, but their hearts were in UK imports. Others signed on with marginal national labels (Beserkley was distributed by Playboy Records, then GRT). Greg Shaw's Bomp! and the Residents' Ralph label created their own specialized network of collector-fans, but functional national distribution for indies was nonexistent through the 1970s. You had

a better chance of finding singles by LA's legendary Dangerhouse bands in London, England, than you did in New York or Chicago. It was not until the early '80s that labels like SST, Alternative Tentacles, Dischord, BYO, and others rose to prominence at the forefront of the hardcore scene. A generation of stellar American '70s punk bands were thus unable to record more than a single or two to document their peak years. The Avengers released just eight songs during their life span, and the Screamers, none.

Independent start-up labels might have had early hits (Zoo, Mute, 4AD) and been taken under the wings of a major à la Stiff and Radar, sometimes for the malign purpose of bolstering a flagging roster. Others, like Step Forward, Fast, and Factory, held steady as profitable indies. A number of others struggled, yet persisted as their owner's folly (Manchester's Object Records, designer Phil Smee's Waldo's label), or simply ran down their musical or financial resources and shriveled up (Mike Stone's punk label Clay, Ron Johnson Records). Another option involved labels linking with stores or distribution, where costs could be defrayed, and life expectancy lengthened, by keeping a greater share of wholesale and/or retail profits in-house (Small Wonder, Rough Trade, Red Rhino, Attrix).

Both the established and start-up UK independent sector was given a spine by Rough Trade's quasi-socialist distribution system, the Cartel. When it collapsed at the start of the '90s, to a large degree so too did the shared ethics and spirit of adventure of a generation. Thereafter "independent" was subsumed by "indie," effectively little more than a pallid, guitar-orientated musical generic. The term became associated with an aesthetic rather than an ideology, which was in stark contrast to the staggering diversity produced by independent labels previously, ranging from the quiescent Marine Girls to the shattering impact of the Birthday Party to the unadorned pop instincts of the Television Personalities.

I WANT YOU—AUTONOMY

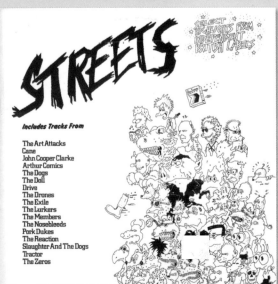

Punk was never just limited to Britain and the US—punk's early cultural hubs may have been centered around London and New York, but others further afield were taking note and were keen to get in on the action. As punk and new wave gained commercial and critical success, together with an attractive notoriety, it was also exported around the globe—both as a product and as an ideology.

Where writers have acknowledged punk's international dimension, they have tended to focus on only a handful of exemplars, many of which were closely associated with the UK and US scenes anyway: the critically acclaimed Metal Urbain (France) and Kleenex (Switzerland) gained a foothold precisely because their records were released (or rereleased) via the Rough Trade imprint, and France's Stinky Toys played at the 100 Club Punk Festival in September 1976 alongside the Sex Pistols, the Clash, and the Damned.

The vibrant Australian scene received some attention, but even its figureheads, the Saints, had to sign to EMI and move to London after only a half dozen shows to achieve that status, prefiguring a flight path that would be followed by the likes of Nick Cave (formerly of Melbourne's Boys Next Door) and others. Canadian bands like the Subhumans and D.O.A. had the distinct advantage of being close to US soil, having a common currency in terms of language, and a relatively easy geography to navigate. A reluctance among English-speaking journalists and scene reporters to engage with the mother tongues of other cultures undoubtedly limited access and the exchange of ideas, and for many, "foreign punk" remained personified by Plastic Bertrand's Belgian novelty single "Ça Plane Pour Moi" (a chart hit in the UK).

By 1977, there were active and distinctive punk outposts throughout Europe. In Germany, the subculture centered on Berlin's SO36 club, with other scenes in Düsseldorf and Hamburg. Switzerland had distinct scenes in both Zurich and Geneva, while in Italy the popularity of early punk and new wave styles soon gave way to the "Furious Years" of extreme hardcore. The Netherlands, too, with a squat culture similar to London's, hosted an active and politically engaged punk scene, with further crossovers between Amsterdam and London. Its most famous exports were the Ex, another band who would benefit from UK distribution of their records via Rough Trade and the Cartel network. Scandinavia, which

hosted a series of 1977 Sex Pistols shows after the villains of the piece fled the UK, was quickly in thrall to punk. Sweden, Norway, and Finland saw an upsurge of homegrown punk "talent" which, like many other international genres, embraced both English and local languages. Even Iceland gained a foothold in the subculture, establishing connections in the early 1980s with some of the more extreme UK post-punk groups such as Crass, Flux of Pink Indians, and Killing Joke, launching the career of a young Björk Guðmundsdóttir in the process.

Eastern Europe, despite the restrictions of freedom enforced by the Soviet state apparatus, had evolved various punk habitats as early as 1977. Yugoslavia, not part of the Soviet Union but signatories to a nonalignment pact and subject to a one-party dictatorship under the Socialist Party, led the way, with groups subjected to routine censorship. Poland's punk scene blossomed from 1978 onward, influenced by reports from the West of the new punk underground, with Hungary and Czechoslovakia following in close order. The political context of these growing scenes should not be underestimated—for many young punks in the former Soviet Bloc, with limited access to direct contact with punk scenes farther west, the new ideology was to be taken seriously as a way of life rather than a passing fashion trend. Restrictions on travel, foreign currencies, and access to even the raw materials considered essential by Western DIY punk labels, ensured that Eastern European punk "products" were difficult to create, and even more difficult to distribute. In Russia itself, the Leningrad Rock Club provided the formative hub and begat its own hardcore punk scene (the divisions between "hardcore" and "punk" being much more strictly delineated in much of Europe than the UK or US). Outside of Europe, Japan was both an enthusiastic early consumer and adopter of punk, witnessed in part by the licensing and marketing of numerous UK and European punk records from 1977 onward, alongside the establishment of homegrown punk artists and clubs.

Early Latin American punk scenes grew up in Mexico, Brazil, and Argentina, but the continent was otherwise comparatively late off the starting blocks—parallel scenes in Peru, Uruguay, Ecuador, and Colombia didn't fully develop until the mid-1980s. A late start was also true of the continent of Africa, with the exception of its southernmost

"We got offers from all over the world to play, but we wouldn't. It came to an obvious head when we were in Düsseldorf or somewhere like that on one of the small European tours we did early on. We were setting up inside the gig, and there was some trouble outside. We went outside, there were a load of punks who hadn't been allowed in yet. And across the road there was a whole row of police cars, with policemen behind the cars, with guns aimed at punks at the front of the gig. We didn't know how to react. In England, I would have very carefully walked over slowly and talked to them. But I couldn't speak German, etc, and then we realized there was a really serious danger we were putting other people into. That's why we decided to stick to mainland Britain."

Penny Rimbaud of Crass on the difficulties of exporting political ideology to countries with less liberal regimes

state, which hosted distinct scenes in Durban, Cape Town, and Johannesburg from the late 1970s onward. Several of these provided an outlet for those disaffected by apartheid on both sides of the racial divide, and were to inform subsequent developments in African music throughout the final days of that regime and beyond.

After a brief flirtation with mainstream commercial success, and following the widely proclaimed "death of punk" in the late 1970s—at least from the point of view of the cultural commentators and hip journalists who were keen to get back to some cleaner forms of "entertainment"—punk splintered and diversified, diving back below the critical radar and becoming more hardened and focused in the process. An alternative, underground network for exchanged gigs, promotion, and distribution grew up in towns and cities across the globe. A political ideology centered on anarchism and libertarian ideals, do-it-yourself pragmatism and free expression married punk to a new era of political and social activism. Whether it be pointed and dialectical or avowedly apolitical, youthful rebellion for youthful rebellion's sake, punk remains a way of saying "no" in a hundred languages and a thousand accents from the desert to the ice shelves.

PUNK SANS FRONTIÈRES

01

_ Björk performing with pioneering Icelandic post-punk group KUKL at the Roskilde Festival, Denmark, 1985. The group toured Europe with Flux of Pink Indians and Crass, and released two albums on the Crass label. On splitting in 1986, members of the group formed the Sugarcubes and found critical success via the label One Little Indian, established by former Flux bass player Derek Birkett. Copyright Per-Åke Wärn.

02/03

Artist Various Artists
Title 10000 Years Punk, Underground China—A Beijing Punk Compilation
Format EP, 7-inch
Label Tian An Men 89, France, 1998
_ Originally housed on a sub-label of Tian An Men entitled Xiandai Gongren Changpian.

04

Artist Malinheads
Title Probegepogt Aus Spandau
Format EP, 7-inch
Label Pogar, Germany, 1983

05

Artist Olho Seco
Title S/T
Format EP, 7-inch
Label Pogar, Germany, 1984
_ An extended play release by Brazilian group Olho Seco, this record was actually released on a German label, demonstrating something of the international reach of punk cooperation.

06

Artist Anti-Everything
Title The International Conspiracy to Push You Down
Format CD
Label Boatshrimp, Trinidad, 2009

01 02 03
04 05 06

Netherlands & Belgium

The relationship between the burgeoning early UK punk scene and developments in the Netherlands and Belgium was a two-way process, with a high degree of collaboration across the North Sea. The Kids recorded "Bloody Belgium" on their eponymous debut album, which became a local anthem and mirrored the Sex Pistols' disaffection with Albion. Like the rest of the album, the song was recorded in English: language was an issue for many European punk groups, with the additional complexity that Belgium, like other European countries such as Switzerland, did not have a single unitary language shared by its populace. Other key bands included early starters Chainsaw, Mad Virgins, and Spermicide, and in the '80s Zyklome A and street punks Funeral Dress (authors of "I'm in Love with Oi!") and latterly pop-punkers Janez Detd.

Meanwhile, the Netherlands was developing its own disparate punk scenes, with early originators such as Ivy Green from Hazerswoude, who recorded a debut album on Warners' punk subsidiary label Pogo, and the Dildos and the Tits from Amsterdam. The latter released a particularly notorious debut single, "Daddy Is My Pusher"/"We're So Glad Elvis Is Dead," on the Plurex label in 1978. The second track established something of a trend—the debut single by the Vopo's from Zwolle a year later was entitled "I'm So Glad the King Is Dead." A widespread squat-based anarchist punk scene preempted a burgeoning hardcore underground (the best-known example being BGK), with groups such as the Ex taking up local political protests to form the basis of a dual-language attack on government and its capitalist infrastructure. The group seized on a range of local and international causes—such as releasing a box set of singles to promote the cause of workers at a local paper factory that was forced to close, with an accompanying poster and booklet giving information about the issue in both Dutch and English. The Ex went on to produce a range of work documenting both contemporary and historical anarchist protest, promoting a political agenda through music and sophisticated graphic strategies and incorporating a widely diverse range of musical approaches from industrial punk to art-house experimentation.

01
Artist Frites Modern
Title Veel, Vet, Goor en Duur
Format LP, 12-inch
Label Boy Bensdorp Platen, Netherlands, 1984
_ Dutch punk band sometimes mistakenly considered to be Belgian by dint of the fact that they took their name from a burned-out french fries stand on a section of the Belgian motorway (and the scorched-out "Friterie Moderne" sign next to it).

02
Artist Pitfall
Title Separation
Format EP, 7-inch
Label Re-Records, self-released, Netherlands, 1982
_ Recordings took place in November 1981.

03
Artist Panic
Title Dertien/ Bereslecht—Live
Format Single, 7-inch
Label Oidipoes, Netherlands, 1980

04/05
Artist The Ex
Title 1936 the Spanish Revolution
Format Double Single Pack, 7-inch, plus book
Label Ron Johnson, United Kingdom, 1986
_ A double single set by leading Dutch anarcho punk outfit the Ex, coinciding with the fiftieth anniversary of the Spanish Civil War. The package features an extensive photographic history of the Spanish Revolution from the perspective of the anarchist CNT.

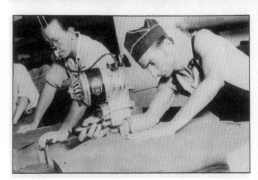

kleding voor de milities - werkplaats "lerenriemenmakerskollektief"
■ clothing for the militias - "tannery-collective workshop"

"het werk is intensief opdat niets ontbreekt aan het front, een ar-
beider smijdt in één keer 120 overalls" uit Solidaridad Obrero
■ "the work is intensive to make sure nothing lacks on the front,
a worker cuts 120 overalls at a time" from Solidaridad Obrero

06
Artist Zyklome A
Title Made in Belgium
Format LP, 12-inch
Label Punk Etc.,
Belgium, 1984
_ In terms of national
metaphor and identity,
the employment of the
"pissing boy" (or
"Manneken Pis" bronze
statuette in Brussels)
is emblematic of both
regional pride and
disassociation.

07
Artist Vopo's
Title Dead Entertainment
Format LP, 12-inch
Label Redlux Foundation,
Netherlands, 1981

08
Artist BGK
Title Nothing Can
Go Wrogn!
Format LP, 12-inch
Label Alternative
Tentacles, USA, 1986
(Licensed from Vogelspin,
Netherlands, 1986)

09
Artist The Kids
Title The Kids
Format LP, 12-inch
Label Philips,
Belgium, 1978
_ Although it follows
album cover design
tradition through the
employment of a group
photo, the eponymous
debut album by the Kids
retains a sense of DIY
aesthetics through its
use of a roughly torn
image mounted with
sticking tape.

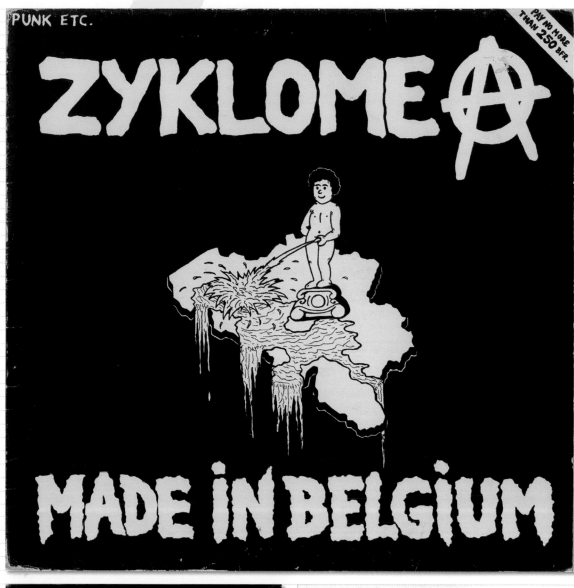

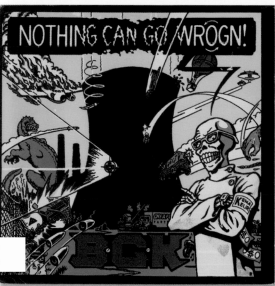

Overlaps between proto-punk developments in the UK and Belgium were to have a major impact on some of the critically acclaimed scene leaders, at least in the UK, as well as elements that were to be less celebrated by the music press. Brian James, founder member and guitarist of the Damned—the first UK punk group to release a record—had developed his chops in proto-punk outfit Bastard. Originally from Sussex, the group relocated to Brussels during late 1975. When James returned to London the following year to join London SS (finishing school for future founders of the Damned, the Boys, Generation X, and the Clash),

the remaining members of Bastard brought in another guitarist and changed their name to Elton Motello, recording "Jet Boy, Jet Girl." The overlap between that song and the international novelty hit "Ça Plane Pour Moi" by Plastic Bertrand was to form the basis for one of the long-standing sagas of European punk. Interestingly, the Damned connection doesn't stop there—when the group first disbanded at the end of 1977, original bassist (and future guitarist) Captain Sensible relocated to the Netherlands and recorded a version of "Jet Boy, Jet Girl" with backing band the Softies.

10
Nieuwe Koekrand fanzine, volume 11, issue 77, Amsterdam, Netherlands
_ Front cover illustration by Jeff Gaither (USA).

11
Artist Too Much
Title Silex Pistols
Format Single, 7-inch
Label Pathé Marconi, France, 1978

12
Artist Hubble Bubble
Title Hubble Bubble
Format LP, 12-inch
Label Sinus Music, Belgium, 1978

13
Artist Hubble Bubble
Title New Promotion
Format Single, 7-inch
Label Sinus Music, Belgium, 1977
_ Group formed by drummer Roger Jouret (Plastic Bertrand) while studying music at the Royal Conservatory in Brussels. Jouret was selected by producer Lou Deprijck to create the image of punk singer Plastic Bertrand for the release of "Ça Plane Pour Moi" in 1977, while continuing to record with Hubble Bubble under the pseudonym Roger Junior.

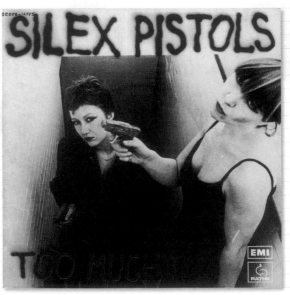

14

Artist Plastic Bertrand
Title Pogo Pogo
Format Single, 7-inch
Label RKM, Belgium, 1977
_ The first release of the single, later reissued with "Ça Plane Pour Moi" as the A-side to international chart success. The record was rerecorded by Elton Motello on the same label with alternative lyrics, accompanied by a strikingly similar cover design (see 15).

15

Artist Elton Motello
Title Pogo Pogo/Jet Boy, Jet Girl
Format Single, 7-inch
Label RKM, Belgium, 1977
_ This single was released in several different territories by Elton Motello, with a UK release on Lightning Records a year later reversing the A- and B-sides. Both songs use the same backing track as Plastic Bertrand's single, with alternative lyrics in the English language for "Ça Plane Pour Moi."

16

Artist Elton Motello
Title Pogo Pogo
Format Single, 7-inch
Label Pinball, Germany, 1977
_ German issue of the first Elton Motello single.

17

Artist Elton Motello
Title Victim of Time
Format LP, 12-inch
Label RKM, Belgium, 1978

18

Artist Plastic Bertrand
Title Ça Plane Pour Moi
Format Single, 7-inch
Label Philips/Nippon Phonogram, Japan, 1978
_ First Japanese release of the Plastic Bertrand single—it was issued again a year later by the Radio City label.

19

Artist Plastic Bertrand
Title Ça Plane Pour Moi
Format Single, 7-inch
Label Vogue, France, 1978
_ This single became an international chart hit, even registering in the US Billboard charts—a highly unusual feat for a song recorded in French. Though attributed to Plastic Bertrand (real name Roger Jouret), the single was actually performed and produced by its composer Lou Deprijck—a fact which remained hidden for over three decades until an acrimonious court case in 2010.

10 11 | 12 13 14 15   16 17 18 19

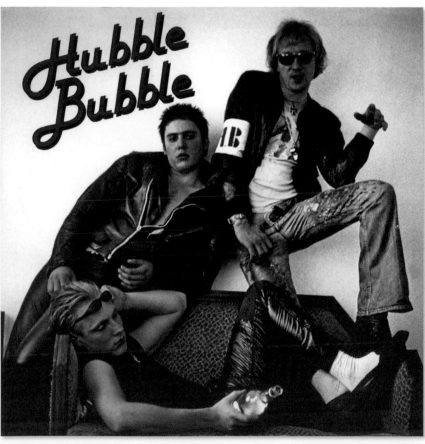

France

Connections between France and the US led to a proto-punk scene in Paris during the early 1970s with a strong allegiance to Lou Reed, the Stooges, and garage rock styles among a group of fans calling themselves Les Punks. Key players included Marc Zermati [see Proto-Punk chapter] and Michel Esteban, who founded the record label Skydog and the magazine *Rock News* respectively. Zermati organized the first European Punk Rock Festival at the Mont-de-Marsan bullring in southwest France on August 21, 1976, featuring an early performance by the Damned alongside local groups Bijou, Il Biaritz, and Shakin' Street. French radical politics, from street-level activism to sophisticated graphic languages of protest, also played a significant part in the development of international punk aesthetics.

Homegrown French proto-punk bands like Metal Urbain and Stinky Toys began performing as early as 1975 and the likes of Marie et les Garçons, Asphalt Jungle, and Gasoline

followed. Their stylistic interpretation of punk displayed a breadth of musical and artistic variety, from new wave, and Stooges-influenced garage rock to more abrasive contemporary styles.

In common with developments elsewhere, the early 1980s saw a fragmentation of styles, with the adoption of a harder edge and a shift toward street punk and hardcore by groups such as Camera Silens, Trotskids, Les Vandales, Rapt, and Kromozom 4. That decade also saw the development of a French alternative scene centered around the groups Bérurier Noir, Ludwig Von 88, and Les Brigades, together with the establishment of stronger links to the international punk underground developed through shared gigs, tours, and low-key record releases. More recently, an emphasis on regional variation has led to a resurgence of punk sung in local languages, including Melmor and Tri Bleiz Die in Breton, Arnapi in Occitan, Bredelers in Alsatian and Haurtzarrak in Basque.

01

Artist Metal Urbain
Title Paris Maquis
Format Single, 7-inch
Label Rough Trade, UK, 1978
_ First record release on the Rough Trade label based at the shop in West London, one of the most important independent labels in the United Kingdom. Metal Urbain were a Paris-based new wave punk group who married punk guitar styles to synthesizer rhythms, though they received little critical support in France.

01 02   04
03 | 05 06

Germany

German punk is an ongoing phenomenon splintered between a series of distinct city-based scenes, with the reunification of East and West adding an additional schizoid element to the mix. In the late '70s the primary scenes were in Berlin, Düsseldorf, and Hamburg. The SO36 club in Kreuzberg was base camp for Berlin punk. Among the first indigenous bands were PVC, formed after watching the Adverts perform in the city. Male, who played SO36's opening night, were front-runners in Düsseldorf. Hamburg's Big Balls and the Great White Idiot (dismissed by purists as hippie infiltrators) were appropriately controversial, with members performing in full Nazi regalia. If in London in the '70s it was shocking to see swastikas, it was tangentially more disturbing still to see German youth revisiting the *verboten* wardrobe. Punk output from East Germany was largely a covert operation prior to reunification, the tale (and cult) of Schleim Keim being the most notable.

Hamburg's ZickZack Records was home to "Neue Deutsche Welle" (New German Wave), including Abwärts, as well as the more commercial Nina Hagen Band. "Deutschpunk" in the '80s was effectively a back-to-basics evolution in response to the artier post-punk set, greatly influenced by Crass and exemplified by Slime, who faced continual censure for their antiauthoritarian stance. The '80s also saw the "Chaostage" (Chaos Days) events where punks congregated in Hannover and Wuppertal and the formation of the Anarchist Pogo Party of Germany, which by the mid-'90s were involved in huge demonstrations that erupted in violence and created headline news.

The most popular band to emerge from German punk was Düsseldorf's Die Toten Hosen, whose Brit-punk influences were acknowledged in an album of cover versions starring many '77-era UK punk vets. More inspired by the American hardcore tradition of Black Flag and Dead Kennedys were Chaos Z from Stuttgart, Vorkriegsjugend from West Berlin, and others, while "fun punk" arrived in the mid-'80s in the shape of Hannover's Abstürzende Brieftauben, Bremen's Die Mimmi's, and Die Ärzte from Berlin. Contemporary German punk remains a diverse entity, with bands drawing from every imaginable tradition, documented by established fanzines and magazines like *Ox*, *Plastic Bomb*, and *Trust*.

01

_ *Trust* fanzine, issue number 7, Hamburg, Germany, 1987. Front cover by Italian artist Dumbo (see Peggio Punx, etc). *Trust* fanzine was crucial to the mid-'80s development of an indigenous "hardcore" scene in Germany, sometimes in opposition to, rather than sympathy with, the parent punk culture.

02

_ *Hamburger Mottenpost* fanzine, issue number 6, Hamburg, Germany, 1988.

01 02 03 | 06
04 05 08 09 07

Artist L'Attentat
Title Made in GDR
Format LP, 12-inch
Label X-Mist Records,
Germany, 1987
_ After the
Zwitschermaschine/
Schleim Keim split
album, this was the
second East German
punk recording to
reach vinyl in the West.
The recordings were
smuggled in on a
cassette tape from the
GDR to West Germany
in 1985. Translated as
"Assassination," the word
L'Attentat had political
overtones, and thus was
a common choice of name.

04
Artist Various Artists
Title Soundstracks zum
Untergang
Format LP, 12-inch

Label Aggressive Rock
Produktionen,
Germany, 1980
_ One of the most
important compilation
LPs in German punk
history; later pressings
are partially
adulterated due to
German censorship laws.

05
Artist Targets
Title Massenhysterie
Format LP, 12-inch
Label Aggressive Rock
Produktionen, Berlin,
Germany, 1985

06
Artist Schleim Keim
Title Drecksau
Format Single, 7-inch
Label Höhnie, East
Germany, 1998
_ Schleim Keim ("Slimey
Germs") from Erfurt—

probably the best-known
East German punk band,
and one of the
originators of the
movement in the GDR.
Vocalist Dieter "Otze"
Ehrlich would later
murder his father with
an ax and die in a
mental institution.

07
Artist Slime
Title Yankees Raus
Format LP, 12-inch
Label Aggressive
Rock Produktionen,
Berlin, 1982
_ Slime were one of
several bands to play
at a youth center in
Norderstedt in 1980
where stage announcements
vilified the Clash for
the ticket prices at
their upcoming Hamburg
Markthalle show. Outrage

at the Clash's "sell-out"
led directly to the riot
that night and Joe
Strummer being arrested
for smacking an audience
member over the head
with his guitar.

08
Artist Operation
Gomorrha
Title Born in Sixty Four
Format EP, 7-inch
Label Gabba Gabba Hey,
Germany, 1984

09
Artist Hermann's Orgie
Title S/T
Format EP, 7-inch
Label Moderne Musik
Schallplatten,
Germany, 1979
_ First pressing of
one of the earliest
self-released records
from Germany.

Punk's notoriety drew media attention wherever it appeared: it was almost inevitable that those outside of the subculture would comment on it as a means to either jump on the bandwagon or for comic effect. Negative publicity for punk in the UK, with stereotypical references in the press to punks vomiting, swearing, and wearing safety pins, zippers and razor blades, led to a nationwide boom in punk parodies and pastiches, from comedians Kenny Everett and the Two Ronnies on national television to records by the Punkettes, Matt Black & the Doodlebugs, and the Water Pistols. The international success of Belgian performer Plastic Bertrand's "Ça Plane Pour Moi" (see pages 130—31) was sure to spark a similar level of interest in the northern European mainland.

One of the earliest European "punxploitation" releases came courtesy of Belgian cabaret group Tjot Idi en de Stipkes in late 1977: Ik Wil Punk (I Want Punk) namechecks the Sex Pistols, just to make the reference absolutely clear, and is performed to an oompah-style brass band backing. Others referred to the Plastic Bertrand song directly—publicity in the Netherlands and Belgium surrounding that release helping to establish a core audience through which to sell a few records while tastes and critical opinions were still being formed, or to stimulate a level of amusement or condescension among baffled outsiders. Punk's natural home often sat somewhere in between those two polarities—the subculture was no stranger to humor and parody itself, nor to a critical internal dialog, and it can sometimes prove difficult to unpack just who is the victim and who is the perpetrator of the "joke."

Visually, parody records tended to make obvious references to the widespread public perception of punk, as described by sensationalist journalists and broadcasters at least. Early punk symbols that had been splashed across the media in salacious accounts of the dangers of this new fashion trend were appropriated and applied on a grand scale— particularly the safety pin, which became a key graphic link to "punk" identity, so much so in fact that it was largely abandoned by punks themselves once the stereotype took hold.

01
Artist Tjot Idi en de Stipkes
Title Ik Wil Punk
Format Single, 7-inch
Label CBS, Belgium, 1977
_ Early comedy release commenting on the new punk craze. The group photograph from the reverse of the sleeve is suitably "punked up" with safety pins, zippers, chains, and a rough photocopy treatment for the front cover. It is interesting to note that this record secured a major label release by CBS Records— the same label that was working hard to promote the Clash as leaders of the punk revolution in the UK.

02
Artist De Kuffers
Title Ik Wil Punk!
Format Single, 7-inch
Label Safety Pin, Netherlands, 1977
_ Further interpretation of the "I Want Punk" theme, with a similarly "crazy" visual aesthetic cashing in on punk media stereotypes. Note the label name, Safety Pin Records—a further attempt to drive the point home.

03
Artist Bobby Ranger
Title Punke Punke
Format Single, 7-inch
Label Monopole, Belgium, 1978
_ Note the use of Letraset "Shatter" typeface—a recent contemporary addition to the range—as the single "punk" reference point in the design.

04
Artist Plastichke
Title Ça Gaze Pour Moi
Format Single, 7-inch
Label Omega, Belgium, 1978
_ Another "comedy" version of the Plastic Bertrand hit "Ça Plane Pour Moi."

05
Artist Benny
Title Bin Wieder Frei (Ça Plane Pour Moi)
Format Single, 7-inch
Label Hansa, Germany, 1978
_ Bizarre though largely faithful reinterpretation of the Plastic Bertrand hit "Ça Plane Pour Moi," this time in the German language. Like Bobby Ranger's Punke Punke (see 03), the cover design does little to indicate any "punk" intent, and the fashion style remains resolutely rooted in the early '70s.

06
Artist De Strangers
Title Punk (Ça Plane Pour Moi)
Format Single, 7-inch
Label Omega International, Belgium, 1978
_ An even stranger take on the Plastic Bertrand hit "Ça Plane Pour Moi," released as an "amusing" parody by Belgian comic outfit De Strangers.

01	02
	03
04	05	06

EURO PUNXPLOITATION

TJOT IDI en de STIPKES

ik WiL punk

BOOKINGS: JAN VIS - HOLLAND - PHONE: 973 - 136444

CBS 5848

DE KUFFERS

IK WIL PUNK!
DE DRUGWALS

SAFETY PIN

ELF 65.129

BOBBY RANGER

new sound BELGISCHE productie

Punke Punke

ik heb lust om te zingen

S.654   MONOPOLE

PLASTIEKE

ça gaze pour moi

UN COUP J'TE VOIS,
UN COUP J'TE VOIS PAS

BENNY

Bin wieder frei

STEREO
15 528 AT

Deutsche Original Aufnahme

Ich sitz' auf einer Kokosnuss

HANSA

DE STRANGERS PUNK

Switzerland & Austria

Alpine punk had one of the most active and fast-moving punk scenes in Europe outside of London, to the extent that numerous bands were formed as early as 1976. The best-known would be Kleenex (subsequently LiLiPUT) who gained a foothold in the UK via the patronage first of John Peel and subsequently Rough Trade, but their contemporaries included Dieter Meier, the Nasal Boys, Mother's Ruin, and TNT, all from Zurich. Sozz from Büren, Crazy from Lucerne, and Geneva's Bastards and Jack & the Rippers were all active by the late '70s.

Unlike many European territories, the audience for punk in Switzerland was generally much wealthier and more inspired to see punk in terms of an art movement. To that end there was a great deal of crossover between the camps, resulting in some stunning visuals (documented in the book *Hot Love*, authored by the compiler of the *Teufelskraut* album illustrated below) as well as less regulated Ramones-derived aural fare. Kleenex were unarguably wonderful, but only a small part of the Swiss punk wave.

Neighboring Austria's scene was smaller and later off the blocks, but just as experimental. The *Wiener Blutrausch* (pictured) compilation captures the meeting space between the Austrian counterculture of the '60s and '70s and the new breed, with bands such as Schund announcing a more recognizable domestic punk style. Contemporary bands include Rentokill and 3 Feet Smaller.

01 02
Artist Various Artists
Title Teufelskraut
Format LP, 12-inch
Label Teufelskraut Ltd.,
Switzerland, 1982
_ Released in St. Gallen,
a Swiss town bordering
on Austria, this
compilation comprises
bands from both
countries.

03
Artist Schund
Title Laut Spielen!
Format EP, 7-inch
Label Self-released,
Austria, 1982
_ Early '80s Viennese
punk.

04
Artist Various Artists
Title Wiener Blutrausch
Format LP, 12-inch
Label FSchnazz-o-phone,
Austria, 1979

_ Early Austrian
compilation designed
by revered artist (and
leader of theatrical
rockers Drahdiwaberl)
Stefan Weber.

05
Artist Sozz
Title Patrol Car
Format Single, 7-inch
Label Farmer,
Switzerland, 1979

06
Artist ME 110-D
Title S/T
Format EP, 7-inch
Label Soilant,
Switzerland, 1982
_ ME 110-D, in step with
much of the World War II
imagery associated with
punk, took their name
from the production
model of the German Bf
110 (its correct name)
Messerschmitt twin-
engine fighter plane.

07
Artist TNT
Title Eine Kleine
Machtmusik
Format LP, 10-inch
Label Another Swiss
Label, Switzerland, 1983
_ Note the ingenious
parody of the aesthetics
of classical music
imagery on the cover;
from main picture to
typography.

01   03 04
02 | 05 06 07

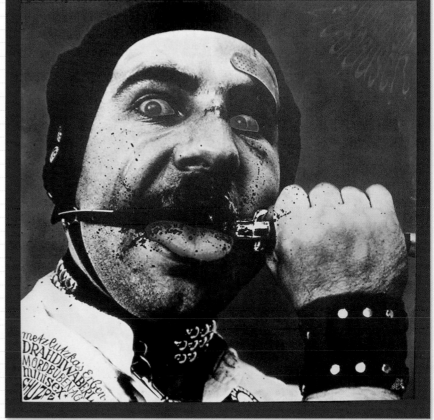

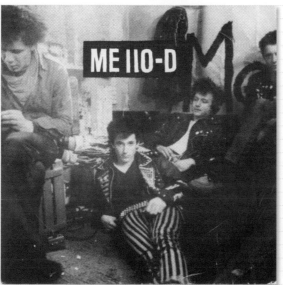

08
Artist Pöbel
Title Es Lebe Hoch
Die Perversion
Format Single, 7-inch
Label Panzaplatte,
Austria, 1981

....

09
Artist Sperma
Title Züri Punx
Format Single, 7-inch
Label Another Swiss
Label, Switzerland, 1979

....

10
_ Alpdruck fanzine,
issue number 1.
An "art" punk fanzine
featuring the work
of graphic designers
and illustrators from
central Europe. Cover
artist Orlando Odermatt.

11
Artist Kleenex
Title Ain't You
Format Single, 7-inch
Label Rough Trade,
UK 1978
_ Foldout picture
sleeve poster.

....

12
Artist Kleenex
Title You
Format Single, 7-inch
Label Rough Trade,
UK, 1979
_ Second single by the
Swiss all-girl group.
The following year they
were forced to change
their name to LiLiPUT
to avoid legal action
by the Kleenex tissue
company.

08 09 10
11 12

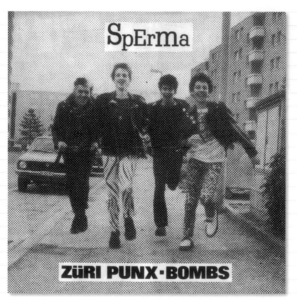

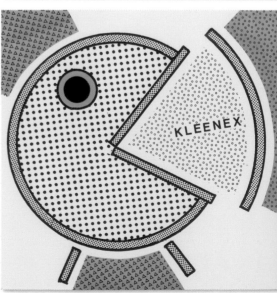

Spain & Portugal

After emerging from the dictatorship of Franco, Spain was primed for punk and as a result swept up portions of both the dispossessed working classes and left-leaning politicos. Although those politics changed from city to city, with an evident division between the Basque regions repressed under Franco and elsewhere, the music initially drew more on American garage rock traditions than '77 Brit-punk. Understandable on all accounts, as unlike other European territories, Spain had to adjust to the arrival of democracy—never mind punk rock. As Stuart Schrader of *Shit-Fi* fanzine would note, "Spanish punk in 1978 did not have a coherent ideology and had no desire to promulgate one. Its unifier was simple: possibility." Kaka De Luxe were the first noteworthy band in Madrid while Barcelona's Ultimo Resorte played their first gig in a psychiatric hospital. Eskorbuto, Korkatu, and La Polla Records (a band, not a record label) represented punk in the Basque region and there was a strong strain of punk/goth crossover with artists such as Desechables and Paralisis Permanente.

Antithetically to Spain, the first wave of punk groups in Portugal, which had itself recently emerged from fascism, were directly influenced by the '77 British punk explosion. Bands such as the Faíscas, Aqui D'el Rock, and Minas & Armadilhas emerged in 1977 and 1978. In 1982, the second wave of Portuguese punk started to reflect diverse punk styles, such as Oi! band Mata-Ratos and hardcore groups Ku de Judas and Crise Total. Whereas the first wave was short-lived, many second-wave bands are still active. In the late '80s the two most influential bands were Peste & Sida and Censurados. Latterly the scene has continued to fragment, as in many countries, between pop-punk exponents such as Aside and a resolutely hardcore creed as exemplified by Inkisição. But trends such as D-beat, crust, straight edge, riot grrrl, and ska-punk are all represented.

01
Artist R.I.P./Eskorbuto
Title Zone Especial Norte
Format Split LP, 12-inch
Label Spansuls, Spain, 1984
_ Legendary early Basque punk record featuring R.I.P. and Eskorbuto (Skurvy).

....

02
_ Poster promoting a joint concert by the bands Xutos & Pontapés (Kicks & Kicks), Aqui D'el Rock (Here the Rock) and Minas & Armadilhas (Mines & Traps), May 5, 1979.

03
Artist Aqui D'el Rock
Title Há que Violentar o Sistema
Format Single, 7-inch
Label Metro-Som, Portugal, 1978
_ The title translates as "There is the need to inflict violence to the system".

....

04
Artist GRB
Title Estoy Tan Contento!
Format EP, 7-inch
Label Self-released, Barcelona, 1986
_ The title translates as "I Am So Happy!"

01 02 03 04

Italy

Italy's first acknowledged entrants were the highly satirical Skiantos, but more legitimate punk fare came from Tampax, Hitler SS, and the all-female Kandeggina Gang—whose Jo Squillo later became a TV host and even had a pop hit duetting with Sabrina. In the early '80s Italian punk was considered almost peerless. The hardcore scene was fueled by domestic political crises and raged against corruption and police brutality, with bands such as Negazione, Upset Noise, Cheetah Chrome Motherfuckers, Raw Power, and Wretched acquiring an international reputation—the best releases matching invention to intensity. Like Holland, the punk community was built around an active squat scene, with the DIY spirit taken to heart in a way that mirrored the UK's burgeoning indie punk output.

Though the likes of Cripple Bastards continued the thread to an extent, the "Furious Years," as they became dubbed, were all but over by 1985. Italy's punk scene has struggled to recapture its stature since, though there was a boisterous engagement with Oi! and street punk thereafter, notably through the auspices of Nabat and Klasse Kriminale.

01
Artist Peggio Punx
Title Ci Stanno
Uccidendo Al Suono
Della Nostra Musica!!
Format EP, 12-inch
Label Peggio Records,
Italy, 1985

02
Pogo fanzine,
issue number 2, 1978,
Milan, Italy

03
Artist Disper-Azione
Title Sempre Immutata
Fede
Format EP, 7-inch
Label Chaos Produzioni,
Italy, 1985

	02
01	03
	04

04
Artist Upset Noise
Title Disperazione
Nevrotica
Format EP, 7-inch
Label Not on Label
(self-released), 1985
_ The cover artist is
Dumbo, also responsible
for the Peggio Punx's
Ci Stanno.

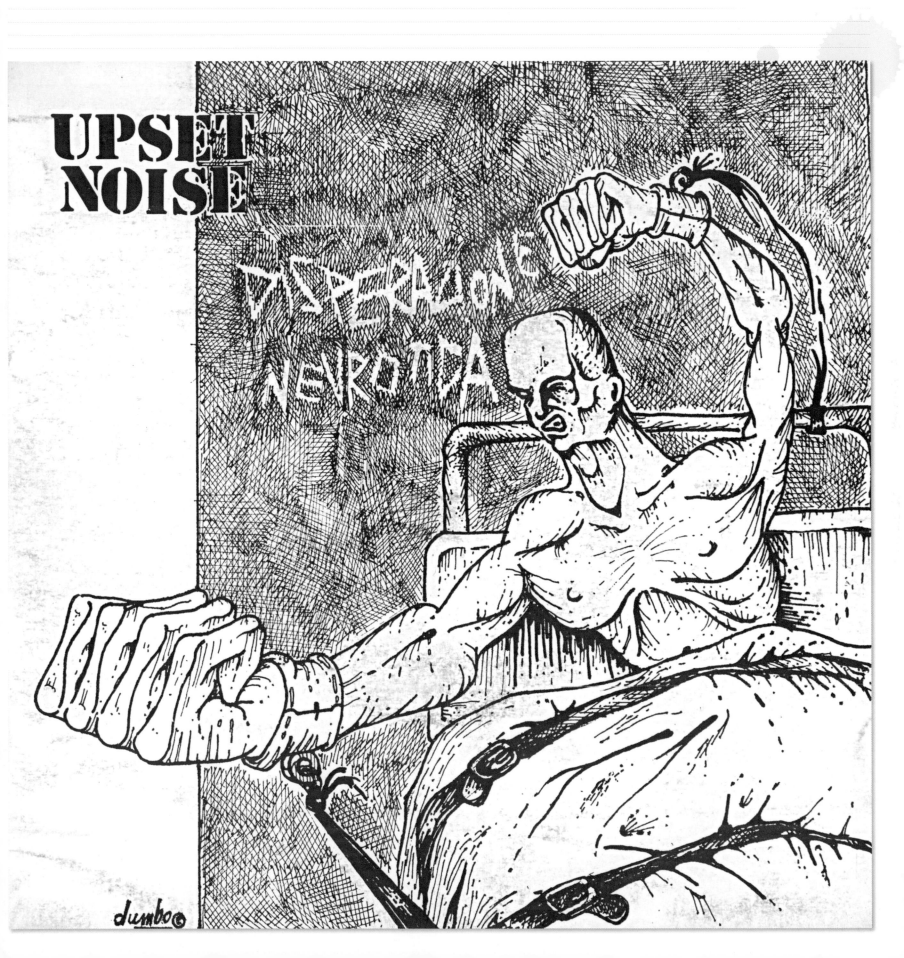

Nordic Countries

Like Italy, Scandinavia and the Nordic nations are famed for the noisy '80s upstarts who helped redefine the concept of hardcore. However, both Sweden and Finland had large early scenes, too. Sweden's thriving '70s punk community boasted Ebba Grön, the Rude Kids, Kriminella Gitarrer, Attentat, Mass Media, and P.F. Commando. The Finnish punk cause was advanced by Karanteeni, Briard, Ratsia, Eppu Normaali, Lama, Widows, and N.U.S.; the latter, the first outlet for scene mainstay Pelle Miljoona. Denmark's Sods and Lost Kids, Iceland's Fræbbblarnir, and Norway's Kjøtt and Hærverk all made their mark.

In Iceland, Purrkur Pillnik and Tappi Tíkarass ("cork the bitch's ass" translated, featuring a young Björk) would eventually coalesce into KUKL. Finland and Sweden, equally, then upped the ante by founding

a hardcore scene that was distinctive and mesmerizingly brutal—Anti-Cimex, Crude SS, Mob 47, and Avskum in Sweden and Lama, 000, Kohu-63, Rattus, Riistetyt, Terveet Kädet, and Kaaos in Finland. Sweden's Asta Kask and Strebers even promulgated a whole subgenre known as Trall ("melodic punk").

If Norway was less prolific initially, subsequent bands of note included Stengte Dører, Bannlyst, Siste Dagers Helvete, Kafka Process, DePress, and Akutt Innleggelse, the latter a nursery for Turbonegro, whose records have been widely licensed internationally. Denmark had the Electric Deads, City-X, War of Destruction, and a '90s straight edge scene based around Kopenhague modeled on Minor Threat (notably Young Wasteners and the tellingly named Washington Disease).

01
Artist Various Artists
Title Hellää Terroria Korville
Format EP, 7-inch
Label Poko, Finland, 1980
_ Compilation of some of the earliest Finnish punk bands on the prolific Poko label, which released scores of punk 45s between 1977 and the mid-'80s.

02
Artist Rattus
Title Uskonto On Vaara
Format EP, 12-inch
Label Poko, Finland, 1984
_ One of the most striking examples of Pushead's early artwork and his international collaborations.

03
Artist Headcleaners
Title Disinfection
Format EP, 7-inch
Label Malign Massacre, Sweden, 1982
_ This is the third or fourth pressing. Originally released in 1981, in Sweden the band was known as Huvudtvätt.

04
Artist Crude S.S.
Title Who'll Survive
Format EP, 7-inch
Label Uproar, Sweden, 1983

05
Artist Peyr
Title Idur Fir Fofa
Format EP, 10-inch
Label Eskimo Falkinn, Iceland, 1981

"Hellää terroria korville"

karanteeni widows

sensuuri loose prick

RATTUS

USKONTO ON VAARA

HEADCLEANERS
disinfection EP

CRUDE S.S.

WHO'LL SURVIVE

Terveet Kädet

UNKIND EP

06
Artist Terveet Kädet
Title Unkind
Format EP, 7-inch
Label Mad Rat, Finland, 1990
_ A later release by one of the preeminent forces in Finnish hardcore, whose popularity extended to commercial US thrash metal bands as well as South American groups such as Sepultura.

07
Artist Kjøtt
Title Et Nytt Og Bedre Liv
Format EP, 7-inch
Label Fleske-Skiver, Norway, 1980
_ One of the most influential of Norwegian punk bands, partially due to their insistence on singing exclusively in Norwegian.

08
Artist T.A.V. (The Aller Værste!)
Title Dans Til Musikken
Format EP, 7-inch
Label Den Gode Hensikt, Norway, 1980
_ "The Worst" were one of the first European bands to embrace the punk/ska hybrid pioneered in the UK.

09
_ Barabbas fanzine, issues 3-4/84, Barabbas, P.O. Box 151, SF-00141 Helsinki, Finland. Finnish punk zine; Barabbas also operated a record label of the same name.

10
Artist The Rude Kids
Title Stranglers
Format Single, 7-inch
Label Polydor, Sweden, 1978
_ A single released as a reaction to the Stranglers' song "Sweden (All Quiet On The Eastern Front)" from their third album *Black & White* in 1978. Swedish punks the Rude Kids ask "if it's quiet why don't you play?" in response to the Stranglers' criticism of their country and canceled 1978 tour.

11
Artist P.F. Commando
Title Rough Sound
Format EP, 7-inch
Label Comm Records, Sweden, 1980

12
Artist Hærverk
Title Produkt Av 70-åra
Format EP, 7-inch
Label Torpedo Plater-produkt, Norway, 1980
_ Hærverk translates as "vandalism" in English— while the cover art for this release is one of the most notorious in Norwegian punk history.

Due to the restrictive Swedish alcohol laws in the '70s, there were hardly any rock clubs or bars offering gigs. The core of the earliest "punk bands" in Gothenburg therefore founded Garageligan. This was a nonprofit, antifashion, antiestablishment, nonhierarchical cooperative of bands with the aim of forging a gig circuit outside of the few commercial venues available. Industrial design student Håkan Sandsjö (drummer in founding band Bruset) was responsible for most of Garageligan's earliest visual output. He drew on pop art, Barney Bubbles, Dada, and Soviet constructivism as influences; the resultant mix he describes as "nostalgic futurism." Most of the posters were done quickly in an analog cut-and-paste collage technique, usually with little more than twenty-four hours from the initial idea to the finished printed product. That provided the opportunity to comment on news issues and politics by including politicians and press cuttings in the images. The inclusion of the Rat character in most of the posters was inspired by Savage Pencil's comic strips in *Sounds* and *NME*. In a deliberate travesty of the use of razor blades in punk imagery, an electric razor was photographed close-up with a repro camera, creating the dotted patterns at the bottom of the Attentat sleeve shown opposite. Håkan nowadays runs his own advertising company, Sandsjö Action.

13
_Poster for a
Garageligan concert at
Frölunda Kulturhus with
the bands Knugens Håf,
Attentat, Mean, and
Slobobans Undergång,
1980. Design by Håkan
Sandsjö.

14
_Poster for a
Garageligan concert at
Sprängkullen with the
bands Slobobans
Undergång, Knugens Håf,
and Zäpo, 1981. Design
by Håkan Sandsjö.

15
_Poster for the first
Swedish Punk Rock
Festival at the park
Slottskogen in 1979,
featuring thirteen bands
including Ebba Grön, TT
Reuter, Grisen Skriker,
Göteborg Sound, Bruset,
Knugens Håf, Attentat,
Liket Lever, and Problem.
Poster design by Håkan
Sandsjö.

16
_Poster for a
Garageligan concert at
Sprängkullen with the
bands Mean and Abstract.
Design by Håkan Sandsjö.

17
Artist Attentat
Title Stila Dej Inte
Format Single, 7-inch
Label Ryckman Records,
Sweden, 1979
_Design and photography
by Håkan Sandsjö.

18
Artist Bruset
Title Ett Fall För John
Drake Rik & Lycklig
Format EP, 7-inch
Label GBG, Sweden, 1979
_Design by Håkan
Sandsjö.

Eastern Europe

Eastern Europe, despite suffering state-imposed artistic restrictions beyond anything encountered farther west, had active punk communities from 1977. In the Balkans, Paraf in Croatia, Pankrti in Slovenia, and Pekinška Patka in Serbia were key. All three faced routine censorship. Pekinška Patka became infamous from the moment they first played Novi Sad's Klub 24 and parodied the "Communist Youth Work Action Song" with new lyrics ("Brigitte Bardot is picking thistles/You can see half of her pussy"). The Baltic states boasted bands such as Estonia's Propeller and Generaator M and the still-active JMKE and Velikije Luki, as well as Latvia's Tsement, Inokentijs Mārpls and Clash-influenced Anglo-Latvians Arvīds Un Mūrsitēji. Foje, hugely popular post-punks from Lithuania, built on a scene developed by Už Tėvynę and Erkė Maiše and hardcore band Turboreanimacija.

Poland's punk scene began with Walek Dzedzej Punk Band, Kryzys, and Deadlock, before a second wave including Dezerter, Moskwa, Rejestracja, and Siekiera. Hungary's prime exports displayed a penchant for acronymical anonymity and included CPg, ETA, VHK (subsequently released on Jello Biafra's Alternative Tentacles label, their full name translating as "The Galloping Coroners"), Qss, and Bikini. The former Czechoslovakia gave us Energie G, the first Prague punk band, whose ranks included famed artist David Cajthaml, A64, FPB (later to find worldwide fame as Už Jsme Doma), Zona A, and Zikkurat. Early Bulgarian punk bands included Novy Tsvety (New Flowers) and VZZU, while Romanian punk only appeared after the fall of Ceauçescu with bands like Pansament, Zob (Broken), and Ura de Dupa Uşa (Anger Behind the Door). The first band to play punk in Albania was Guttersnipe in 1992.

Leningrad's Rock Club (and its "just do it" spirit of "Tusovka") was midwife to Russia's punk scene. Early performances came from Aquarium and Kino, the latter formed after Viktor Tsoy left Avtomaticheskiye Udovlyetvoritely (Automatic Satisfiers), the city's first punk group. (Leader Svin "Pig" Panov, considered the "father of Russian punk," took up the baton after reading a Russian newspaper column criticizing the Sex Pistols.) Tsoy, all but canonized by the Russian rock scene following his death in August 1990, was "punk as fuck and the first Russian musician to top the charts with a protest song" ("Mama Anarkhiya") according to expert Bryan Swirsky. Grazhdanskaya Oborona (Civil Defence), from Omsk in Siberia, were hugely influential—and remained so after leader Yegor Letov's death, despite conflicting advocacies of anarchy, communism, National Bolshevism, and Russian Orthodox Christianity that went against the grain of secular Western punk. His first musical/life partner, the late Yanka Dyagileva, is considered by some as Russia's foremost poet. The gypsy-punk crossover popularized by expat Ukrainian/Russians Gogol Bordello and Yugoslavs/Bulgarians Kultur Shock is mirrored in former Eastern Bloc states by folk punk bands such as Moldova's Zdob şi Zdub, Ukraine's Gaydamaki and Perkelaba, and Serbia's No Smoking Orchestra. Even with far greater freedoms, however, punk retained its antiauthoritarian vigil. Currently Russian art-lab punks Voyna are managing to push envelopes (and the authorities' patience) ever further with their art installations. Their *Fuck for the Heir of Little Bear* exhibition, featuring live sex, revived memories of Throbbing Gristle's *Pornography* show at London's ICA.

Further afield in the former Soviet empire, punk is represented in Kazakhstan through Adaptatsiya, in Uzbekistan through Tupratikon's, and appeared in Tajikistan with Zlo. The first punk band in the Caucasus was Georgia's Retsepti, followed by Armenia's NATO (National Amorality of Third Orgasm). In Azerbaijan, Overkill for Profit flies the flag for hardcore.

01
Artist Grazhdanskaya Oborona
Title Попс
Format 2-LP, 12-inch
Label Золотая Долина, Russia, 1992
_ This is a double album compilation of previously released material. Grazhdanskaya Oborona were hugely influential, by some way the biggest punk voice in Russia, and came from Omsk in Siberia. Their leader, Yegor Letov, passed in 2008, but he remains revered both in punk and rock circles throughout Eastern Europe.

02
Artist Visací Zámek (VZ)
Title Hymna Šibeničních Bratří
Format EP, 7-inch
Label Supraphon, Czechoslovakia, 1988
_ This was the only official punk rock release in the former Czechoslovakia under the communist regime and was housed, as a necessity, in a ready-made "standard" sleeve—referred to as the Posloucháte větrník edition. The band was also instructed to shorten its name (which translates as "Padlock") to VZ.

03
Artist Dezerter
Title Underground out of Poland
Format LP, 12-inch
Label Maximumrocknroll, USA, 1987
_ An influential archival document compiling previously recorded Dezerter material. This was a project coordinated by Joey Keithley (aka Joey Shithead) of Canada's D.O.A. Only it wasn't meant to look this way. The band, conscious to avoid clichés about their "repressed" nation, sent over specially designed artwork. It got lost in the mail. They were allegedly mortified when they saw what MRR had come up with, barbed wire notwithstanding.

04
Artist Zóna A
Title Potopa
Format LP, 12-inch
Label Opus, Bratislava, CSFR, 1990
_ Songs written from 1983 to 1989 and recorded in 1990. This was the band's first release, but they remain active.

05
Artist Moskwa
Title S/T
Format LP, 12-inch
Label Pronit, Poland, 1988

06
Artix TZN Xenna
Title Dzieci Z Brudnej
Ulicy
Format Single-EP, 7-inch
Label Tonpress, Poland,
1985
_ Released on the
state-owned Tonpress
label.

....

07
Artist Termiti
Title Ploča 'Vjeran pas
Format CD
Label Dallas Records
1996, Croatia
_ Complete discography
of legendary Croatian
punk band extant from
1978 to 1982.

08
Artist(s) Control/New
Generation (split
release)
Title BG Rock 1
Format LP, 12-inch
Label Балкантон
(Balkanton), Bulgaria,
1989
_ The color scheme and
"artistic values" on
this sleeve imply that
Control had one foot in
the new wave camp, as
the music duly attests.

09
Artist Tožibabe
Title Dežuje
Format EP, 7-inch
Label FV Založba,
Yugoslavia (Slovenia),
1986
_ Slovenian all-female
hardcore/punk band
active during the '80s.
One of the very few
Yugoslavian female bands
of the hardcore era.

06
07
08 09

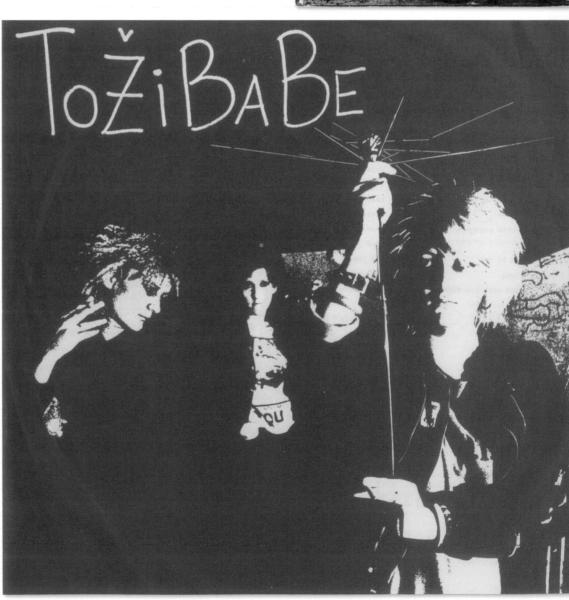

Greece & Turkey

Although there were precedents, Greek punk took shape in its capital Athens in the early '80s, with a host of bands including Panx Romana, Stress, Anti-Humans, and Adiexodo establishing a network for independent venues and releases. The second wave mirrored the advance of hardcore across Europe, with key exponents being Gulag, Ksehasmeni Profitia, and Deus Ex Machina. While the core of an anarcho independent scene remains, there is also a conflicting subgenre of bands—as there is in many European territories—invoking nationalist imagery and politics, including Hellgrinder and Pogrom.

Tünay Akdeniz & Çığrışım are widely acknowledged to have released Turkey's first punk record, though the vinyl itself betrays more of a debt to the New Seekers than the new wave. More legitimate punk artifacts include releases by Istanbul's Rashit, active from the early '90s, Dead Army Boots, Leş, Athena (a ska-punk band that appeared on Eurovision), Radical Noise, the Headbangers, and the Spinners from Ankara, the first Turkish all-female punk band. Deli, meanwhile, provided evidence of the continued restrictions in the country when they were arrested for "insulting the state" over a song that critiqued the examination board behind the national university entrance paper. "Three hours, 180 questions / May God protect my mind," ran the offending lyric.

01
Artist Tünay Akdeniz & Çığrışım
Title Mesela Mesele
Format Single, 7-inch
Label Pardon, Turkey, 1978
_ Marketed as "punk rock," though it sounds like absolutely nothing of the kind.

....

02
Artist Panx Romana
Title Αντάρτες Πόλεων
Format LP, 12-inch
Label Wipe Out!, Greece, 1989
_ Panx Romana chose a photograph of the Tiananmen Square "tank man" incident from the year of release as a cover shot—an image still largely blocked from Chinese eyes by "the Great Firewall of China"—in an act of political solidarity.

03
Artist Rashit
Title Kapak Güzelleri
Format LP, 12-inch
Label Darbouka Records (France), Turkey, 2003
_ This album cover makes strong visual references to both Andy Warhol's *Marilyn* screenprints and Jamie Reid's "God Save the Queen" graphics.

....

04
Artist Κουμπότρυπες Α.Ε.
Title Η Καινούργια Επανάσταση/Καθημερινές Καταστάσεις
Format Single, 7-inch
Label Happening, Greece, 1983
_ The first punk record with Greek lyrics.

05
Artist Gulag
Title Big Talk (Μόνο Λόγια)
Format EP, 7-inch
Label Wreck-Age Records (Germany), Greece, 1989

01 02
03 04 05

In the late '70s, the preeminent UK punk artists, all of whom with the exception of the Damned had signed to major labels, were bartered to foreign markets, licensed either to subsidiary outlets or third parties. In many cases, artwork was altered, sometimes in small typographical detail, perhaps signified only by the presence of foreign-language notation on the label. Sometimes the original approach was jettisoned entirely. This of course made them extremely collectible—smarter operators realized this quickly—and within two years the initial flurry of 45rpms triggered by the independent record label boom was accompanied by "import" racks in record stores for the fan who "had to have everything."

Among the most intriguing examples were the Stranglers. With an Anglo-French bass player immersed in Japanese martial arts cultures and a lead vocalist who had spent years studying in Scandinavia, they were far more worldly than some of their peers. Hence French versions of several songs and, from their third album *Black & White*, "Sweden (All Quiet on the Western Front)" was issued as a single in the country that provided titular inspiration, with a rerecorded Swedish vocal. Later, Hagsätra punk band the Rude Kids repaid the compliment, cutting the song "Stranglers" and opening for them.

The most prized foreign releases were generally those issued in Japan, whose reputation for design and packaging was highly regarded (even if the lyric sheets, and their accompanying translations, were a little more haphazard). Many of these records were also pressed on "super vinyl," using a purer compound produced by JVC in Japan that reduced surface noise and was extremely durable. Just as attractive, however, was their design studios' willingness to radically reinterpret the original design concepts.

Notable foreign sleeves include the New Zealand version of the Pistols' "Pretty Vacant," utilizing photography from their Screen on the Green show rather than the conventional shattered glass image. The German pressing of the Clash's "Train in

Vain," not even released as a single domestically, featured Mick Jones in performance as well as *London Calling*-styled typography. Siouxsie & the Banshees' "Israel" abandoned the group's high-end art concepts for a color group picture on its German pressing. The Jam, that most English of punk era exports, had multitudinous foreign editions of their singles, ranging from a Greek "pop art" box set to a Spanish "Eton Rifles" (emblazoned with the legend "No. 1 en Inglaterra" added, which was a bit of a fib, as it peaked at number three). There were six separate international versions of "All Around the World" and around the same number of "Strange Town." Again, here the Japanese edition stood out—the sleeve featuring two businessmen walking down a street in twilight, rather than the standard "hitcher" version.

The independents were at it, too; the very first UK punk single, the Damned's "New Rose," was widely licensed, including a version in a unique picture sleeve, and featuring a different B-side, on the Dutch Ariola Benelux imprint. Lesser lights such as London (the band, rather than the city) had no picture sleeve at all for the UK release of "Everyone's a Winner," but did have three different ones for the German, Italian, and French markets. Slaughter & the Dogs' 1979 German release of "I Believe," meanwhile, with impeccably awful art direction, was actually a recording by subsequent band the Studio Sweethearts.

If this all seemed like a rather one-way cultural exchange, that was largely true. American punk, while hardly in its infancy, was not nearly as commodified at this stage (though there were several variations of Ramones sleeves in Spain, Japan, and elsewhere). Mainland European artists didn't have sufficient followings to sell punk product back to Britain, with rare exceptions. And thus was born the foreign pressing niche, which became an obsession among certain punk record collectors for several years before a combination of the Internet, music industry takeovers, format consolidation, oil prices, and, just perhaps, common sense, did for it.

"I ended up looking after the international situation, doing the licensing deals. I managed to coax the French and the Germans and Scandinavians and Japanese and Australians, and get a great network of licensees for Stiff. And that's what I did . . . There was a point when being on Stiff meant there wasn't a moment when we didn't have a single in the Top 40. It just seemed every week it was like that and it was more a case of keeping the Europeans up to speed with how successful we were being in the UK."

Alan Cowderoy on how foreign licensing helped keep the Stiff Records ship afloat

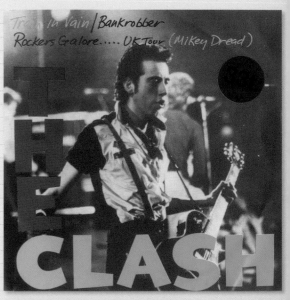

WHO WANTS
THE WORLD?

01
Artist The Clash
Title Train in Vain
Format Single, 7-inch
Label CBS, Germany, 1980
_ Originally recorded as a promotional track to be given away on a free flexi disc, "Train in Vain" became a late addition to the album *London Calling*, appearing as an uncredited extra track. The EP was not released in the UK, but became extremely popular as an import item.

02
Artist Siouxsie & the Banshees
Title Israel
Format Single, 7-inch
Label Polydor, Germany, 1980
_ German release: the single was housed in a plain gold die-cut sleeve on its original UK issue.

03
Artist The Stranglers
Title N'Emmènes Pas Harry
Format Single, 7-inch
Label Liberty United, France, 1980
_ French issue of the single "Don't Bring Harry," sung in French by Anglo-French bass player Jean Jacques Burnel.

04
Artist The Stranglers
Title Duchess
Format Single, 7-inch
Label United Artists, Japan, 1979

05
Artist The Stranglers
Title 5 Minutes
Format Single, 7-inch
Label United Artists, Germany, 1978

06
Artist The Stranglers
Title Sverige (Jag är insnöad på östfronten)
Format Single, 7-inch
Label United Artists, UK, 1978
_ The Stranglers' song "Sweden (All Quiet On The Eastern Front)" rerecorded in Swedish. Singer Hugh Cornwell had studied in Sweden prior to the formation of the group in 1974. After the Stranglers canceled their 1978 Swedish tour, the Rude Kids released an answer single with a parody artwork entitled "Stranglers (If It's So Quiet, Why Don't You Play?)"

07
_ German poster advertising the Sex Pistols' "God Save the Queen" single. The text reads "The incredible single from England's most notorious band—now available here."

| 01 | | 04 | 05 | 03 06 |
| 02 | | 07 | | |

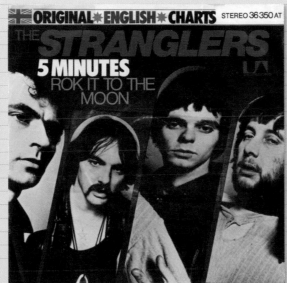

Australia & New Zealand

The Australian response to punk was proportionally as creative and gripping as that of the UK or US. Sydney's Radio Birdman (featuring Detroit refugee Deniz Tek) ran a close second to Brisbane's Saints, whose "(I'm) Stranded" predated both the Pistols' and the Damned's debuts and remains as exhilarating today as on its original release in September 1976. However, as demonstrated by *Tales from the Australian Underground* (2003), one of the finest archive regional compilations ever, both dissidence and dissonance ensued. Melbourne's The Boys Next Door, featuring a young Nick Cave, and Kim Salmon's Scientists in Perth were just two of the notable bands establishing a national scene that would eventually encompass acts such as the Celibate Rifles, New Christ, and Lime Spiders. Throughout, however, Australian punk remained more in thrall to the Stooges-MC5 riff-dominated garage rock aesthetic than its UK variant.

In New Zealand, the founding fathers were the Scavengers, Suburban Reptiles, and the Enemy. The latter, though unrecorded at the time, saw the debut of Chris Knox, a huge influence on the development of the "Dunedin Sound" and subsequently the US's lo-fi tradition through his work with Toy Love and Tall Dwarfs. The Clean were equally important in that regard, while over in Auckland, Simon Grigg's Propeller Records documented the North Island's punk and post-punk scene.

Small-island scenes of pop-punk (or perhaps, surf punk) appeared in the Pacific in the '90s with Snocud in Tahiti (later to become Joli Rouge), Mutants Love Chicken in New Caledonia, and Felix and the Cats in Fiji.

01
Artist Kryptonics
Title Land That Time Forgot
Format Single, 7-inch
Label Easter Records, Australia, 1987

02
Artist James Freud & the Radio Stars
Title Modern Girl
Format Single, 7-inch
Label Mushroom, Australia, 1980

03
Artist The Rocks
Title You'r So Boring
Format EP, 7-inch,
Label Small Axe, Australia, 1996 reissue (originally Point Blank Records, Australia, 1978)
_ While the original pressing stated "Point Blank Records" instead of "Small Axe Records" on the sleeve, it's notable that this reissue retained the original grammatical mistake in the title.

04
Artist Seminal Rats
Title Omnipotent
Format LP, 12-inch
Label What Goes On (UK), Australia, 1987

05
Artist The Clean
Title Boodle Boodle Boodle
Format EP, 7-inch
Label Flying Nun, New Zealand, 1981
_ Chris Knox of the Enemy, Toy Love, and Tall Dwarfs fame drew this cover based on a promotional photograph of the band. It became Flying Nun's most important early success, helping create the notion of the "Dunedin Sound" and establishing the record label as the most important and durable New Zealand independent record label.

06
Artist Fun Things
Title S/T
Format EP, 7-inch
Label Machine Music, Australia, 1980
_ Featuring brothers Brad and Murray Shepherd, who respectively went on to Hoodoo Gurus and Screaming Tribesmen, among others.

07
Artist The Saints
Title This Perfect Day
Format Single, 12-inch
Label Harvest, UK, 1977
—

08
_ *Rise Above* fanzine,
issue number 2, 1985

09
Artist Desperate
Measures
Title S/T
Format EP, 7-inch
Label Desperate Times,
New Zealand, 1982
_ Featuring future *Big
Cheese/Vive Le Rock!*
editor Eugene Butcher on
vocals, who remembers
"hand-printing all
three hundred copies!"

10
Artist Lime Spiders
Title Out of Control
Format Single, 7-inch
Label Citadel,
Australia, 1985

Canada

"Oh Canaduh," sang the Subhumans in 1978 on the B-side to "Death to the Sickoids," in what was effectively an alternative punk rock national anthem later covered by scene veterans NoMeansNo. Canadian punk first took root in Toronto with the Diodes and Viletones—both were playing CBGB by the summer of '77, the former having set up their city's first punk club, Crash 'n' Burn, while the latter's singer Nazi Dog would earn a reputation as the Great White North's Iggy. Other early movers included the Curse, the Poles, and the Dishes, together with Hamilton's Teenage Head and Forgotten Rebels and the Skulls in Vancouver, whose cast included both Joey "Shithead" Keithley, later of D.O.A., and Brian "Wimpy" Goble, who subsequently formed the Subhumans.

In common with its US cousins, by the early '80s the locus of punk shifted as a counter to the new wave boom. D.O.A.'s *Hardcore '81* is considered by many to have given this new subgenre its first titular reference. Canada's punk output in the '80s was as prolific as it was varied, much of it attended by a sense of humor (particularly notable in the output of Stretch Marks and Dayglo Abortions) that encompassed not only lyrics but artwork. Edmonton's skateboarding hardcore protagonists SNFU (Society's No Fucking Use) released their debut album *. . . and no one else wanted to play* in 1985, appropriating a 1962 photograph of a young boy with a toy hand grenade (by celebrated photographer Diane Arbus) for the cover. Following a legal dispute, the cover was withdrawn and replaced with a hand-drawn image bearing a strikingly close resemblance to the original, only to fall foul of copyright and be withdrawn yet again.

Other notable exponents included Toronto's Youth Youth Youth, Direct Action, and the irascible Bunchofuckingoofs. A French-Canadian scene developed separately in the '80s under the influence of the French "alternative wave." Bands like Banlieue Rouge positioned themselves on the left wing of street punk. Propelled by political activism, the Quebecois scene continues to thrive with bands like Les Ordures Ioniques and Les Flokons Givrés.

01
Artist Dayglo Abortions
Title Feed U.S.A. Fetus
Format LP, 12-inch
Label Fringe Products, Canada, 1986
_ Design by Rancid.

02
Artist The Subhumans
Title Incorrect Thoughts
Format LP, 12-inch
Label Friends, Canada, 1980
_ Despite having been one of the finer punk bands to walk the planet, the Subhumans probably remain best-known for their connections to Direct Action and "The Vancouver Five"—which led to original member Gerry "Useless" Hannah spending five years in jail. Design by Bob Mercer (photo "ORAF").

03
Artist Forgotten Rebels
Title In Love with the System
Format LP, 12-inch
Label Star Records, Canada, 1981

04
Artist D.O.A.
Title Hardcore 81
Format LP, 12-inch
Label Friends, Canada, 1981
_ The album that gave an entire movement its name. Design by Bob Mercer.

05
Artist D.O.A.
Title Bloodied but Unbowed
Format LP, 12-inch
Label CD Presents, USA, 1986
_ A compilation of early recordings by Canada's

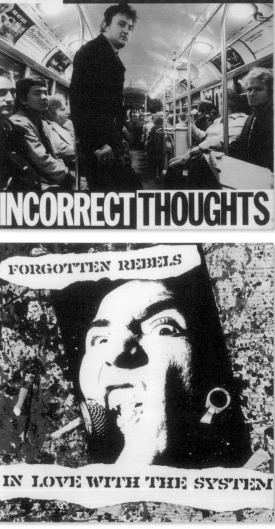

most celebrated punk band, D.O.A., featuring Mount Rushmore as a backdrop (as with Dayglo Abortions, the extent to which they were reacting to US rather than native Canadian politics is clear).

06
Artist The Diodes
Title S/T
Format LP, 12-inch
Label CBS, Canada, 1977

07
Artist Bunchofuckingoofs
Title Theres No Solution So Theres No Problem
Format 2-EP, Double 7-inch
Label Back Alley, Canada, 1986
_ The Goofs' self-released first vinyl—a band who were synonymous with antifascist violence and excessive drinking in Toronto, but whose logo once graced a Sotheby's catalog (Kieran Plunkett of UK punk band the Restarts, who studied art in Vancouver, had spray-painted it on the Berlin Wall just weeks before it came down, and the "block" was later exhibited in Switzerland and New York before auction).

08
Artist Stretch Marks
Title Who's in Charge
Format EP, 7-inch
Label Head Butt, Canada, 1983

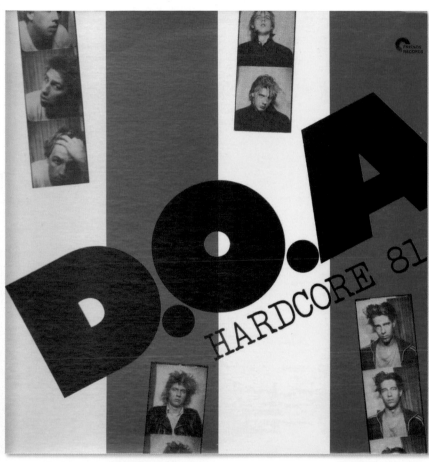

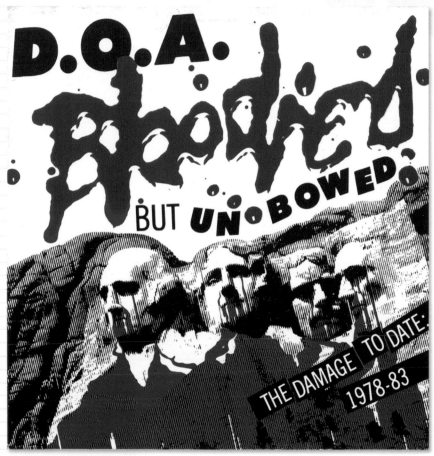

Japan & Asia

Home to some of the most musically accomplished and brutal, lightning-fast hardcore punk, Japan's prime movers were originally SS, followed by Anarchy, Star Club, the Stalin, Typhus/Gauze, and scene titans Gism. Confuse, Lip Cream, street punks Cobra, Systematic Death, Kuro, Death Side, and the Comes flew the flag into the '80s. While much of Japan's punk stable betrays a greater debt to metal than is commonplace elsewhere, the output is also notable for its variety, encompassing D-beat, anarcho punk, pop-punk, grindcore, and fertile Oi! and street punk scenes.

China now has a punk scene large enough to compete, from early movers He Yong, Underbaby, and Catcher in the Rye in Beijing to more contemporary bands like Brain Failure, SMZB (from Wuhan), No Name (from Xi'an), Anarchy Boys, Gumbleed, and Misandao. Punk in Taiwan appeared in 1988 with Double X. Hong Kong was home to '80s expat bands like the Rebel Rockers and the Convicted, and in parallel, to the legendary libertarian band Blackbird, influenced by Crass, Patti Smith, Chinese folk, and blues, with songs sung in Cantonese.

The Philippines nurtured the second oldest punk scene in Asia, with veterans Third World Chaos and Ocean Zoo appearing in the early '80s, followed by bands on early label Twisted Red Cross. It was closely followed by Malaysia (pioneers Hijrah, the Pilgrims, and Mallaria) and Singapore (first-known band Opposition Party in 1988). Thailand had punks in the '80s and currently hosts a fully grown scene,

street punks Bangkok Alcohol plying the bars of Khao San Road. A large punk scene in Indonesia was birthed in Bandung in the mid-'90s, but has since spread all over the archipelago, from Aceh to Sulawesi. In Jakarta, it is centered around bands like Anti Squad, Brigade of Bridge, and skinheads the End. Much South-East Asian output was captured primarily on cassettes, long after the format had been superceded in the West; often this would mean that aural artifacts were bedecked in covers that were individually hand-drawn rather than replicated by machine.

Punk appeared in South Asia in the mid-'90s; in Nepal with Jilkey and the Rockers, and later in India with Messiah and Tripwire, and in Pakistan with Cornhole and Korrupt'd. The earliest punks in the Middle East were spotted in the '80s in Lebanon and Israel (Rami Fortis' first album was highly acclaimed, while the first-known anarcho punk band Noon Mem's demo *The Final Ada* caused a stir) and in the early '90s in Iran and Jordan.

01
Artist Ghoul
Title Oi! Oi!
Format Flexidisc, 7-inch
Label Hold-Up, Japan, 1985
_ Flexidiscs were common among punk and hardcore releases from Japan during the '80s long after their brief popularity in the West had receded.

02
Doll Super Rock Magazine, issue no. 251, July 2008.
_ Legendary Japanese magazine *Doll*. This edition included extended articles on early Swiss punk rock and Defiance from Portland, Oregon.

03

Artist Warriors
Title Wild Cherry
Format EP, 12-inch
Label S.F.X, Japan, 1986
_ Known as Nickey & the
Warriors or simply the
Warriors at various
points in their career.

04

Artist The Stalin
Title Mushi
Format Picture LP, 12-inch
Label Climax, Japan, 1983

05

Artist The Star Club
Title The Very Best of
Kings of Punk
Format Picture LP, 12-inch
Label Club the Star
Records, Japan, 1987
_ Tenth anniversary
special-edition release.
In common with so many
Japanese releases, the
supposed "grubbiness"
of punk is opposed by
high-end design and
production standards.

06

Artist Lip Cream
Title Kill Ugly Pop!
Format LP, 12-inch
Label Captain/Dynamite,
Japan, 1985

07

Artist Various Artists
Title Outsider
Format LP, 12-inch
Label City Rocker
Records, Japan, 1982
_ Note the use of almost
identikit Crass logo
and imagery from their
Bullshit Detector various

artist releases,
including "pay no
more than" legend
and stencil typography—
but in a twist of the
UK band's "anarchy and
peace" coda, which is
replaced herein with
"anarchy and violence"
in the central circle,
signifying not only
regional but also
aesthetic and
philosophical
dissonance from the
original template.

01 02 | 03 04 05 | 06 07

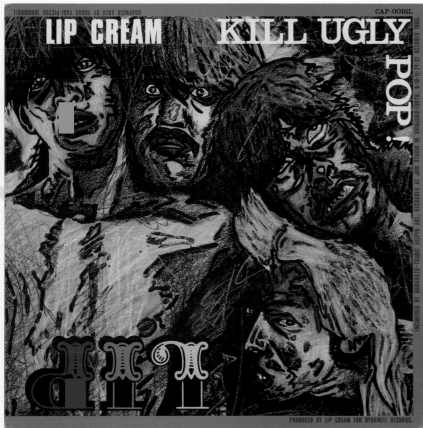

Latin America

The original punk scene in Brazil, pioneered by Restos de Nada and later Olho Seco and Cólera, dwarfed all others on the continent. They were followed by Los Violadores, Los Laxantes (later Todos Tus Muertos), and Alerta Roja from Argentina, as the subculture spread throughout South America. Though punk is now hugely popular in Brazil, it is also deeply factionalized; subgenres such as riot grrrl and straight edge compete for attention. Peru's first widely distributed punk band Leusemia formed in 1983. Though Uruguay had a proto-punk/garage rock scene with bands like Mother's Worries, its domestic punk scene only effectively got underway in the mid-'80s (as did those of Ecuador, Colombia, and Venezuela), eventually leading to the rise of Trotsky Vengarán. Chilean punk appeared just before the fall of the dictatorship

with Los Presioneros and Oi! band Ocho Bolas. In Central America, Panama and Costa Rica had pioneering scenes in the early '90s. In the Caribbean and outside of safe European homes, Anti-Everything released the first hardcore punk album from the Caribbean in 2009. Operating out of Port of Spain, Trinidad, their most famous song, "Trinidad Sucks," mixed straight punk hollering with patois, while other songs employ steel drums. Even Cuba boasts its own punk band Porno Para Ricardo, following in the hard-fought footsteps of veterans Joker and Los Detenidos, and again not without some struggle. Leader Gorki Águila spent several years in jail on vague charges of "dangerousness" and was only released after international pressure on the Cuban authorities.

01
Artist Kaoz
Title Ayacucho
Format EP, 7-inch
Label(s) Sintemores Records, Odio Los Discos Records, and Discos Huayno Amargo Peru, 2008 (collaboration release between three Peruvian labels)
_ Kaoz formed in 1986 in Lima, Peru. The tracks were recorded in 1989.

02
Artist Cólera
Title Dé O Fora
Format EP, 7-inch
Label Hageland, Belgium, 1986
_ From São Paulo, Cólera were arguably Brazil's most important early punk export, alongside Olho Seco. Both bands saw releases on various international imprints.

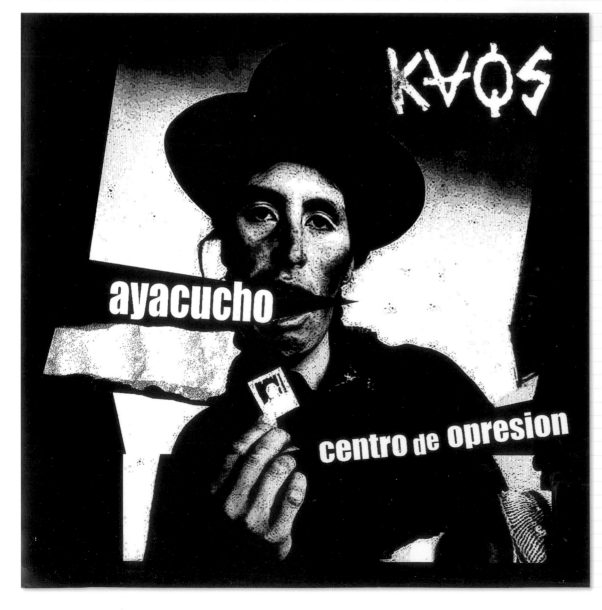

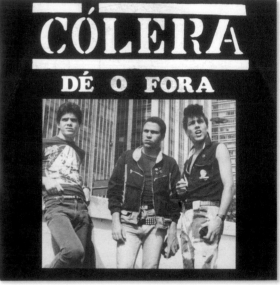

Artist Various Artists

Title Grito Suburbano (Suburban Scream)

Format LP, 12-inch

Label New Face, Brazil, 1984

04

Artist Bastardos Sin Nombre (BSN) (Bastards Without a Name)

Title Guerra Bacteriológica

Format EP, 7-inch

Label Discos Fuentes, self-released, Colombia, 1991

05

Artist Inocentes

Title Pânico em SP (Panic in São Paulo)

Format EP, 12-inch

Label WEA Discos LTDA, Rio de Janeiro, Brazil, 1986

_ A rare major label

"punk" release from South America with a cover managing to indicate the band's distance from "DIY" values while retaining the mystique of the ghetto.

06

Artist Ratos de Porão (Bilge Rats)

Title Crucificados Pelo Sistema (Crucified by the System)

Format LP, 12-inch

Label Punk Rock Discos, Brazil, 1984

07

Artist Various Artists

Title Ataque Sonoro (Sound Attack)

Format LP, 12-inch

Label Ataque Frontal, Brazil, 1985

01 02 05
03 | 06 07
04

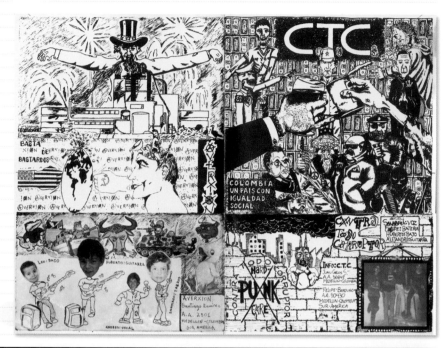

Important International Collaborations

The cross-proliferation that occurred in international punk in the early '80s was built on the curiosity of the likes of the UK's Andy "Shesk" Thompson of Xcentric Noise and Chris BCT (Borderless Countries Tapes) in the US. Blown away by the explosive hardcore they found ready-formed in scenes in Sweden, Italy, Brazil, and further afield, they documented their discoveries on duplicated cassette tapes bedecked in impromptu DIY art (or in Xcentric Noise's case, secured the use of some of Pushead's earliest drawings).

01–03

Artist Various Artists
Title Raw War—The World of Punk (see also *Grevious Musical Harm*)
Format Cassette
Label Xcentric Noise Records, Beverley, North Humberside, UK, 1983
_ Andy "Shesk" Thompson's Xcentric Noise was one of the earliest cassette labels to spread the word about the vitality and energy of international punk. *Raw War* (01), the fourth in the series, introduced listeners to such important bands as Olho Seco (Brazil), 5° Braccio (Italy), Wannskrækk (Norway), Rattus and Terveet Kadet (Finland), Funeral Oration (Holland), as well as domestic UK bands (Cult Maniax) and underground American acts (the New York Ravers, Neos). Artwork came from the then unheralded hardcore punk/metal graphic artist Pushead, who also drew XNT's first international vinyl single by the Headcleaners (02) and the cover for *Grevious Musical Harm* (03). "It was only years later that I realized I'd spelt 'grievous' wrong," notes Andy.

04

Artist Various Artists
Title Welcome to 1984
Format LP, 12-inch
Label Maximumrocknroll, USA, 1984
_ A year later, some of the bands featured on cassettes like *Raw War* eventually reached vinyl (including Olho Seco, Terveet Kadet, and Ratus) via this hugely significant *Maximumrocknroll*-sponsored release—named after Jello Biafra's declamatory, and timely, line in "California Über Alles."

Artist Various Artists
Title I've Got an
Attitude Problem
Format EP, 7-inch
Label Loony Tunes and
BC Tapes & Records joint
release, UK and US, 1987
_ A combined release
by Scarborough's Loony
Tunes and San Diego's
BCT—primarily focusing
on Italian and Swedish
hardcore bands.

06
_ Verbal Assault (US),
Negazione (Italy), and
Original Disease (France)
poster for a gig in
Zurich: evidence of
the way in which
international

collaboration occurred
between bands from
different continents.

07
Artist Various Artists
Title Ahhhh... Italian
Punk
Format Cassette
Label BCT, San Diego,
USA, 1983
_ Like Xcentric Noise,
BCT distributed
worldwide punk to the
West and further afield.
This, its fourth release,
sold for just $4 and
contained thirty-two
songs over its C-60
format, mining Chris's
beloved Italian
hardcore. "Yeah,"

he acknowledges, "the
Xcentric international
comp tapes were huge
in exposing me and
other punks I knew to
non-US/UK hardcore
bands. When we formed
BCT we decided that
since there was no limit
to who we could have on
our comps that we'd try
to reach out to anywhere
in the world and ended
up doing Finnish,
Italian, Spanish, and
Brazilian comp tapes."

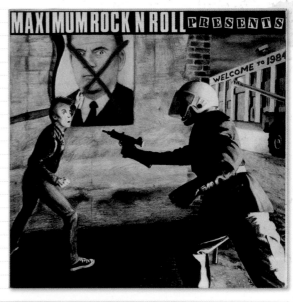

CHRIS BCT

3 Tapes, from San Diego, released a slew of compilation cassettes (and later records) from the early '80s onward that helped spread the word about the thriving European and world hardcore scenes that had been brewing underground with little attention for years.

1 Kaaos – Totaalinen Kaaos
7-inch EP (Propaganda Records, 1982, Finland)
_ Kaaos may be my favorite Finnish hardcore band and it's hard when there were so many incredible ones. They just get to the core of HC and blast through.

2 Various – Russia Bombs Finland
LP (Propaganda Records, 1982, Finland)
_ I could never particularly tell who was who when I listened to this but it was all pure Finnish HC, some of the finest on earth.

3 Various – I Thrash, Therefore I Am
Cassette (BCT, 1985, various countries)
_ One of my top two favorite all-time non-US/UK HC comps. When we put it together, as with all our comps, we only used the songs that ripped.

4 Various – Last White Christmas Vol I
Cassette (BCT/Cessophena Records, 1984, Italy)
_ Antonio, bassist for Cheetah Chrome Motherfuckers, was my first world-punk visitor and he came a week after this gig, around July '83. GDHC, the independent punk collective in Italy, decided that BCT could release it. CCM explained to me when they did their one LP later in 1986 that Italy had no rock history to speak of, so the punks' creative base was unrestrained. I feel there's some jazz seepin' in there.

5 Peggio Punx – Disastro Sonoro
7-inch EP (Peggio Dischi, 1982, Italy)
_ These guys have what sounds to me like a punk mandolin—totally unique.

6 Wretched – In Nome Del Loro Potere Tutto
Stato Tatto
7-inch EP (self-released, 1983, Italy)
7 Wretched/Indigesti Split 7-inch EP (self-released, 1983, Italy)
_ The first three Wretched records—two 7-inches and their 10-inch—are some of the finest Italian HC ever; fierce, intense, unrelenting.

8 Various – Sub
LP (Estúdios Vermelhos, 1982, Brazil)
_ Brazil had a great scene and most of the great bands (Ratos de Porão, Cólera, Psykoze, Fogo Cruzado) are on this comp.

8 Various Singles and LPs
(circa late '80s/early '90s, Japan)
_ Brain Death, Outu, Systematic Death, Sob, Rose Rose, Deathside, Deathless Muss, Lip Cream—any 7-inch or LP by any of these Japanese bands from the late '80s/early '90s.

9 Various – Really Fast Vol. I
LP (Really Fast Records, 1983, Sweden)
_ We marveled at this comp when it came out (featuring Missburkama, Anti-Cimex, Asta Kask, Huvudtvätt, and others). A classic representation of Swedish bands.

10 Appendix – Ei Raha oo Mun Valuuttaa
LP (Propaganda Records, 1983, Finland)
_ Great Finnish hardcore from 1983.

LUK TAM

Luk Tam has written for punk fanzines since 1986, including *Maximumrocknroll*, and run the not-for-profit Tian An Men 89 Records since 1993. The label issues vinyl punk records from "non-Western" countries, especially those lacking pressing plants. He has traveled to more than 120 countries searching for punk and underground music, holds an MD in ethnology and degrees in English, Psychology, and Cinema, and speaks French, German, Chinese, Russian, and several other languages.

1 Demokhratia – Bled El Petrol Takoul Lekhra
7-inch EP (Tian An Men 89 Records, 2009, Algeria)
_ The first Algerian hardcore punk band blasts the global scene with their political songs in the local Algerian Arabic dialect and announces the birth of the Middle East punk scene in the twenty-first century.

2 Various – 1382 The Persian New Waves (Majd-e Now-e Farsi)
LP (Tian An Men 89 Records, 2004, Iran)
_ Twenty-five years after the Islamic Revolution, and the death of the first wave of Iranian rock bands, punk and alternative styles help rebirth Persian rock 'n' roll.

3 Various – 10000 Years Punk
7-inch EP (Pangke Wansui) (Tian An Men 89 Records, 1998, China)
_ The first ever Chinese punk vinyl, presenting the second wave of Bejing punk bands (after the first "grunge"-inspired wave) featuring Oi!, punk, and ska-punk.

4 Yegor i Opizdenevshiye – Prig-Skok
LP (GrOb Records/Zolotaya Dolina, 1992, Russia)
_ Side project of the late Yegor Leytov, vocalist and mastermind of Grazhdanskaya Oborona, legends of Siberian punk. Most albums were recorded clandestinely at home during Soviet times. Epic Russian punk with folk and psych influences.

5 Sweety Punk – Soa Ity Painky
7-inch EP (Tian An Men 89 Records, 2001, Madagascar)
_ First band to put Madagascar on the punk map; a hidden, struggling punk scene.

6 Sound of Ruby – From Under the Sands of the Desert
7-inch EP (Tian An Men 89 Records, 2011, Saudi Arabia)
_ First Saudi punk band craftily mixing punk, folk, and psych.

7 Termiti – Ploca Vjeran Pas
CD (Dallas, 1996, Croatia)
_ Reissue of this classic Yugo punk band; killer melodic '77 punk laced with synth.

8 Raikoris – Himalayan Frostbite
7-inch EP (BatAttak, 2003, Nepal)
_ Melodic, political Nepali punk with female vocals; the pioneers of the DIY Katmandu scene.

9 Sepia – Two Eggs
CD (Bakery Music, 1995, Thailand)
_ Crazy, insane punk-driven mix from the Kingdom of Siam.

10 Various – We Are the Punx in Korea
CD (Skunk, 2002, South Korea)
_ Top-class compilation of the second wave of Korean punk; a blistering mix of street punk, hardcore, and pop-punk.

WORLDWIDE PUNK TOP TENS

JOSEF LODERER

Josef Loderer currently lives in England but grew up in Slovakia, Switzerland, and Canada. He ran Zurich Chainsaw Massacre Records in Switzerland, promoted tours by the likes of Rattus as well as running a long-running punk radio show from Zurich.

1 Crazy – No Chance
LP (Moderne Musik Tonträger, 1980, Switzerland)
_ I spent most of my life in Switzerland and no other band could have done a better job at describing lyrically my feelings about this little country in the center of Europe.

2 Rattus – WC Räjähtää
LP (Poko, 1982, Finland)
_ Rattus produced many fine records, but this one was their best.

3 G.I.S.M. – Detestation
Mini-LP (Dogma Records, 1983, Japan)
_ Brutally executed hardcore with a guitarist in love with himself; extraordinary release and band.

4 The Kids – self-titled
LP (Phillips, 1978, Belgium)
_ One of the best '70s punk records ever produced.

5 So Much Hate – How We Feel
LP (X-Port Plater, 1987, Norway)
_ In my opinion one of the most important late '80s hardcore acts and maybe the last band that mattered in that decade.

6 Gauze – Equalizing Distort
Mini-LP (Selfish Records, 1986, Japan)
_ If someone asked me to describe Japcore, then this record answers all.

7 Razors – Banned Punx
Mini-LP (Konnekshen, 1982, Germany)
_ Razors were from Hamburg and played superb UK-influenced punk straight from the streets.

8 Terveet Kädet – Ääretön Joulu
7-inch EP (Poko, 1982, Finland)
_ Just like Rattus, TK produced more than one good record but this one stands out in terms of production and eight short, sharp songs.

9 Camera Silens – Réalité
LP (self-released, 1984, France)
_ In the late '70s France didn't really produce many great punk records. Hardcore never seemed to have had much of an impact and so it is not surprising that in the '80s bands like Camera Silens played hard yet melodic chorus-laden punk rock.

10 Ultimo Resorte – self-titled
7-inch EP (Flor Y Nata Records, 1982, Spain)
_ A smasher of an EP from Barcelona in 1982.

ANDY THOMPSON

Andy Thompson's Xcentric Noise was a (primarily) tape label run from North Humberside that was instrumental in the spread of worldwide punk in the early '80s. He currently works as a photographer in London.

1 EU's Arse – Questa E' La Loro Speculazione Di Morte!
Split 7-inch EP with Impact (self-released, 1983, Italy)
_ Just raw, heartfelt passion with extended growling screams and great cover; raw and powerful as hell.

2 Various – Grito Suburbano
LP (Pogar Records, 1982, Brazil)
_ Featuring Olho Seco, Cólera, etc.

3 Headcleaners – Disinfection/Infection Grows
7-inch EPs (Malign Massacre Records, 1981, and Xcentric Noise Records (UK), 1983, Sweden)
_ Classic early Swedish hardcore.

4 Rattus – Fucking Disco
7-inch EP (Hilipili Records, 1981, Finland)
_ And some classic early Finnish hardcore.

5 Massmedia – Das Jazz
7-inch (Massproduktion, 1979, Sweden)
_ Apparently the distortion or effects box didn't work hence the guitar sound; only adds to it for me!

6 Agent Orange – Your Mother Sucks Cocks in Hell
7-inch EP (Graaf Hendrick 1983, Netherlands)
_ Better than the illustrious Californian band, and definitely more punk.

7 Razar – Task Force (Undercover Cops)
7-inch (Able Label, 1978, Australia)
_ Never did manage to get the picture sleeve, unfortunately!

8 PF Commando – Manipulerade Mongon
LP (COMM Records, 1979, Sweden)
_ Includes a compulsory song about the Raggare (gangs of Swedish rockers who were often violent toward punks).

9 Lama – Väliaikainen
7-inch EP (Johanna, 1981, Finland)
_ Or pretty much all of their earlier stuff.

10 Terveet Kädet – TKII
One-sided 7-inch EP (Ikbal, 1981, Finland)
_ Finnish punk kings.

PETER CRAVEN

Peter Craven is globe-trotting editor of Brighton's Zonked fanzine, and has been attending hardcore and punk shows in far-flung countries for more than two decades. He also runs marathons.

1 Cólera – Suburbio Geral
(taken from various artists LP Grito Suburbano, Punk Rock Discos, 1983, Brazil)

2 Rattus – Miks Haluat Tapella
(taken from WC Räjähtää LP, Poko, 1982, Finland)

3 5° Braccio – Repessione
(originally released on their Vanchiglia demo tape, 1982; Italy)

4 Raw Power – Fuck Authority
(from self-released, self-titled cassette, 1983, Italy)

5 Olho Seco – Isto É Olho Seco
(from self-titled 7-inch EP, Pogar Records (Germany) 1984, Brazil)

6 Terveet Kädet – Outo Maa
(from the Ääretön Joulu 7-inch EP, Poko, 1982, Finland)

7 Kidnap – No SS
(taken from various artists LP Apocalypse Chaos, Chaos Productions, 1982, France)

8 Civil Dissident – That Was This Is
(from bonus 12-inch with Cleanse the Bacteria various artists album, Pusmort (US), 1985, Australia)

9 G.I.S.M. – Endless Blockades for the Pussyfooter
(from Detestation 12-inch mini-album, Dogma, 1983, Japan)

10 Upright Citizens – Swastika Rats
(from Make the Future Mine & Yours 12-inch LP, H'art Musik, 1983, Germany)

ANARCHO
PUNK, OI!
& HARDCORE

Protest and Survive
For all the gray tones of punk's dawning days, in the UK at least, recession, social upheaval, and the Winter of Discontent had yet to chill the populace. By the turn of the decade things were much worse—the economy in meltdown as the country entered the most fearful recession for decades. The Labour Party was routed in the election of May 1979, and the rampant "free market" agenda of the incoming Conservative government reigned unchecked. Whole industries were asset-stripped or closed, the Cold War escalated, and the prospect of global nuclear conflagration seemed closer by the day. The USSR invaded Afghanistan at the beginning of 1980, Ronald Reagan entered the White House later that year, and the Doomsday Clock inched several minutes closer to midnight.

While the Punks of '77 protested vehemently, the anger was often adolescent, borne of everyday disenchantments, boredoms, predictabilities, and thwarted lusts. Now, however, punk's passions were patently more earnest and focused—if no longer, perhaps, as personal.

Interest had also reawakened in anarchism as a practicable political philosophy—in contrast to its Fleet Street/Malcolm McLaren equation with most anything grossly contrary to the British way of life. The popular media had lazily divorced the subject of Lydon's lyrical decree, "No Future . . .", from its explicit conclusion ". . . in England's dreaming" and associated the whole affray with simple nihilism. Crass offered a breathtakingly sincere retort to that assumption, and, against all odds, the commune-dwelling Epping refuseniks succeeded wildly at propagating their model of activism and opposition, building particularly on widespread dissatisfaction with some of the compromises accepted by the Clash and other first-wave bands.

Crass' strident polemical message, encompassing fragments or whole tracts of anarchist theory and literature, gathered an audience that proved receptive and eager to engage. Alongside fellow travelers Poison Girls, they set an agenda that fused pacifism, women's rights, and animal liberation with anarchism's upending of societal norms and conventions.

They took endless flak for their perceived sermonizing and lack of humor, but Crass were stoically unapologetic. They served as moral anchors and stern but kindly uncles to an eruption of loosely like-minded activity, and while slapdash copycat-ism was certainly rife, the bands that took their anarchist credo to heart—Zounds, the Mob, Rudimentary Peni, the Cravats, Chumbawamba—pushed punk's envelope ever further. Singer/artist Gee Vaucher's arresting graphic style, meanwhile, became an overnight global brand, as much part of punk's visual lingua franca as the safety pin, razor blade, mohawk, or markered "X"s on the backs of mosh pit hands.

California Über Alles
There was no coherent "second generation" of late '70s punks in the US—nor was there anything like a stateside counterpart to Oi! Instead, smaller cities seemed to celebrate their own, sporadic "year zeros" well into the '80s—with the "punk" bands in attendance just as varied as the Roxy generation of '77.

San Francisco's Dead Kennedys, Washington, DC's Bad Brains, and Canada's D.O.A. toured incessantly, establishing an underground gig network outside of the traditional live circuit and playing ever faster, louder, and more visceral music. And in their collective wake came hardcore. The most influential of the new groups on the block, DC's Minor Threat (née Teen Idles), were directly inspired by Bad Brains' jaw-dropping live shows. But the renewed intensity was only partially fueled by these musical and logistical innovations. The true soundtrack to American hardcore, ever chattering in the background, was the nightly television news.

Ronald Reagan's landslide victory in November 1980 profoundly reshaped the US and its dreaming. The economy was in broad decline and inflation was at a postwar high, both aggravated by the oil crisis occasioned by the overthrow of the Shah of Iran. When Islamist militants stormed the US embassy in Tehran in late 1979 and US citizens were taken hostage, candidate Reagan's promise of a more muscular administration and an escalation of military strength proved irresistible. The new right-wing governments on either side of the Atlantic found common cause in tough talk and scapegoating, and the Thatcher-Reagan juggernaut fueled musical resentments around the planet. One result was an immediate, unprecedented (and rapidly stultifying) unanimity of protest lyrics across every imaginable genre—but it also propelled hardcore to rise and spread more widely and rapidly even than punk.

Although things ended badly for Faulty Products in the US, it was their LA-based national distribution network (1980—82) that opened doors for a new model of punk record label that could reach beyond its own local scene. Many were formed and run by band members, including SST (Black Flag), Alternative Tentacles (Dead Kennedys), BYO (Youth Brigade), Epitaph (Bad Religion), New Alliance (Minutemen), Friends Records (D.O.A.), and Dischord (Minor Threat). With these dawned the golden age of American hardcore, spurred on nationally by *Flipside* fanzine, the skateboarding periodical *Thrasher*, and the emergence of *Maximumrocknroll* in 1982. In distinct contrast to the often homogenizing tendencies of the British music press, the fanzines' hardcore scene reports and relentless calls to self-inspection and justification encouraged divergent and robustly competitive trends not only across North America, but worldwide.

Hardcore identity was further enriched in the US by local artists. Some came in through skateboard sticker culture, tattoo parlors, and T-shirt concessions, and there were continuing connections with underground art and comic book culture dating back to proto-punk days—in strong contrast to the UK where even those who'd survived "year zero" in turn became tarred by their visual associations with the ancient history of '77. Also, many US and Canadian bands simply had more money to spend on graphics.

Several American artists who came to the fore substantively reinvented the iconography of punk. Raymond Pettibon's "narrative cartoons" for Black Flag and the Minutemen were stark but idiosyncratic depictions of the margins of American society, in the tradition of a political cartoonist. Winston Smith's work with Dead Kennedys was didactic but whip-smart funny, in keeping with long-term collaborator Jello Biafra's lyrical currencies. Pushead (Brian Schroeder) spearheaded the appropriation of horror imagery in hardcore (a still powerful motif). Others such as Randy Biscuit Turner, Shawn Kerri, Mad Marc Rude, Jaime Hernandez, and Sean Taggart became either established artists or cult heroes, even if neither was their original career plan.

Hardcore was powerfully (and idiosyncratically) embraced across Northern Europe—above all in Scandinavia—but dynamic scenes exploded in countries and continents where "punk" had gained only the barest toehold: Japan, Brazil, Italy, and along the rusting fringes of the Iron Curtain. Hardcore's broader musical exertions were matched with a worldwide outpouring of ever more intense visual imagery in flyers, T-shirts and sleeve art. These designs were often blunt, rudimentary, and bracingly extreme—and frequently far more eloquent than any of the shouting.

NATURAL SELECTION— ANARCHO PUNK, OI! & HARDCORE

Artist Crass
Title Yes Sir, I Will
Format LP, 12-inch
Label Crass, UK, 1983
_ Reverse of sleeve.
Design by Crass.

BE WARNED!
THE NATURE OF YOUR
OPPRESSION
IS THE AESTHETIC
OF OUR
ANGER

CRASS RECORDS.PO BOX 279.LONDON N22.CATALOGUE NUMBER 121984/2.

UK82 New Punk & Hardcore

The first obituaries for UK punk had surfaced as early as the Jubilee summer in 1977, when Queen Elizabeth celebrated the twenty-fifth anniversary of her accession. The question "What is punk?" began to be asked more searchingly. New wave was already offered as a cleaner, safer umbrella genre, but even if the energy persisted, any monolithic notion of punk was indeed at an end. Bands like Wire, the Adverts, Adam & the Ants, and Subway Sect had been universally accepted as punks, but when Gang of Four came to prominence in 1978, they were . . . something else.

The death of Sex Pistols' bassist Sid Vicious in February 1979 had already been noted by many as a sign to move on, and changing decades always give pundits an excuse to herald the "new" over the "old." A newer generation, however, were less keen to see punk co-opted into the mainstream, or consigned to fashion history. Drawing inspiration from the original lo-tech ethos of the first wave, and hard-hitting second-generation British groups such as Sham 69, UK Subs, the Ruts, and Stiff Little Fingers,

the new punk and hardcore groups adopted harsher and more aggressive stylistic approaches, both musically and visually.

Margaret Thatcher had been elected Prime Minister in May 1979, following the notorious Winter of Discontent, and a shift to the right saw huge rises in unemployment and widespread poverty. The political climate continued to sharpen as inner-city riots erupted in Bristol, Liverpool, and London, and racial tensions everywhere ran high. The preeminent punk label of the day, No Future, favored cheerily loutish sing-along melodies that did not always betray political or genre affiliation. The Riot City label was more tendentious, but revved-up pop songs remained the norm. Discharge, contrastingly, reimagined punk as aural and thematic warfare, with any concept of melody lost in the first charge.

01
Artist Chron Gen
Title Puppets of War
Format EP, 7-inch
Label Gargoyle, UK, 1981
_ The group's name is an abbreviation of "Chronic Generation."

02
Artist The Partisans
Title Police Story
Format Single, 7-inch
Label No Future, UK, 1981

03
Artist Discharge
Title Realities of War
Format EP, 7-inch
Label Clay, UK, 1980
_ Design by Martin H.

04
Artist Vice Squad
Title Living on Dreams
Format EP, 7-inch
Label Riot City, UK, 1980

_ "Considering our limited budget," notes Vice Squad drummer Shane Baldwin, "the final package was quite elaborate. A former schoolfriend of Dave [Bateman; guitar] and Mark [Hambly; drums], Glenn Johnson, drew a suitably apocalyptic design for the sleeve depicting the four of us in the smoking rubble of a nuclear explosion. Danica Gacesa, a friend of Simon [Edwards; Heartbeat/Riot City Records], did a foldout insert. I designed the 'Shatter' Riot City logo, and we chose a nice gold effect for the label."

01 02 03   07 08 09
04 05 06 | 10 11

I FUCK GOATS

I HATE PEOPLE

PEOPLE HATE ME

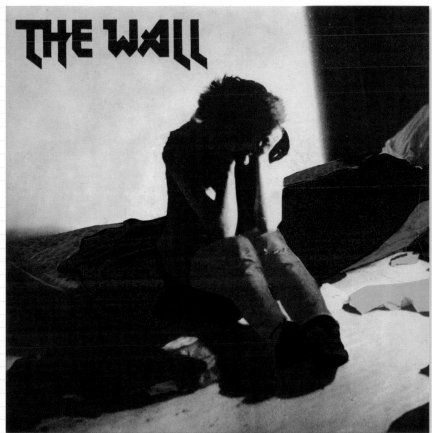

Discharge were derided in the UK even by lonesome advocate for third-generation UK punk Garry Bushell, who noted variously that they had " . . . all the grace and appeal of a syphilitic sore . . . Crassland refugees from grim old Stoke . . . a series of painful bursts of indistinguishable noise . . . "

Yet the band's combination of Motörhead-inspired sonic thuggery and Crass-influenced abstentionist/pacifist politics found a ready audience and, strangely, one whose international dimension eventually dwarfed their reception in the UK. Their material was revisited by the likes of metal megabrands Anthrax, Sepultura, and Metallica, who all cited the band as a primary influence. But their enduring impact is better measured in the worldwide proliferation of "D-beat" bands.

When Tezz Roberts minted the original Discharge beat on "Realities of War" (all seventy seconds of it), he had no conception of what he was setting in motion. Termed D-beat only in retrospect by Rich Militia of Sore Throat at the turn of the '90s, by then Discharge's influence on the worldwide hardcore stage was self-evident. (There are points when D-beat is taken to be shorthand for, or synonymous with, "hardcore punk.") So, although not known as D-beat contemporaneously, Sweden's Anti-Cimex and Mob 47 and Crucifix, Final Conflict, and Diatribe from the US have all been cited as D-beat. Genre expert Tony Gunnarsson points to Discard, a side project from Mob 47, as the first D-beat band proper, with Disaster the first UK entrants.

"Before Discharge there was no raw punk, period. The almost hypnotic D-beat along with Cal's vocals is the reason why Slaktattack and many other bands in Scandinavia and worldwide still keep doing this (or dis!). It spread since it's so timeless and awesome. It's like Motörhead, it will always be true, raw, and powerful."

Yxan, of contemporary Swedish D-beat band Slaktattak

Thereafter D-beat became a phenomenon, especially in Sweden, supported by Finn and Distortion Records and the associated *Sika Äpärä* fanzine and Dischange was the most popular band in a scene in which, according to Gunnarsson, "anything other than Discharge and Anti-Cimex was considered shit." In Japan, Disclose and their charismatic leader Kawakami ruled the scene, alongside Final Bloodbath, D-Clone, and Contrast Attitude, who have kept the flag flying since Kawakami's death in 2007.

In South America, "hardcore" was initially popularized through Finnish band Rattus. Ratos de Porão and Besthöven, "the poorest punk band in the world" according to leader Ofão, became leading lights of Brazilian D-beat, with a regular wave of new contenders such as Unidos Pelo Ódio and Desastre, with Disnube from Argentina and Sistemas de Aniquilacion from Peru emerging. In the '90s, Recharge from Hannover held the D-beat down in Germany—proliferation across numerous European territories ensuing, including Belgium's Visions of War and Holland's Terror Defence. Dishammer, Destruccion, and MG15 flew the flag for Spain. Russia's principle D-beat export remains Distress, from St. Petersburg. The genre was or is represented in Indonesia by Ashes of Death, in France by Four Monstrous Nuclear Stockpiles, in Serbia by Dishumanity, in Australia by Pisschrist, and in Ireland by Bacchus.

In keeping with the visual aesthetic pioneered by Discharge, most D-beat releases, regardless of country of origin, are routinely monochromatic. They often feature Crass-like line drawings or photographs cut from books about World War II, maintaining a link with Discharge's own obsessions with war generally and that conflict in particular (one trait is visual allusion to or actual physical representations of the Holocaust). There are, of course, exceptions. Sweden's Warvictims employed color on their *Domedagen* album, but this was based on a 1942 Waffen-SS Dutch recruitment poster.

BUPP – U –DUPP – U – DU...

"I have no idea how to describe it. It was just one of those things that happened. I stumbled on playing the drums. I couldn't play them correctly anyway. As a drummer I wasn't inspired by anyone, really. We weren't planning to make anything sound like anything. It's just what turned out. Me and my brother [guitar player Tony 'Bones' Roberts] grew up on stuff like Black Sabbath from our elder brother. It was me and my brother seeing how we could make music, and that's what we felt comfortable doing. It wasn't until the single 'Realities of War' took off—we didn't really think it was all that—we didn't even realize how different it was."

Tezz Roberts, originator of D-beat

D-beat even has its own manifesto, written by Jan "Jutte" Jutila, of Time Square Preachers. (Legend has it that Jutila once made a pilgrimage to Discharge's old studios in Stoke-on-Trent to breathe in its ambience.) But it also has a sense of humor.

Demarche's singer Splinter formerly played in the Czech band Dis Means War, who specialized in "D-beat cliches," while Scarborough's Active Minds satirised the deluge of Discharge clones with their single "Dis Is Getting Pathetic . . ."

The simple drum pattern patented by a percussion novice that traveled the world and led to the formation of a thousand bands remains one of punk's most bizarre legacies.

THE STRANGE JOURNEY OF D-BEAT

01 | 02
03 04 05
06 07

01

_The musical notation for "D-Beat," as set out by enthusiast Jan "Jutte" Jutila, drummer of Time Square Preachers.

02

Artist Discharge
Title Fight Back
Format EP, 7-inch
Label Clay, UK, 1980

03

_The gravestone of Kawakami, the famed leader of Japanese D-beat legends Disclose, in full Discharge regalia.

04/05

Artist Active Minds
Title Dis Is Getting Pathetic
Format EP, 7-inch
Label Looney Tunes, UK, 1995
_The artwork for Discharge's second EP would later be reinterpreted by Active Minds, whose 1995 EP *Dis Is Getting Pathetic* reflected on the slew of D-beat bands proliferating worldwide. The sleeve artwork featured the *Fight Back* parody as its front cover and the rear of Discharge's first release, *Realities of War*, with "Your Face Here" cutouts, on the reverse, to emphasize the point.

06

Artist Warvictims
Title Domedagen
Format LP, 12-inch
Label Crucificados Pelo Sistema (Germany), Sweden, 2009
_The cover artwork is appropriated from a 1942 German recruitment poster appealing for Dutch fighters to join the Waffen-SS in order to fight the Bolsheviks on the Eastern Front. The SS helmet insignia from the original poster has been altered to an inverted antiwar symbol.

07

_Discharge's first photo session, conducted by Mike Stone, boss of Clay Records.

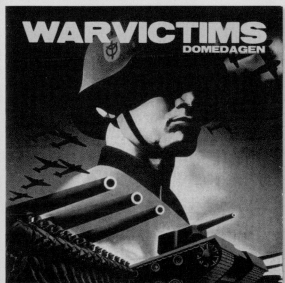

Where Have All the Bootboys Gone?

The second-generation punk bands held to an ostensibly narrower musical identity, as did many '77 bands that made major label signings in '78: Lurkers, 999, UK Subs, Stiff Little Fingers, etc. But it was with the Cockney Rejects and Angelic Upstarts, who like the Ruts were both indie-to-major graduates in 1979, that a "street punk" identity coalesced. Alongside Sham 69 and Cock Sparrer (who first recorded for Decca two years previously), they were cited as godfathers of the "Oi!" movement, zealously promoted by Garry Bushell in *Sounds* as an attempt to realign the punk initiative. A new cohort of bands, including the 4-Skins and the Business, mixed soccer chants with robust hymns to the alienation felt by a working class that punk had either romanticized or ignored. But the genre's inevitable appeal to skinhead culture did not play well with a suspicious (and overwhelmingly middle-class) media, and several bands made little attempt to distance themselves from the far right, who in turn recruited actively from the scene.

01
Artist Blitz
Title All Out Attack
Format EP, 7-inch
Label No Future, UK, 1981
_ One of the definitive images of a "punk" and "skinhead" alliance within the same band.

02
Artist The Adicts
Title Viva la Revolution
Format Single, 7-inch
Label Fallout, UK, 1982
_ The Adicts were the most prominent of the UK third-wave bands to adopt visual imagery from Stanley Kubrick's film *A Clockwork Orange*.

03
Artist Various Artists
Title Oi! The Album
Format LP, 12-inch
Label EMI, UK, 1980
_ First of the Oi! compilations compiled/promoted by *Sounds* journalist Garry Bushell. The second, *Strength Thru Oi!*, achieved widespread infamy when it was revealed its cover star was notorious neo-Nazi Nicky Crane. Design by Shoot That Tiger!

04
Artist 4-Skins
Title One Law for Them
Format Single, 7-inch
Label Clockwork Fun, UK, 1981

05
Artist The Oppressed
Title Never Say Die
Format EP, 7-inch
Label Firm, UK, 1983
_ Design by Roddy Moreno.

06
Artist Various Artists
Title Punk and Disorderly III—The Final Solution
Format LP, 12-inch
Label Anagram, UK, 1983
_ Design by Jim Phelan.

07
Artist Anti Pasti
Title Live at the Lyceum
Format LP, Cassette
Label Chaos Tapes, UK, 1981

08
Artist Chaos UK
Title Burning Britain
Format EP, 7-inch
Label Riot City, UK, 1982

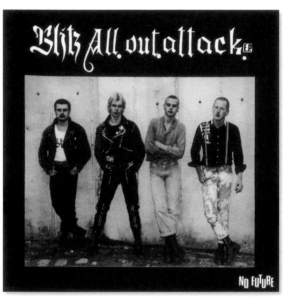

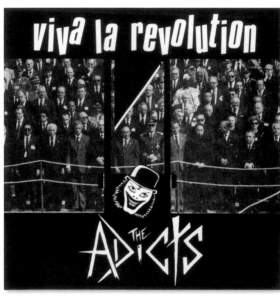

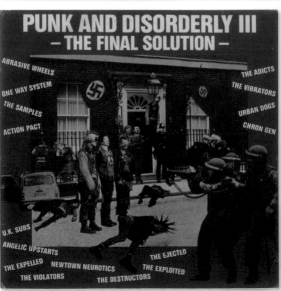

Artist G.B.H.
Title Give Me Fire
Format Single, 7-inch
Label Clay, UK, 1982
_ The name Charged G.B.H.
was inspired by original
bassist Sean McCarthy's
trial for grevious bodily
harm, though the prefix
was usually dropped.
Design by Mike Stone.

10
Artist Action Pact
Title People
Format EP, 7-inch

Label Fallout, UK, 1983
_ Cover design by
Augustus D'Arcy, a
pseudonym for music
journalist and later
ZigZag editor Mick
Mercer. "Augustus D'Arcy
(Gussy to his mates,
I suddenly find myself
recalling) was a monocled
berk from the *Tom Merry*
series of public
schoolboy stories
originally published in
Gem comic, a rival to the
Billy Bunter stories."

The cover photo is
a still from *Psycho*.

11
Artist The Exploited
Title Rival Leaders
Format P, 7-inch
Label Pax, UK, 1983

12
Artist Riot Squad
Title Fuck the Tories
Format EP, 7-inch
Label Rondelet, UK, 1982

01 02 03   08 09 10
04 05 06 | 11 12

Bloody Revolutions: Crass Records

Crass formed in 1977 as a response to the rise of the punk movement. Based at the communal Dial House in Epping, on the outskirts of London, the group included a number of participants who had been involved in earlier art and underground hippie movements, and they set about interpreting the radical anarchist message of punk on literal, rather than purely gestural, terms. The members of this strongly ideological group formed a punk band to relay their anarchist message. Their media interruptions—incorporating records, books, films, events, concerts, posters, and a widespread graffiti campaign—employed a distinctive visual style and an overt anarchist rhetoric, paving the way for an entire subgenre of anarchist punk bands. Adopting a strategy of (low) maximum price details on their record sleeves and foldout posters, the group's graphic output

was designed to communicate consistently strong political messages. Following the success of their debut album *Feeding of the Five Thousand*, originally released by Small Wonder in 1978, Crass set up their own label for subsequent group releases, going on to issue debut recordings by a number of allied groups whom they felt a political or ideological affinity with.

Crass's visual work was self-produced, with art direction credits going to Crass and G Sus (Gee Vaucher), though the group's first circular visual was designed by Dave King some time before the formation of the group. Its original purpose was the frontispiece of a self-published book by drummer Penny Rimbaud (an adopted pseudonym for Jeremy Ratter) in 1976, which was entitled *Christ's Reality Asylum*.

"Both Gee [Vaucher] and myself trained as graphic artists. Both of us prior to Crass had brought money into the house by doing book design and that sort of stuff. And part of training as a graphic artist wasn't just learning type[setting], it was also thinking in terms of marketing; a lot of the projects at college were: 'This is the product, how do you design and market it? How do you create a corporate idea?' Even Naomi Klein credited us with being one of the first logos. And it was. It was very much the idea of creating a corporate identity . . . It was a very distinct policy that things should have an instantly recognizable image. So we developed a format into which anything could slip; in most cases the bands were left to do the artwork, BUT the artwork had to fit into the circle that went on the front."

Penny Rimbaud, Crass drummer and founder member

19454U
enola hallo
AN.OK?521984
pay no more than 45p

01
Artist Crass
Title Reality Asylum
Format Single, 7-inch
Label Crass, UK, 1979
_ Design by Dave King/
Crass.

02
_ Poster foldout, Crass
Penis Envy album, 1981.
Design by Gee Vaucher.
The third album by
Crass took on the
theme of feminism and
the role of women, an
often controversial
topic within a heavily
male-dominated
punk scene.

03
_ Crass postcard, 1981.
Design by Gee Vaucher/
Crass.

04
_ Poster insert, Crass,
Christ The Album, 1984.
Vaucher's complex
aesthetic reached a high
point on this poster.
The image features a
wide range of prominent
figures from global
politics, religion,
business, and the
entertainment industry.

03   01 02 | 04

AN INSTITUTION IS THE LENGTHENED SHADOW OF ONE PERSON

05
_ Poster foldout, Crass, *Yes Sir, I Will*, 1983. Design by Crass. The image, and its caption which provided the album title, were taken directly from *The Sun* tabloid newspaper, December 1982, and depict Prince Charles welcoming home soldier Simon Weston, after he had been horrifically injured on the ship *Sir Galahad* during the Falklands War.

06
_ Poster foldout, Crass, *Feeding of the Five Thousand—Second Sitting*, 1979. Design by Crass. The use of a strong war photograph with the well-known phrase taken from a 1914 recruiting poster originally featuring Lord Kitchener, together with the ironic use of the hand as a prominent feature, creates a particularly powerful, but blunt, message.

07
Artist Crass
Title Feeding of the Five Thousand—Second Sitting
Format LP, 12-inch
Label Crass, UK, 1979
_ Design by Gee Vaucher.

08
Artist Crass
Title Penis Envy
Format LP, 12-inch
Label Crass, UK, 1981
_ Design by Gee Vaucher.

09
Artist Crass/Poison Girls
Title Bloody Revolutions/ Persons Unknown
Format Joint Single, 7-inch
Label Crass, UK, 1980
_ Gee Vaucher's gouache illustration for the record cover and foldout poster is based on a publicity photograph of the Sex Pistols from 1977, reconfigured with individuals' heads substituted with those of the Queen, Pope John Paul II, the statue of justice, and Margaret Thatcher. This complex image works on a number of levels: primarily, it satirizes the Sex Pistols themselves as figures of authority and the state, passing an ironic comment on their failure—and that of the punk "establishment"—to live up to a "revolutionary" ideal, while also attacking those figures themselves. Crass strongly critiqued the failure of the punk movement in terms of political engagement, with the Clash, the Sex Pistols, and other punk "heroes" attracting their ire in both lyrics and artwork.

10
_ Antiwar cloth patch, insert for the Crass single "Nagasaki Nightmare," 1980.

11
Artist Various Artists
Title Bullshit Detector Two
Format LP, 12-inch
Label Crass, UK, 1982
_ *Bullshit Detector* compilation albums were an attempt by Crass to promote and publicize the

"Get well soon," the Prince said. And the heroic soldier replied: "Yes, sir, I will."   THE SUN, Thursday, December 2, 1982

YOUR COUNTRY NEEDS **YOU**

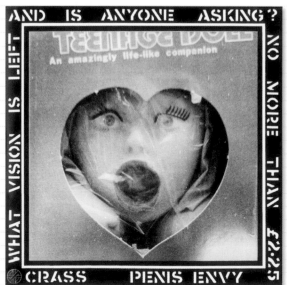

myriad new anarcho punk groups following in their wake. While the Crass label released records by individual groups (almost always as a oneoff deal that sought to allow those groups to launch their own careers from thereon in), they also received hundreds of demo tapes from others, which formed the backbone of three volumes of *Bullshit Detector*.

Production levels were, by consequence, variable. Design by Your Funeral/Crass.

12
Artist Flux of Pink Indians
Title Neu Smell
Format EP, 7-inch
Label Crass, UK, 1981
_ Design by Flux/Crass.

13
Artist Conflict
Title The House that Man Built
Format EP, 7-inch
Label Crass, UK, 1982
_ Design by Conflict/Crass.

14
Artist Anthrax
Title Capitalism Is Cannibalism
Format EP, 7-inch
Label Crass, UK, 1982
_ Design by Anthrax/Crass.

05   06   11
07 08 09 | 12 13 14

10

Where Were You?

Punk had long fought a battle for authenticity, both externally in the face of a critical media and hostile public reception and internally as those involved played out sometimes bitter rivalries. The notion of what constituted a "real" punk identity—in particular, who was maintaining the strongest link to a pure punk ideology and who was "selling out"—remained high on the agenda as the subculture developed.

The initial umbrella assimilation of punk's diverse range of individual attitudes and interests was as much a defence mechanism as it was an ideological flag to rally around. From ragged do-it-yourself amateurs to rehashed pub rock opportunists and polished new wavers, little distinction was made at the time of punk's early inception. However, the prospect of commercial success and financial reward invariably interferes with such simple egalitarian social structures, and it wasn't long before the rivalry of internal competition upset the equilibrium.

By mid-'77, punk was hot property in the UK, and major record labels were scouring clubs and small venues in order to secure a deal with the next heirs apparent. Although the punk style had been widely vilified in the national press, record labels saw huge potential in the combination of raw and basic rock 'n' roll music, cheap production methods, widespread media attention, and a growing and perhaps increasingly less discerning audience.

Punk's global development through commercial new wave and post-punk to hardcore, Oi!, and a variety of other "points of difference" led to further contrast, in musical execution, lyrics, fashion, and dress styles. Authenticity was by this time often equated to the length of an individual's personal punk credentials ("where were you in '77?" was a common lyrical refrain in the early '80s) as much as their hair, which under "year zero" rhetoric had decreed a swift visit to the barber. Also under the credibility microscope were lifestyle choices that displayed outward signs of punk visual permanence (i.e., not just dressing up at weekends).

Rival Tribes

The fissures developing between the avant-garde, new wave, and punk traditionalists had led many to drift away from "punk" definitions altogether, while others retreated further into a more closely guarded "real punk" arena, continuing what they saw as a lineage of authentic punk ideology, fashion, and musical styles. This split was highlighted in sections of the music press, with many critics keen to show support for "progressive" post-punk groups while distancing themselves from the burgeoning hardcore and Oi! scenes which were dismissed as hidebound and conservative. Many involved in the latter camp saw this split as more than stylistic, citing negative press reporting as a further example of class prejudice. Similarly, political differences—particularly between the anarcho punk ideologues and their street punk and Oi! rivals—led to some very public disagreements.

A heightened level of internecine squabbling was the result, sometimes veering beyond lyrical barbs to artwork and design. The title of the Exploited's 1981 debut album *Punk's Not Dead* was a direct response to the Crass song "Punk Is Dead" from their *Feeding of the Five Thousand* two years earlier, itself a rebuke to the previous punk generation's immersion in what Penny Rimbaud dubbed "the rock 'n' roll circus." The cover of "new punk" stalwarts Special Duties' "Bullshit Crass" single, complete with Crass-style typography, visually parlayed the ideological divide.

Rivalries could equally be based on regional identities. The influential 1982 hardcore collection *This Is Boston Not L.A.* made no concession to diplomacy, particularly in the Freeze's title track and its closing line, "This is Boston, fuck L.A." It served as a riposte to Dangerhouse's 1978 West Coast compilation *Yes L.A.*—which itself contained the Bags' "We Don't Need The English" (" . . . telling us what to wear, telling us to dye our hair . . ."). Regional compilations had been a staple product of the early independent labels—an opportunity to collate a cluster of local groups, tapping into an overlapping fan base as a direct market for the album. But the trend in hardcore was more often a mark of aesthetic or tribal difference to outsiders, a more aggressive, insular message to the outside world as well as a show of local pride.

In the UK, Sham 69 had attempted to heal wounds, particularly through unity anthems such as "If the Kids Are United." Ironically, their performances were cursed by pitched battles between sections of the audience—in many cases, such rivalries were extensions of both pre-existing soccer team allegiances and attempted infiltration by the far right. There were also self-evident tensions, and sometimes accommodations, between skinhead and punk factions. Scotland's Oi Polloi originally bridged both the Oi! and anarcho punk camps and similarly exhorted punks and skins to unite together in common cause.

Oi Polloi's sense of political identity is also evident in their contribution to the 1998 compilation EP *Bare Faced Hypocrisy Sells Records*, released in response to anarcho punk group Chumbawamba signing to EMI, a label the group had been extremely critical of in the past, particularly in regard to its parent company's links with arms manufacture. The title was a parody of Chumbawamba's 1986 debut album *Pictures of Starving Children Sell Records*, itself a direct response to the Live Aid charity concerts, while the détourned cover graphic was from their *Never Mind the Ballots* follow-up.

The response was no surprise—links to EMI had earlier seen New Model Army fall foul of their peers, as articulated by Conflict on 1986's *Only Stupid Bastards Help EMI* album, which parodied that band's puritanical attitude (they routinely wore T-shirts proclaiming "Only Stupid Bastards Use Heroin" at this time). Chumbawamba were not averse to genre-baiting themselves, recording "I'm Thick" under the pseudonym Skin Disease, mailing it to Oi! evangelist Garry Bushell and duly collapsing in hysterics after it appeared on the *Back on the Streets* EP (front cover, almost inevitably: a close-up photograph of a pair of Doc Martens "bovver" boots).

If punk's rigid divisions in the UK helped inform such spats, infighting in American hardcore, alongside genre and geographical saber-rattling, was generally a more satirical affair—with noone escaping censure. Spokespersons such as Jello Biafra were lampooned in the Necros/White Flag's *Jail Jello* EP at the height of the *Frankenchrist* furore, while Poison Idea titled one of their records *The Ian MacKaye EP*; its front cover a close-up of a giant spread rectum, mocking hero worship of the Minor Threat front man.

PUNK FACTIONS

01

Artist Oi Polloi
Title Punks 'N' Skins
Format EP, 7-inch
Label Fight 45 Records,
France, 1996

02

Artist Various Artists
Title This Is Boston
Not L.A.
Format LP, 12-inch
Label Modern Method,
USA, 1982

03

Artist Killroy
Title 99 Bottles
Format Single, 7-inch
Label Ghetto-Way,
USA, 1983
_ Mod-baiting cartoon
cover from one of the
first Californian punk
bands to respond to the
British Oi! movement.

04

Artist Special Duties
Title Bullshit Crass
Format Single, 7-inch
Label Rondelet, UK, 1982

05

Artist Conflict
Title Only Stupid
Bastards Help EMI
Format LP, 12-inch
Label Modern Army,
UK, 1986

06

Artist Chumbawamba
Title Never Mind the
Ballots
Format LP, 12-inch
Label Agit Prop, UK, 1987
_ The cover illustration
references the anonymous
poster *Le Vote Ne Change
Rien, La Lutte Continue*
from the 1968 protests
in France.

07

Artist Various Artists
Title Bare Faced
Hypocrisy Sells Records
Format EP, 7-inch
Label Propa Git Records,
UK, 1998

01
02 03 04
05 06 07

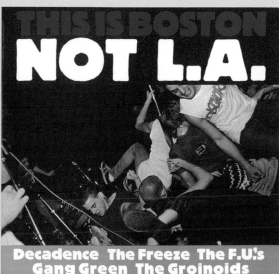

Anarcho in the UK

In response to the literal call to arms offered by Crass, a second generation of anarcho punk groups sprang up across the UK—particularly in more remote, and often less urban, environments. Crass, Poison Girls, and others toured widely and made a point of playing in unconventional venues. Many of these events raised funds for a range of political causes, from the Campaign for Nuclear Disarmament (CND) to the Animal Liberation Front, as well as smaller local campaigns. Book and record stalls at venues provided access to the underground and anarchist media, and gigs were sometimes scheduled for afternoons without a bar licence in order to admit a younger audience. The incorporation of local opening acts across different regions also allowed a platform for audience members inspired to take up the mantle themselves. Many of these groups were not just copycat attempts to jump the growing anarcho punk bandwagon and emulate the scene leaders: groups such as the Subhumans, Flux of Pink Indians, Zounds, and the Mob pursued their own ideological and aesthetic direction.

01
Artist Subhumans
Title Demolition War
Format EP, 7-inch
Label Spiderleg, UK, 1981
_ One of the most successful of the next generation of anarcho punk groups, the Subhumans pursued an avowedly personal and humanitarian political agenda.

02
Artist Subhumans
Title Reason for Existence
Format EP, 7-inch
Label Spiderleg, UK, 1982

03
Artist Subhumans
Title Religious Wars
Format EP, 7-inch
Label Spiderleg, UK, 1982
_ Design by Nick Lant.

04
Artist Subhumans
Title Evolution
Format EP, 7-inch
Label Bluurg, UK, 1983
_ Design by Nick Lant. "Nick wrote to us to get some info in 1983, and at the bottom of his letter was an intricate doodle of a punk's head, and at the time we needed a cover for the *Religious Wars* EP, so I sent him the lyrics and wondered, and a week later he sent the cover! Amazing imagery—he did the *Day the Country Died*, *Evolution*, and *Rats* record covers as well, with increasing depth and detail, and if we hadn't lost touch we'd still be asking him for more! [Does anyone know where he went?]"—Dick Lucas, Subhumans.

05
Artist Subhumans
Title Rats
Format EP, 7-inch
Label Bluurg, UK, 1984
_ Design by Nick Lant.

06
Artist Subhumans
Title The Day the Country Died
Format LP, 12-inch
Label Bluurg, UK, 1983
_ Design by Nick Lant.

07
Artist The Mob
Title The Mirror Breaks
Format Single, 7-inch
Label All the Madmen, UK, 1983
_ Design by Wilf.

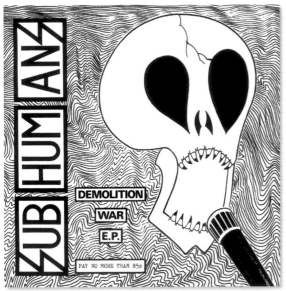

Artist Zounds
Title Demystification
Format Single, 7-inch
Label Rough Trade,
UK, 1981
_ Linda Robinson took
the original photograph.
"My memory," recalls
singer Steve Lake,
"is that the cover
concept was originally
by Laurence [Wood;
guitarist]. Despite
having many annoying
character traits,
Laurence often had some
very good ideas. He was
also a great guitar
player. We actually got
a friend of ours (Gooji
Pete) to be the guy
tearing off the blindfold
on the concourse of
King's Cross station.
He didn't have the right
expression though, so we
decided to superimpose

my ugly mug on his body.
The thought of my brain
in Gooji Pete's body
still sends shivers
down my spine."

09
_ Poison Girls at
Alexandra Hall,
Portsmouth, October 31,
1981. A generic poster
that leaves space
to list details of
individual venues and
times. The text at the
bottom highlights the
national Campaign for
Nuclear Disarmament
march in London that
same month.

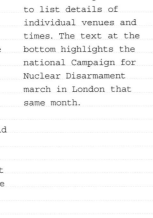

Weathered Statues: Icons of American punk

After Winston Smith's DKs symbol, the most recognizable visual "trademarks" of American hardcore punk were Raymond Pettibon's "four-bar flag" Black Flag logo and the Misfits' "skull" emblem and typography. No ownership was ever claimed for Minor Threat's soon-to-be ubiquitous "straight edge" symbolism (an "x" drawn on the back of a hand which originally denoted to bartenders that the bearer was underage, but was quickly co-opted as a badge of honor). Amended again, to the large "x" were added "HC" for hardcore and the two-letter state abbreviations as symbols of turf and allegiances to scenes around the nation. Other hardcore graphic identities often denoted the name of the band's initials in a simple circular design easily replicable via spray-paint or stencil.

01
_ 1981 poster for a Bad Brains show, opened by Bad Religion, the Lewd and JFA, drawn by Shawn Kerri, one of the most noteworthy artists of her generation (and one of the relatively few female graphic artists represented in hardcore). Note the legend "From Washington D.C." in relation to Bad Brains, though they were shortly to relocate to New York.

02
Misfits Skull Logo patch
_ Based on a poster for *The Crimson Ghost* '40s horror series, and designed by singer Glenn Danzig (other claims for authorship include Mad "Marc" Rude, who worked on several key releases by the band), the Misfits skull first appeared on their "Horror Business" single. It has since become one of the key icons of punk, as has the band's typography.

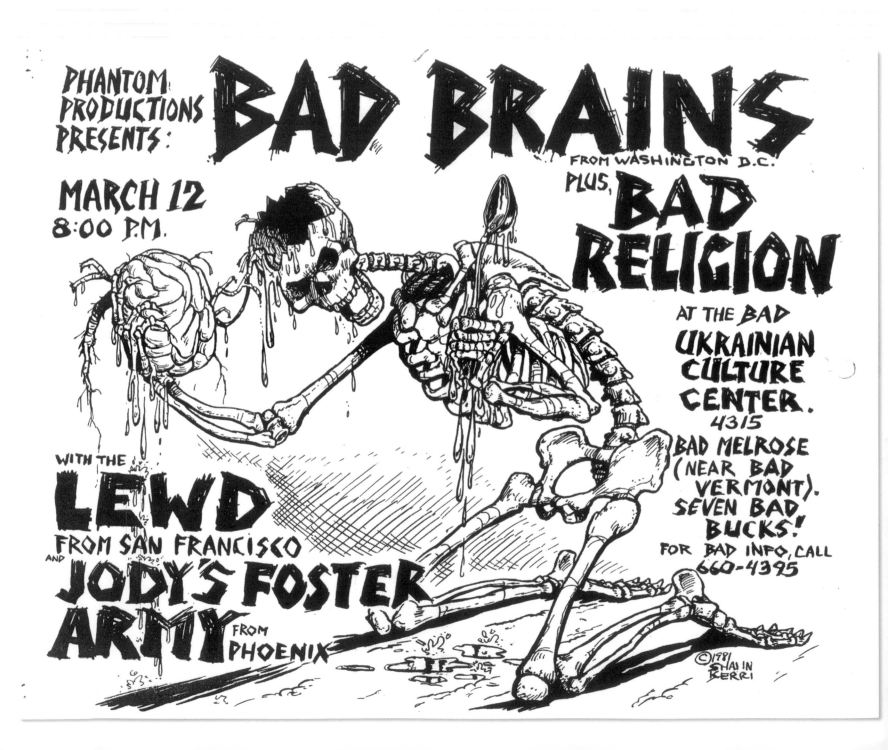

03
Artist Bad Religion
Title S/T
Format EP, 7-inch
Label Epitaph, USA, 1981
_ The first release
by Bad Religion; also the
first on the still-extant
Epitaph Records, run by
the band's guitarist
Brett Gurevitz.

04
Artist Black Flag
Title Six Pack
Format EP, 7-inch
Label SST, USA, 1982
_ Design by Raymond
Pettibon.

05
_ Misfits "The Undertaker
and his Pals" poster.
The titles and line art
in the foreground are
taken directly from
a poster for a 1966 B
movie of the same name.

06
Artist The Teen Idles
Title Minor Disturbance
Format EP, 7-inch
Label Dischord, USA, 1980
_ This posthumous EP
release from a band
featuring both Jeff
Nelson and Ian MacKaye,
later of Minor Threat,
incorporated the
straight edge "cross"
markings as its central
visual concept. It was
also the first release
on Dischord Records.
Design by Jeff Nelson/
Susie Josephson.

07
Artist Minutemen   02
Title Paranoid Time   03 04 05
Format EP, 7-inch   01 | 06 07 08
Label SST, USA, 1980
_ Design by Raymond
Pettibon.

08
Artist Minor Threat
Title Out of Step
Format EP, 12-inch
Label Dischord, USA, 1983
_ Design by Jeff Nelson.

How Low Can a Punk Get? The Rise of Hardcore

The evolution of American hardcore, wherein punk values hardened as the music's tempo accelerated, has variously been traced to either Dead Kennedys' 1981 mini-album *In God We Trust, Inc.* or Canadians D.O.A.'s *Hardcore '81*. However, as elsewhere, the join was never clear, with groups such as Black Flag and Bad Brains predating hardcore's proliferation but rapidly becoming figureheads. Hardcore's rise, much maligned by some original American punks for its perceived uniformity and machismo, coincided with the development of a network of independent labels such as SST, Dischord, and Alternative Tentacles, but was also notable for its regional idiosyncrasies. Scenes in Washington, DC (which gave rise to the "straight edge" phenomenon wherein participants refrained from drinking and drugs) and Boston contrasted to the beach punk ethos of California and a steadfastly working-class New York variant exemplified by Agnostic Front, while smaller local variations sprang up in other cities across the US. ROIR (Reachout International) was a cassette-only label specializing in unreleased material by local bands going back to No Wave stars James Chance and Lydia Lunch. It issued two hugely important albums in 1982—the debut by Bad Brains and the compilation *New York Thrash*, before moving on to document the widening underground scene.

01
_ Volume 2 of Flipside's "video fanzine," 1983.

02
_ *Flipside* fanzine, issue 32, May 1981.

03
_ *Maximumrocknroll* fanzine, no. 9, October 1983.

04
Artist Various Artists
Title New York Thrash
Format LP, Cassette
Label ROIR, USA, 1982
_ The prime artifact from the "Loud Fast Rules" generation of New York bands, featuring Bad Brains, Kraut, Nihilistics, Heart Attack, and a pre-rap Beastie Boys. Design by Bob Giordano/Dave Hahn.

05
Artist Bad Brains
Title S/T
Format LP, cassette
Label ROIR, USA, 1982
_ Bad Brains were highly capable jazz musicians turned on to punk by the Ramones, who relocated from their native Washington, DC to New

York City in 1979. Their quicksilver hardcore-punk hybrid, alongside stabs of dub reggae, galvanized the entire New York punk scene. Design by Dave Lee Parsons (aka "Mir") whose Rat Cage Records label was central to the *New York Thrash* generation of bands, releasing the debut Beastie Boys 45, among others.

06
Artist Even Worse
Title Mouse or Rat?
Format Single, 7-inch
Label Worse Than You, USA, 1982
_ This version of the New York band (also documented on *New York Thrash*) included DJ Tim Sommer, later of Hugo Largo, *Big Takeover* zine editor Jack Rabid, and Sonic Youth's Thurston Moore (though Moore did not play on this record).

07
Artist Ism
Title A Diet Fit for Worms
Format LP, 12-inch
Label S.I.N, USA, Long Island, New York, 1983

08
Artist Agnostic Front
Title Victim in Pain
Format LP, 12-inch
Label Rat Cage, USA, 1984
_ Agnostic Front's debut album was the moment when a much more brutal take on New York hardcore arrived. Design by "Mir" (Dave Lee Parsons).

09
Artist Sado-Nation
Title S/T
Format EP, 7-inch
Label Trap, USA, 1980
_ Early US hardcore from the Pacific Northwest (Portland).

10
Artist Various Artists
Title The Big Apple Rotten to the Core
Format LP, 12-inch
Label S.I.N., USA, 1982
_ A vinyl companion to the *New York Thrash* compilation, drawing on bands who played regularly at the A7 club in the East Village, and notable for Squirm's "Fuck You Brooke Shields" and "John Hinckley Jr. (What Has Jodie Foster Done To You?)" by Ism, who ran the label.

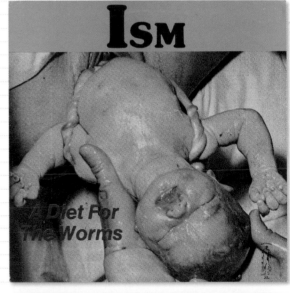

Hardcore—and the flyer art that announced it—flourished in nations untouched by punk, in the unlikeliest strip-malled suburbs, and in the grayest "planned communities" and "new towns" but its visual assault took place on other levels as well—high art, low art, and no art at all.

The American hardcore scene involved a number of artists and designers who are routinely cited among the key artists of the late twentieth century. Their work, both within and outside the genre, is celebrated in exhibitions and documented in high-end art books that stand in the starkest contrast with what were often rush-photocopied original creations. Raymond Pettibon, Winston Smith, Shawn Kerri, Sean Taggart, Jaime Hernandez, and Pushead all developed followings within hardcore but were only part of a subculture wherein amateur graphic artists played leading roles in intensifying their scenes and helping to give a "brand" to the music: empowering, taunting, promoting, boasting, even satirizing.

David Ensminger's recent book *Visual Vitriol* explored the phenomenon of US flyer art, arguably the signature representation of American hardcore in the '80s. Ensminger establishes a link between the philososphy of the movement and its implementation through this apparently simple medium: "Punk's meaning, taken literally, suggests an insurgence, a critique, or aim—to be authentic, to be playful, to be utilitarian, to be DIY, to be a seizure, and to seize space and create or disrupt media. If we imagine flyers as a convenient means to an end, to be used as a platform for dates, times, venues, and bands, what is said is perfunctory. But even minimal information invokes a sense of economics (the punk and DIY economics of scale), technological apparatus (paper quality, Xerox machine quality), aesthetic biases (to edit or not to edit), and resource management (make thousands of copies, like Black Flag, or a dozen)."

In LA the SST label produced massive quantities of flyers for their bands in an attempt to "become the media," rankle the scene, and bridge boundaries between the city, the beaches, affluent suburbs, and the Inland Empire. In some cases, more than a thousand pieces of Pettibon flyer art were distributed. Elsewhere bands with catchphrases like the Big Boys' "Now go start your own band" catalyzed fans: for any one gig, the Big Boys' Tim Kerr and Randy "Biscuit" Turner might produce a flyer, even more than one, and then fans would press into the neighborhoods brandishing their own as well. It was still cheaper to mass-produce flyers using offset press when there were two hundred copies or more, but smaller photocopy runs were easily within reach of all but the most penniless in the hardcore community.

The more basic flyers collaged group logos and artwork from record sleeves or press reports alongside photographs and hand-rendered or Letraset transfer text, usually struggling for position as the by now standard multiple group billing necessitated the combination of disparate graphic elements within the same space. Most were initially laid out at full size on one standard, US Letter-sized sheet of paper, to be run off in multiple at the local copy shop (or better still, the local school, office, or community center Xerox while noone was looking). In terms of reproduction, line art worked best for the format since photo gradients became blotchy without the benefit of a halftone screen. High contrast and instantly hard-hitting images were the order of the day; Pettibon's illustrations for Black Flag, along with that group's simple but highly effective logo, were perfect for the medium. The most primitive lettering of all—roughly-formed capital letters made with vigorous back-and-forth strokes of a Magic Marker—became the graphic signature of the most influential hardcore label of all, D.C.'s Dischord.

"It's hard to explain the whole ritualistic process that used to go into show promotion . . . We really had to go out and target that audience, usually in the flesh . . . The use of X-ACTO knives, rubber cement, the trip to Kinko's—all a lost art I'm afraid! And then there was the distribution of the flyers, hitting the local record stores and hangouts, shuffling up the stacks of flyers by the door to make sure yours ended up on top! Of course, when you came back by the store a day later, your flyers were now on the bottom of the stack, or worse, in the trash already! When it came to actual street action, the staple gun was the weapon of choice. To this day, if you look closely at any telephone pole lining Hollywood Boulevard they resemble some mutant strain of cacti, sprouting rust-colored needles up to the reach of an eighteen-year-old bassist! My least favorite method of distribution was manning the gauntlet outside someone else's gig. Oh, the humiliation of having some fifteen-year-old punkette take one of the offered flyers, take one look at it, inform you that your band still sucks, and then dropping it to the ground as if it were a diseased pigeon. It's no wonder bands today (us included) make digital flyers, post them online, and with a click of the mouse send out to five thousand spam folders. But then, what are these things? Virtual works of art, a mixture of ones and zeroes? They don't really exist, do they? I'd challenge any young band to click print, and then go and hand the flyer to the next kid coming out for a smoke!"

Mike Magrann, Channel 3

BECOME THE MEDIA—
HARDCORE FLYER ART

Small Parts Isolated and Destroyed

Much of UK punk's outer garb in the '80s instantly signaled a band's precise social position and likely outlook. Musical boundaries and expectations were similarly constrained. In contrast, across the US and Canada, "hardcore" served as a generic identifier for a hugely diverse population of bands and scenes. Black Flag, Minor Threat, Bad Religion, Circle Jerks, Fear, (Vancouver's) Subhumans, the Big Boys, Bad Brains, Effigies, Social Distortion, Suicidal Tendencies, Youth Brigade, TSOL, The Dicks, Hüsker Dü, Really Red, the Misfits, Government Issue, 7 Seconds, et al. were all "hardcore." Yet all were clearly distinct from their peers.

An array of subgenres multiplied: skate-punk, metal-core, straight edge, "Youth Crew," fuck straight edge, emo ("emotional hardcore," though it had a long way to travel before it became recognizable as the entity that exists today), and right-wing variants of the above. "Post-hardcore" mirrored the post-punk moniker of an earlier generation, as exemplified by Naked Raygun, Big Black, and others. Then, at the turn of the '90s, riot grrrl brought another counter-revolution.

01
Artist 7 Seconds
Title Skins, Brains & Guts
Format EP, 7-inch
Label Alternative Tentacles, USA, 1982
_ Bill Gilliam, Alternative Tentacles' label manager in the UK, passed on releasing this record due to its sleeve. "The US 7-inch had this guy with what is now an extremely fashionable haircut, but in those days would have been interpreted as a skinhead . . . having spent a couple of years with Sham 69, I knew about skinheads. I just figured it was something that Alternative Tentacles didn't need to do."

02
Artist Flipper
Title Get Away
Format Single, 7-inch

Label Subterranean, USA, 1982
_ Rear cover, with Flipper's take on the song "There Was an Old Lady Who Swallowed a Fly." Design by Jacy Webster.

03
Artist Social Distortion
Title Mommy's Little Monster
Format LP, 12-inch
Label 13th Floor, USA, 1983

04
Artist Youth Brigade
Title Sound & Fury (second version)
Format LP, 12-inch
Label Better Youth Organization, USA, 1983
_ Second version of their debut LP, which they had withdrawn over

quality issues. The Stern brothers pooled bar mitzvah money to establish the still-extant Better Youth Organization record label; the art design here was by their stepmother, Kandy Stern.

05
Artist Gang Green
Title Skate to Hell
Format Single, 7-inch
Label Taang!, USA, 1985
_ Gang Green emerged as a full tilt rebuttal of early Boston hardcore's fervent political edge by announcing themselves as a party band, addicted to skating, whose songbook consisted to a large extent of eulogies to their favorite brewery, Budweiser.

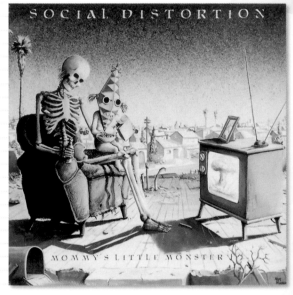

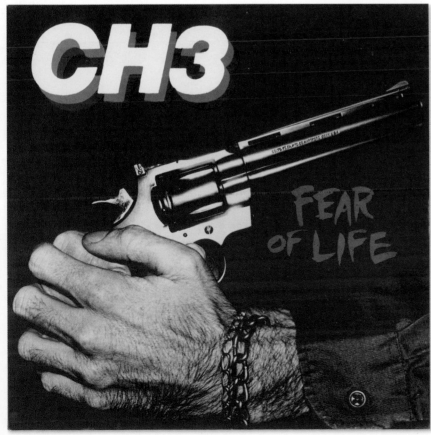

Sound & Fury

Two thematic constants in the development of American hardcore have been its political, antiauthoritarian dimension, and also its humor and love of offence. Custodians of the sarcasm tradition within the genre include the Angry Samoans (whose *Back to Samoa* featured such epics as "They Saved Hitler's Cock" which, like many of their lyrics, was chosen with the particular goal of horrifying LA's dominant DJ, tastemaker, and gentle soul, Rodney Bingenheimer). Tesco Vee's the Meatmen, meanwhile, broke the Midwestern taste-ometer with relentless innuendos and the likes of "Crippled Children Suck." While GG Allin pushed everyone's buttons, there were a series of records offering lewd and juvenile commentary on rock stars or celebrities of the day dating back to the Rotters' "Sit on My Face Stevie Nix" from 1979. Some bands straddled both sarcasm and politics, notably Dead Kennedys, but the hardcore scene saw an avalanche of records attacking Ronald Reagan and the Republicans, or broader tirades against authority, the police, American foreign policy, and big business.

01
Artist Angry Samoans
Title Back to Samoa
Format LP, 12-inch
Label Bad Trip, USA, 1982
_ Design by Ron Spencer.

02
Artist GG Allin & the Scumfucs/Artless
Title S/T
Format Split LP, 12-inch
Label Holy War, Germany, 1985
_ The most outré performer of all time, Allin was famous for everything up to and beyond onstage defecation as well as the ingestion of copious quantities of hard drugs leading to his inevitable OD. This split LP with Artless is one of the tamer record sleeves produced in his name.

03
Artist The Meatmen
Title Crippled Children Suck
Format EP, 7-inch
Label Touch & Go, USA, 1982

04
Artist Hüsker Dü
Title Land Speed Record
Format LP, 12-inch
Label New Alliance, USA, 1982
_ Design by Fake Name Grafx (alias for drummer Grant Hart).

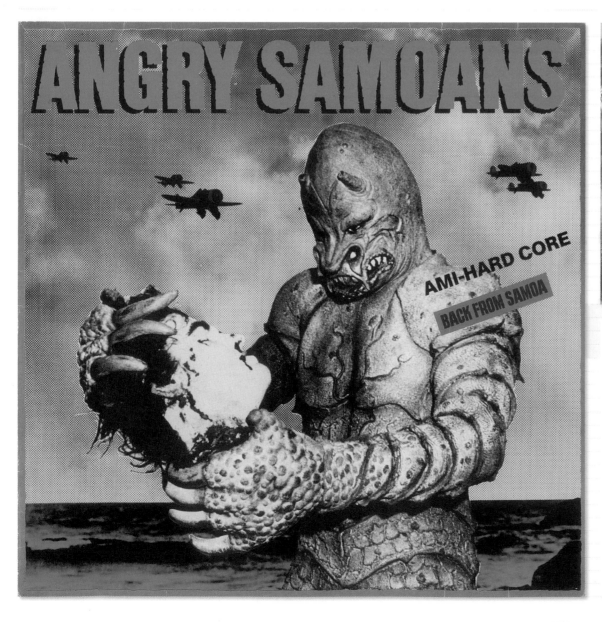

05
Artist SS Decontrol
Title The Kids Will
Have Their Say
Format LP, 12-inch
Label X-Claim!/Dischord,
USA, 1982
_ Design by Bridget
Burpee.

06
Artist Anti
Title I Don't Want to
Die in Your War
Format LP, 12-inch
Label New Underground,
USA, 1982
_ Design by Dan Phillips,
Ed Colver, Gary Kail.

07
Artist Battalion of
Saints
Title Second Coming
Format LP, 12-inch
Label Nutrons, USA, 1984
_ Design by Mad Marc Rude.

08
Artist Government Issue
Title Make an Effort
Format Single, 7-inch
Label Fountain of Youth,
USA, 1983

09
Artist Reagan Youth
Title Youth Anthems for
the New Order
Format Mini-LP, 12-inch
Label R Radical, USA,
1984
_ Design by Reagan Youth.

10
Artist The Fartz
Title Because This
Fuckin' World Stinks
Format EP, 7-inch
Label Fartz, USA, 1981
_ Later rereleased on
Alternative Tentacles.

11
Artist Various
Title Let Them Eat
Jellybeans
Format LP, 12-inch
Label Alternative
Tentacles, USA, 1981
_ The album that
announced the US punk
explosion to the UK
and Europe. Compiled
by Jello Biafra of
Dead Kennedys, it was
released on Alternative
Tentacles after the
group's UK record label
Cherry Red passed,
thinking the new punk
styles were a passing
fad with which it didn't
want to be too closely
identified. Design
by Jello Biafra and
Winston Smith.

Forest Fire

Because of the sheer geographical expanses
involved and the lack of national distribution,
few of the first American punk bands were
able to release more than a fraction of their
material—no matter how brightly their stars
shone at home. The mold was emphatically
broken by Dead Kennedys, Jello Biafra's highly
literate, politicized, scornful San Francisco
punk band who released their debut album on
British independent Cherry Red. The group
managed to court controversy and legal
entanglement on a scale hitherto and hereto
unsurpassed. Much of this was attributable
to Biafra's lifelong commitment to "pranks."
Some of it was payback against the band
from those they had manifestly annoyed.

01
Artist Dead Kennedys
Title California
Über Alles
Format Single, 7-inch
Label Fast Product,
UK, 1979
_ This is the UK version
of the single. The
original US version had
a black-and-white cover
featuring the more
familiar "political
rally" image on its
inner sleeve. Design
by Bob Last and Bruce
Slesinger (aka Ted,
the band's drummer).

02
Artist Dead Kennedys
Title Holiday in Cambodia
Format Single, 7-inch
Label Cherry Red, UK, 1980
_ The Cherry Red version
of the single, later
superseded by "flaying
torture" and "burning
monk" versions. Design
by Annie Horwood.

03
Artist Dead Kennedys
Title Kill the Poor
Format Single, 7-inch
Label Cherry Red, UK, 1980
_ Design by Greg Wright.

04
Artist Dead Kennedys
Title Nazi Punks Fuck Off
Format Single, 7-inch
Label Alternative
Tentacles/Subterranean,
USA, 1981
_ A direct response to
punk audiences who
continued to flirt with
fascism for shock value.
Came with a portmanteau
armband as ironic
artifact.

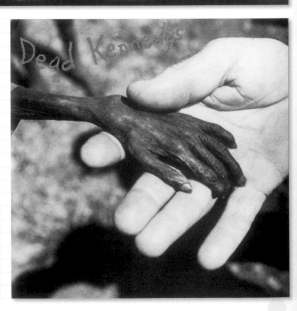

05
Artist Dead Kennedys
Title Plastic Surgery
Disasters
Format LP, 12-inch
Label Static, UK, 1981
_ Photo by Michael Wells.

06
Artist Dead Kennedys
Title Too Drunk to Fuck
Format Single, 7-inch
Label Cherry Red, UK,
1981
_ The single which caused
major controversy in the
UK when it became the
first record to break
the Top 40 using the
titular expletive.
Arrests followed for
those wearing the T-shirt
bearing the slogan.

07
Artist Dead Kennedys
Title Frankenchrist
Format LP, 12-inch
Label Alternative
Tentacles, USA, 1983
_ The photo of a Shriners
(think Freemasons, only
slightly weirder) rally
is arguably the funniest
image ever reproduced on
a punk rock cover.

Again, it resulted in a
court case, but on this
occasion the band had
cleared the image with
its owners, Newsweek.
Design by Jello Biafra,
Newsweek photo
(Lester Sloan).

08
_ Poster for Jello
Biafra's 1979 San
Francisco mayoral
campaign—he finished
fourth. His platform,
among more esoteric
interventions, included
making the police stand
for reelection and
demanding that downtown
businessmen dress in
clown suits during
working hours.

09
Title Work 219:
Landscape XX.
_ The poster given away
with Frankenchrist,
often nicknamed "Penis
Landscape," would cause
ever-greater trouble for
Dead Kennedys, ultimately
resulting in a charge of
"distributing harmful
matter to minors." It
was originally a 1973
painting of airbrushed

acrylic on paper-covered
wood by acclaimed Swiss
artist H. R. Giger. The
image, widely perceived
as a suitable metaphor
for "everyone's fucking
everyone else" American
capitalism, became one
of the most celebrated
and controversial pieces
of punk art, even though
it essentially belonged
to a different era.

The intervention of
Tipper Gore's PMRC
(Parents Music Resource
Center) led to the
"stickering" of
records and face-offs
on the Oprah Winfrey
Show. Biafra and
other defendants were
eventually acquitted
of the charge on a
split jury.

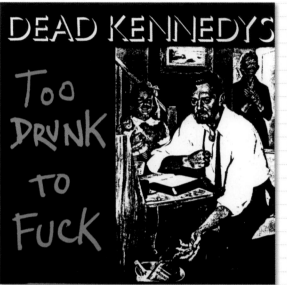

So You're Skeptical?

BIAFRA® for MAYOR
Campaign Fund Raiser

7:30 P.M.   ADMISSION $2
SYMPTOMS
ANTI-BODIES   FREE BUFFET
EYE PROTECTION
VS. JARS
CONTRACTIONS
PINK SECTION
DEAD KENNEDYS

SEPT. 3   LABOR DAY   MABUHAY

A look at how two very different disciplines—collage and figurative cartoons—became the two most celebrated evocations of the visual identity of American punk.

Winston Smith

It's not hard to draw parallels between Winston Smith and Jamie Reid. James Morey, who fittingly took his adopted name from the protagonist in George Orwell's *1984* and cites himself as a "graphic wise-cracker" or "punk art surrealist," has employed similar cut-up and collage techniques to satirize the consumer, business, and religious worlds.

In the late 1960s, Smith was a bored seventeen-year-old in Oklahoma when he decided he'd had enough of sterile, inward-looking America and hightailed it to Florence, Italy, to study art. On his return seven years later, he relocated to San Francisco and ended up roady-ing for groups including Journey, the Tubes, Neil Young, Crosby, Stills & Nash, Santana, and other local and national bands performing in San Francisco in the mid-'70s.

He began to collaborate with fellow artist Jayed Scotti (later of the Feederz) in 1977, resulting in the self-published *Fallout* magazine. They also produced a number of flyers for local bands—many fictitious. A few of the supposed venues were located a half-mile past the coast, somewhere out in the Pacific Ocean.

A lot of this artwork drew on the "safeness" and domesticity of postwar America, reveling in its triteness and sublimating the popular iconography of white picket fence USA by juxtaposing more brutal or stark images to provide an ominous subtext. Throughout, and in common with fellow traveler and friend Gee Vaucher of Crass, his preferred working methodology was to painstakingly handcraft each image.

Smith was working on graphics for a magazine produced by the San Francisco chapter of Rock Against Racism when a mutual friend introduced him to Jello Biafra. During their first encounter, Smith showed the Dead Kennedys' singer the composition "Idol," an image of Jesus on a crucifix made out of dollar bills with bar codes forming the background. It would eventually adorn the cover of the band's mini-album *In God We Trust, Inc.* (though an equal treat was the rear cover artwork of elderly ladies in a car approvingly gesticulating toward a KKK cross burning).

In 1980, Smith would design Dead Kennedys' logo (and later that of Alternative Tentacles) and became a frequent collaborator with Biafra across several albums and singles, one of the most affecting being 1982's *Plastic Surgery Disasters*, which as well as the striking cover image included a twenty-eight-page "libretto" of Biafra's lyrics. "After Biafra gave me a stack of his handwritten lyrics for each song on the album (including a few that never made it on the record in the final cut), I spent a couple weeks on my own creating about half of the compositions. Then Biafra came up to the ranch where we spent the next six or seven days and nights working on the rest of them. We burned more kerosene in one week than I usually went through in a month. Then we went back to San Francisco and worked on the last few pieces till dawn for a couple days. The results were well worth all the toil but the final printing was terrible. The US version was all washed-out and whole multitudes of images dropped out totally. Even I can't tell what they were supposed to be. But the UK version had a much higher resolution—only THEY managed to cut off about an inch all the way round each image! It's always something, ain't it?"

Aside from his (still ongoing) collaborations with "partner in crime" Biafra, Smith has designed record covers for Burning Brides, Ben Harper, and most famously, Green Day's *Insomniac* (a piece titled "God Told Me to Skin You Alive" after the opening line in Dead Kennedys' "I Kill Children"). His work has been exhibited widely and has appeared in publications ranging from *The New Yorker* to *Playboy*.

Raymond Pettibon

Raymond Ginn was an economics graduate working as a high school math teacher before rising to prominence in first the punk and then the art world as Ray Pettibon, adopting a childhood nickname given to him by his father. The tipping point came when his brother Greg formed Black Flag in 1977. (The name was his suggestion after the discovery that their initial moniker Panic was already taken.) Pettibon, who immersed himself in zine culture as a way of self-publishing his creations, beginning with *Captive Chains* in 1979, was Black Flag's original bass player.

One of his first innovations was the four-bar logo that would accompany Black Flag's subsequent releases. As well as its obvious provenance in terms of the black flag of

"If you gave an assignment to one hundred illustrators to do a logo for a group named Black Flag, in the same context, as we know them, half would likely do almost exactly the same logo, except better. I don't have any of the skills of a commercial artist. The height of the bars were never even. Most flags, if they're illustrated, are waving lines."

— Raymond Pettibon

anarchism, it had the singular appeal of a bar code stamp, as witnessed by its widespread use as a tattoo. As well as Black Flag, he would be closely involved with several other releases on his brother's SST label, notably the Minutemen, and later Sonic Youth and Foo Fighters. But it's his stark cartoon line drawings for Black Flag records and flyers, reflecting what he has termed their "aesthetic of realism," that are still seen as his trademark.

The figures that populate Pettibon's drawings—sometimes realized in monochromatic india ink, sometimes with color—are usually imbued with a duality or sense of enigma or entropy. They are often authoritarian archetypes (Reagan, policemen) or slightly unhinged outsiders—whores and priests, drunks, surfers, or baseball stars. Scenarios have the familiarity of TV shows or popular comic books, often featuring action or violence, especially gunplay. They can be accompanied by lifted text, sometimes altered, either framing the visuals or subverting them. The fact that he has made live animations of his drawings is unsurprising, capturing as they do the feel of a sketchbook or movie storyboard. His depiction of America's underbelly, full of the detritus of empty beer bottles, beat-up cars and television sets, has been compared variously to Robert Crumb and William Blake, but also as analogous to literary figures from James Joyce to Tennessee Williams and Raymond Carver.

Even though he's found time to return to his punk roots, working with Brooklyn's Cerebral Ballzy, these days Pettibon is venerated in the upstream art world, his output exhibited everywhere from London's Tate to New York's MoMA, his work collected by celebrities. But then as he has stated, "Punk rockers don't buy art . . . They never did. I could've asked for 50 cents for any drawing; it would have been too much."

Since punk had been consigned to history's garbage can by the majority of cultural commentators before the 1970s wore out, there was some surprise when Green Day's major label debut *Dookie* hit number two in the US Billboard charts in the spring of 1994. International success followed, with the album hitting the number one spot in Australia, New Zealand, and Canada, and charting highly in the UK and Europe. Either a commercial punk revival was underway, or the music business had at last found a way to market it, or perhaps tastes that once lagged behind the initial punk explosion had finally caught up. Either way, "pop-punk" was now with us, for good or bad.

Green Day had started out as a teenage Californian punk group, part of the fiercely independent DIY punk scene based at 924 Gilman Street in Berkeley, California, where they played alongside the likes of local ska-punk stalwarts Operation Ivy and the Offspring (from Huntington Beach). After signing to local independent Lookout! Records, where they shared a roster with Screeching Weasel, the Mr T. Experience, and New Hampshire vets the Queers, the group built a steady following, to the point where their 1992 second album, *Kerplunk*, sold fifty thousand copies in the US and brought them to the attention of the major labels. Operation Ivy, meanwhile, had split in 1989, with guitarist Tim Armstrong and bassist Matt Freeman moving on to form the hugely influential Rancid, who recorded one EP for Lookout! before signing to Epitaph, a label run by Bad Religion guitarist Brett Gurewitz. The Offspring were also signed to Epitaph, and replicated Green Day's breakthrough with their third album, *Smash*, in April 1994. Their combined success paved the way for a revival of mainstream interest in punk, both at home in the US and internationally.

From 1995 onward, pop-punk saw a widening of punk's traditional audience and a recalibration of its demographic, with the traditional SoCal sound being polished and refined in a manner that was analogous to the way new wave had remodeled punk's rough edges twenty years earlier. Some of the elder statesmen of the hardcore generation were thus brought into the fold, with NOFX and Bad Religion among those benefiting by association and numerous namechecks. Rancid released the era-defining . . . *And Out Come the Wolves* in 1995, further cementing Epitaph's reputation as a globally successful independent label, and raising a few grizzled punk eyebrows in the process. In the time-honored tradition of punk battling for "authenticity" and rejecting the mainstream, this commercial resurgence led to something of a backlash. Ironically though, the massive international success of pop-punk bands such as Blink-182 fostered interest in the "genuine" subculture,

reinvigorating a fan base for the wider punk underground as a new audience dug back deeper into history.

Hardcore had itself continued to diversify and adapt through the 1980s and 1990s. The US thrashcore crossover scene, including bands such as DRI, merged the grassroots urgency of hardcore with the virtuosity of metal, just as authentically metal bands such as Metallica in turn attuned themselves to the speed of the thrash-punk phenomenon. The evolution was interlaced with skate-punk bands such as Suicidal Tendencies (skating sharing some of its rebellious stature, being a pastime long associated with American punks). In the UK, Nottingham's Earache Records embraced ever further extremes through releases such as Napalm Death's 1987 debut *Scum*, an album containing twenty-eight tracks of superfast hardcore including "You Suffer," its running time exactly one second. Crossovers with metal and the industrial avant-garde led to increasingly abstract subgenres including grindcore (Sore Throat's forty-five song debut 7-inch EP, *Death to Capitalist Hardcore* being a founding influence), doom, and crust punk.

In the early '90s, the grunge explosion, led by the unexpected success of Nirvana and the Sub Pop label bands, returned guitar-based rock to the wider public consciousness, with a parallel impact on punk—particularly as the punk credentials of Kurt Cobain, Krist Novoselic, and Dave Grohl, the latter a veteran of DC hardcore band Scream, were repeatedly emphasized. The eruption of further authenticity debates was perhaps inevitable. In this context, it was notable that for their final album Nirvana recruited producer Steve Albini, a veteran of Chicago's Big Black (subsequently Shellac) and a ferocious champion of the punk underground.

Punk was the pivotal influence on the development of goth, at first termed "positive punk" in the early '80s, which enjoyed its own migration to the mainstream and in turn became a dominant thread in youth culture, not to mention a variety of other subgenres ranging from psychobilly to riot grrrl to cowpunk to taqwacore. It is beyond the remit of this book to annotate these further, but the stylistic intrigues evolving under the punk umbrella show no sign of abating.

Punk, then, despite the omnipresence of its visual symbolism, from Ramones T-shirts to John Lydon's butter ads, is clearly more than legacy music. More than forty years after the proto-punk progenitors of Detroit and New York unconsciously launched an underground revolution, and after untold premature obituaries, it appears that punk—in terms of music, philosophy, and graphic identity—remains in rude health.

OVERGROUND—FOR IDENTITY

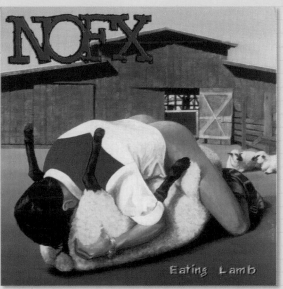

Statements of Intent

As a commercial proposition, punk had been called into question by the music industry from the outset, but as the late '80s merged into the '90s, the death knells were starting to sound more loudly. The entrepreneurship and innovation offered by the DIY punk pioneers had unwittingly led to the success of "indie" music—a definition more widely used to describe a particular aesthetic style rather than a measure of intent, or even independence. Dance music had also found its renaissance through house and techno, and rap, hip-hop, and R & B dominated popular culture.

A number of punk subgenres did, however, offer the prospect of a few green shoots of recovery, from the gradual but steady international rise of street punk, through the extreme noise of Napalm Death and the

Earache Records roster, to crossovers with dance, dub, techno, and industrial music. Ex-Minor Threat singer Ian MacKaye's new group Fugazi pioneered an ethical DIY stance that combined low ticket pricing for concerts and independent record distribution with an open hostility toward traditional music industry practices. Steve Albini pursued an equally autonomous agenda, developing a crossover hardcore/industrial sound with Big Black and Rapeman, before forming "post-hardcore" legends Shellac in 1992 and gaining a high-profile reputation as a producer. Meanwhile, Rancid began their journey to underground punk stardom in 1991, gaining a level of critical credibility by refusing to sign to a major label, unlike their contemporaries Green Day and the Offspring, even when their third album . . . *And Out Come the Wolves* hit the international charts in 1995.

01
Artist Big Black
Title Songs about Fucking
Format LP, 12-inch
Label Touch & Go, USA, 1987

02
Artist Rapeman
Title Two Nuns and a Pack Mule
Format LP, 12-inch
Label Touch & Go, USA, 1988

03
Artist Fugazi
Title S/T
Format EP, 12-inch
Label Dischord, USA, 1988
_ Cover photograph of Fugazi guitarist/vocalist Guy Picciotto in action by Adam Cohen. Design by Kurt Sayenga.

04
Artist Rancid
Title Time Bomb
Format EP, 7-inch
Label Epitaph, USA, 1995

05
Artist Rancid
Title . . . And Out Come the Wolves
Format LP, 12-inch
Label Epitaph, USA, 1995
_ Design and photography by Jesse Fischer.

06
Artist The Offspring
Title Americana
Format LP, 12-inch
Label Columbia, USA, 1998
_ Illustration by Frank Kozik.

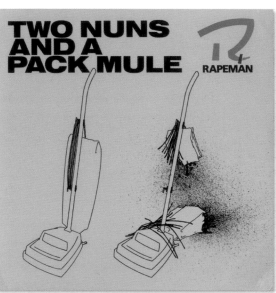

07

Artist Cock Sparrer

Title Running Riot in '84

Format LP, 12-inch

Label Syndicate, UK, 1984

08

Artist Blaggers ITA

Title United Colors of Blaggers ITA

Format LP, 12-inch

Label Words Of Warning, UK, 1992

_ Design by S.I.T. Inc & Karl WOW.

09

Artist Snuff

Title Not Listening

Format EP, 7-inch

Label Workers Playtime, UK, 1989

10

Artist Stupids

Title Violent Nun

Format EP, 7-inch

Label Children of the Revolution, UK, 1984

_ Did the Stupids' very un-PC sense of humor ever give the band problems? "Sort of, I guess, in a very minor way. Our record label asked for 'Waltz of the New Wavers' to be removed from *Violent Nun* because of the line 'all new wavers are queer,' which we thought terribly unfair. I think *Retard Picnic* upset a few folk, but Jesus H. Christ, what can you do? I'm not going to sit here and drum up some excuses for anything we did. It wasn't to be offensive, it was in celebration." (Tommy Stupid). Design by Tommy Stupid.

11

Artist Napalm Death

Title Scum

Format LP, 12-inch

Label Earache, UK, 1987

_ Design by Jeff.

Underground Network

Hardcore continues to operate in something of a parallel existence to the mainstream music industry, with groups self-releasing and co-releasing material, or joining forces to support tours, distribution networks, venues, and collaboratively run DIY labels. Models of operation developed through the '80s hardcore scene, themselves drawing upon earlier approaches within the DIY and anarcho punk communities, and have become adopted as standard practice. The graphic languages of earlier punk subgenres live on, too, through stark monochrome imagery of war, death, and violence.

Disrespect, from Minneapolis, Minnesota, drew heavily on UK82 icons such as Discharge and Crass, as well as lesser-known contemporary groups on the Riot City label, for both musical and graphic inspiration. Their records were released on the local Profane Existence label, part of the DIY punk collective of the same name. Profane Existence also produce a regular anarchist punk magazine, the largest of its type in North America, covering a broad range of topics including veganism, animal rights, women's and minority rights, antifascist action, and the punk lifestyle. In 1992, the collective copublished the first edition of *Book Your Own Fuckin' Life*, a regional directory of bands, distributors, venues, and houses where "touring bands or traveling punks could sleep and sometimes eat for free" with *Maximumrocknroll* fanzine.

> **"Profane Existence Magazine is a product of the DIY (Do-It-Yourself) Punk Community. We believe in having as much control over the production and distribution of our magazine as possible. We work closely with literally hundreds of like-minded DIY bands, labels, publishers, distributors, and other organizations."**

Profane Existence: Making Punk a Threat Again!

01
Artist Disrespect
Title Wartorn
Format EP, 7-inch
Label Profane Existence,
USA, 2005
_ Veteran members of
the Minneapolis punk
scene, released on the
Profane Existence
label—a hardcore
punk DIY collective
also responsible for
the fanzine of the
same name.

02
Artist Diskelmä
Title Burning Dreams
Format EP, 7-inch
Label Kämäset Levyt,
Finland, 2009

03
Artist Disrespect
Title S/T
Format EP, 7-inch
Label Profane Existence,
USA, 2004
_ The sleeve's close
resemblance to the
first Discharge EP
is continued with an
ironic parody on a
foldout poster.

04
Artist Tolshock
Title The Heritage
of Violence
Format EP, 7-inch
Label Farewell, Germany,
1998
_ Swedish crust released
by a German label.
Design by Janne and
the Revolutionary
Noise and Scribble
Board Collective.

05
Artist Asfixia
Title S/T
Format EP, 7-inch
Label 213 Records/
Contraszt!, Spain, 2006
_ Debut EP by this band
from Bilbao in the
Spanish Basque Country.

06
Artist Immured
Title S/T
Format EP, 7-inch
Label Fake Vomit Inc.,
Germany, 2007

07
Artist War of
Destruction
Title Normalisering
Format EP, 7-inch
Label Hjernespind,
Denmark, 2008
_ Legendary early 1980s
hardcore group from
Århus, Denmark.

08
Artist Aus Rotten
Title Fuck Nazi Sympathy
Format EP, 7-inch
Label Havoc, USA, 1994
_ Hardcore punk from
Pittsburgh, featuring
a foldout poster sleeve
and a copy of Rotten
Propaganda, vocalist
Dave's anarchist
newspaper.

09
Artist Skitkids/
Nightmare
Title S/T
Format EP, 7-inch
Label Hate, Germany, 2007
_ Split EP featuring
Skitkids from Sweden and
Nightmare from Japan.

01	02		04	05	06
	03	|	07	08	09

Luk Tam89 has been writing for various punk fanzines since 1986, including *Maximumrocknroll*, and running the not-for-profit Tian An Men 89 Records since 1993. The label issues vinyl punk records from "non-Western" countries, especially those that lack pressing plants, or from bands without the financial wherewithal to see their music documented otherwise. Luk TAM89 particularly focuses on Asia, Africa, the Middle East, and the former Soviet Union states. Luk's extensive travels have taken him to more than 120 countries in his search for punk and underground music. He authored the extensive *Eastern European Punk Music Discography 1977–1999* and maintains the Asian punk discography online resource. He holds an MD in ethnology and various degrees in English, Psychology, and Cinema, and speaks French, German, Chinese, Russian, and a few other languages.

"My covers are a mix of ideas and concepts. Some come from me, some from the bands, and some from a friend who is a graphic designer (usually after I give him some ideas and basic graphic materials from the country). I like it when the art makes a reference to the country of origin, just like I like it when a band uses the local language for their lyrics. This is not always the case. The cover art for the Chinese compilation was designed by the bands, and makes no reference to China, title aside. The same applies to the Madagascar release [fig. 07], which was a band design, and so too our Azerbaijan record. The latter was again a band design, but there is a heavy local reference with the oil derricks. This one I did not like as much and I really wanted to improve the colors, the fonts, etc. I was ready to do a full-color cover: the bands did not want to negotiate, at all . . . so there! With Algeria [fig. 04], again the band did the full design (and again,

used a derrick!). For the Saudi Arabian release [fig. 02] I used the cover of an old Saudi 7-inch as the basis. We had to avoid anything that could have been deemed political or offensive to avoid problems with the authorities. But again, derricks won the day, even though I do like this retro kind of design.

The Tajik cover [*Dushanbe Punkers & Rockers*; not featured] is based on the design of a local cigarette brand, Pamir. It was designed by my friend Lem. The *Pank Federatsiya 1* cover I did myself, based on a poster of the Soviet 'Civil Defence' organization (which trains civilians for war conditions) which I found in a Riga bookshop in 1992. The cover [fig. 03] of the Uzbek compilation (the Combine Harvesters in cotton fields) fits, I think, very well with the title. 'Paxta' in Uzbek means 'cotton,' 'paxtakor' means the 'cotton worker' and it's a word you see everywhere in propaganda design in that country. The photo comes from an old Soviet Uzbekistan propaganda album and was chosen and arranged by Lem.

So essentially different cases apply for the origins of the artwork. The Chinese bands adamantly refused to have anything related to China on the cover. The Azeris and Algerians did it without any input from me. I think that given the very particular kind of music I release (especially in terms of geographic coverage), it helps to have art that both looks 'punk' (whatever that means) and relates to the country of origin of the bands. I also like the idea of experimenting with 'punk design' in/about countries where this might not really have been done before, as my records are almost always the first punk vinyl to originate from that country."

01
Artist Various Artists
Title Underground Kyrgystan: Bishkek is Burning!
Format EP, 7-inch
Label Tian An Men 89, France, 2004
_ The first ever Kyrgyzstan punk compilation.

02
Artist Sound Of Ruby
Title From Under The Sands Of The Desert
Format EP, 7-inch
Label Tian An Men 89, France, 2011
_ The cover design incorporates an image of an old Saudi Arabian single release to disguise its punk content.

FROM THE STEPPES TO THE ICE SHELVES

03
Artist Various Artists
Title Underground
Uzbekistan: Paxta-Core
Format LP, 12-inch
Label Tian An Men 89,
France, 2006

04
Artist Demokhratia
Title Bled El Petrole
Takoul Lekhra
Format EP, 7-inch
Label Tian An Men 89,
France, 2009
_ Highly politicized
hardcore from Algeria
sung in Arabic.

05
Artist(s) Ghost Rider/
The Ants
Title Anthology of
Myanmar Punk Rock Vol. 1
Format EP, 7-inch
Label Tian An Men 89,
France, 2000
_ All songs recorded in
the Myanmar language.

06
Artist(s) Zuby/Vitamin
Rosta
Title Underground
Tatarstan: Underground
Kabardino-Balkaria
Format EP, 7-inch
Label Tian An Men 89,
France, 2001
_ Split release combining
two groups from
different republics of
the Russian Federation.

07
Artist Sweety Punk
Title Underground
Madagascar: Soa Ity
Painky
Format EP, 7-inch
Label Tian An Men 89,
France, 2001
_ The first ever
Madagascan punk record.

01		03	04
02		05	06	07

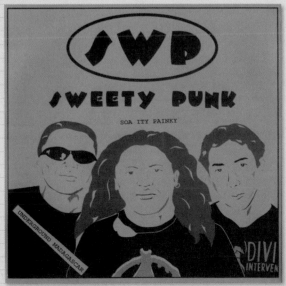

Out of Step (With the World)

The critical reappraisal of punk history since the turn of the century has extended further, casting light on international underground scenes that have in the past remained invisible to the outside world. Shaun Jefford's documentary study of contemporary Chinese punk subculture, *Beijing Punk*, centers on a small club called D-22, which has become the meeting point for young Chinese musicians who have adopted a punk lifestyle in the face of an often overbearing political regime. In a country where the Internet and YouTube are blocked by the government, such audacious behavior is a clear cultural and political statement. Featuring a number of Beijing punk groups including Oi! outfit Misandao, Demerit, and Hedgehog, the film reveals an active local scene and demonstrates that the language of punk music is universal, adopting local idiosyncrasies through cultural filters as it crosses borders and continents.

In a similar vein, though with a greater historical focus, Keith Jones and Deon Maas's film *Punk in Africa* charts the progress of the subculture across the African continent, from small local scenes in Durban and Johannesburg to the crossover ska, dub and traditional African music groups who led the fight against apartheid in the late '70s and '80s. South Africa's first punk group to release a record, Durban's Wild Youth, are featured, along with political hardcore outfit Power Age, multiracial punk-reggae group National Wake, the antiestablishment Asylum Kids, and a burgeoning post-punk and crossover scene that spread across Africa, taking in aspects of local culture as it went.

01
_ Poster promoting the documentary film *Beijing Punk* by Australian filmmaker Shaun Jefford, featuring groups from the Chinese punk underground during the buildup to the Beijing Olympics in 2008. Design by Fineline Creative.

02
_ *Punk in Africa*, a documentary film by Keith Jones and Deon Maas exploring the history of punk in South Africa, Mozambique, Zimbabwe, Namibia, and Kenya. Design by DJ Zhao.

03

Artist Porno Para Ricardo
Title Rock Para Las Masas… (Cárnicas)
Format LP, CD
Label La Paja, Cuba, 2002
_ Debut album by Cuban underground group Porno Para Ricardo (Porn for Richard). Singer Gorki Águila was jailed in 2003 on charges of supplying drugs, and since his release in 2007 has been an outspoken critic of the Cuban regime, leading to further difficulties with the authorities.

04

Artist Rai Ko Ris
Title Himalayan Frostbite
Format EP, 7-inch
Label Batattak, USA, 2003
_ Second Nepalese punk record, released via a US label collaboration.

05

Artist Various Artists
Title Sevdasiz Hayat Ölümdür
Format EP, 7-inch
Label Tian An Men 89, France, 1994
_ Turkish underground punk compilation on the TAM89 label.

06

Artist Various Artists
Title We Are the Punx in Korea
Format LP, CD
Label Skunk, South Korea, 2002

07

Artist Various Artists
Title Illegal by Choice
Format EP, 7-inch
Label De:Nihil, Sweden, 2011
_ A Benefit Record For Hidden Refugees, featuring Meanwhile, Asta Kask, Victims, Kvoteringen, Alert! Alert!, and Demenzia Kolektiva.

08

Artist Big CYC
Title Zadzwoncie Po Milicje!
Format LP, CD
Label Universal Music, Poland, 2011
_ The group's name translates as Big Tit and the album title as Call the Police! A tribute to the bands that had been active throughout the period of martial law in Poland, who were persecuted, beaten, and imprisoned. Design by Jo Mirowski.

Modern Action: Contemporary Punk

One significant legacy of the DIY punk and independent boom was the establishment of business models that could remain small-scale and fine-tuned toward specific target markets. Many early independent punk releases were only produced in small quantities, with a clear aim to balance production with potential demand. Lo-tech and handmade production methods were often labor-intensive and impossible to replicate on a large scale, precluding them from the mass-production approach of the major labels. Interestingly, these "business practices" still prevail today in an underground, independent, collector-led market for do-it-yourself boutique labels. Modern Action Records, based in Sonoma, California, has earned a reputation as a leader in the field through their handcrafted, silkscreen-printed, stenciled, and stickered releases, with extremely limited multiple-format editions that would be the envy of a label like Stiff thirty years earlier. The debut album by the Sharp Objects, released on October 31, 2011, boasted an impressive range of different formats, including twenty-five numbered copies of a special Halloween "jack-o'-

lantern" edition: "Pressed on Black vinyl with a red center label. Covers are plain black with a white Sharp Objects logo spray painted on the front. A pumpkin face was carved outta the front cover, revealing the red spray-painted dust sleeve. Comes with a printed 2-sided dust sleeve w/lyrics/photos, an 11 x 17 poster from the record release show and an 8.5 x 11 record release poster."

No Front Teeth, a UK independent label, follows in a similar vein, incorporating limited-edition, hand-printed, die-cut, stamped, and painted sleeves—a sophisticated use of materials and innovative stenciling techniques by Marco No Front Teeth, a London-based artist and member of the Gaggers, who has become one of the most prolific contemporary punk designers in the country. NFT issued the Strap Straps' *Invisible Knife* debut album in 10-inch format, with two alternative "regular" sleeves and two different limited editions featuring ". . . laser-cut covers so the knife and the letters are all actually cut out, so you can see the record through the gaps and can use the cover as a stencil too."

01
Artist The Gaggers
Title You Ain't No Fun
Format EP, 7-inch
Label No Front Teeth,
UK, 2010
_ Design by Marco No
Front Teeth.

02
Artist Germ Attak
Title Death to Cops
Format EP, 7-inch
Label Loud Punk,
USA, 2010

03
Artist Kissin' Cousins/
Clorox Girls
Title S/T
Format Split EP, 7-inch
Label Beat Generation,
Spain, 2006

04
Artist Straitjacket
Title Enemy
Format Single, 7-inch
Label Jonny Cat,
USA, 2004
_ A kind of double
détournement, as
Straitjacket
reappropriate and mash
up Linder Sterling and
Malcolm Garrett's classic
Buzzcocks cover design.

05
Artist Smogtown
Title Audiophile
Format EP, 7-inch
Label Hostage, USA, 2000

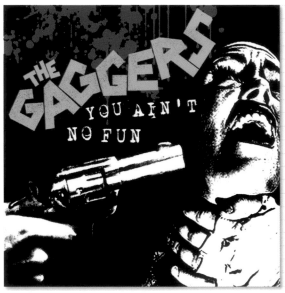

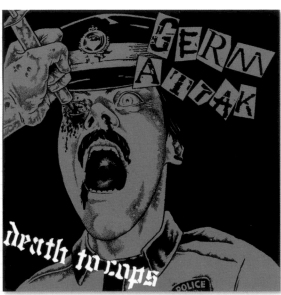

01 02 03   07 08
04 05 06 | 09

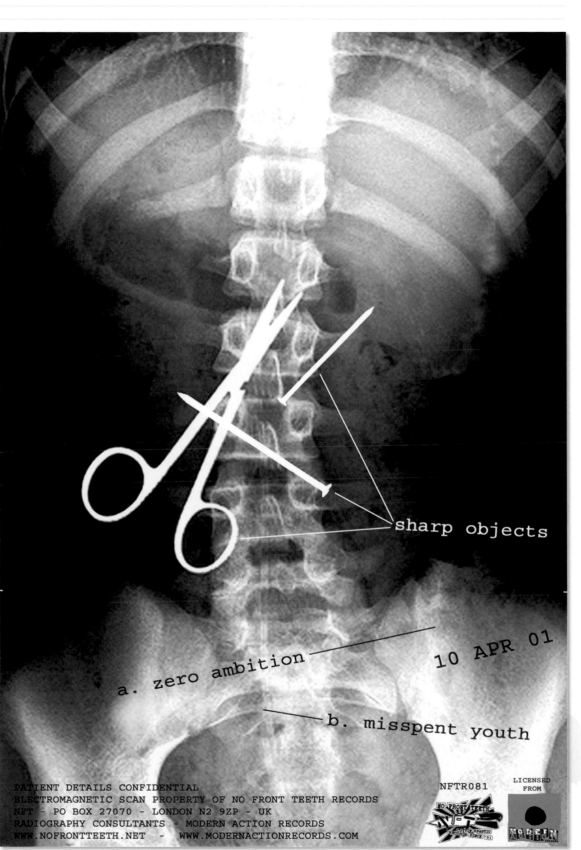

a. zero ambition

b. misspent youth

sharp objects

10 APR 01

NFTR081

LICENSED
FROM

The spirit of rebellion has long been an attractive theme for businesses targeting the youth market—after all, Malcolm McLaren and Vivienne Westwood's first ventures into fashion centered on radical styles aimed at disenchanted subcultures, from teddy boys to rockers to the first wave of punks. In the process, they tapped into a heritage of rebel images going back through the early rock 'n' rollers to a much earlier canon of subversive artists, writers, political agitators, and public antiheroes from Robin Hood to Bonnie and Clyde. It should come as no surprise that McLaren's chosen introduction to the Sex Pistols' film *The Great Rock 'n' Roll Swindle* centered on the Gordon Riots of 1780, deliberately locating the group in a lineage of populist radical subversion dating back two centuries.

As it was increasingly vilified in the media, punk grabbed the public's attention to an extent that hadn't been witnessed since the early days of rock 'n' roll. The histrionic disgust and outrage expressed at the antics of spitting, vomiting, foul-mouthed youth with safety pins through their faces, appalling hygiene, and attitudes to match—whether that was perception or reality—was a surefire way to sell papers or attract listeners and viewers. Businesses were quick to catch on—stylized cartoon "punk" characters could be written as simple shorthand for an idle and stupid proletariat that "we" could rise above, or a dangerous "other" that we should seek protection from—for a price, of course.

Stylized "punks" made an appearance in popular television, as anarchic villains in the police dramas *Quincy* and *CHiPs*, or as figures of ridicule in British sitcoms and the dubious characterizations of comic impressionists. Such antagonism, however, is bound to elicit some sympathy, or at least some interest in the subject, and for many young viewers anything that was offensive to their parents must be something to pursue further. Ever since the early days of cinema, the villain has held a curious attraction, often eliciting more interest among audiences than the supposed forces of good. Music is no different—Jerry Lee Lewis, Johnny Cash, Hank Williams, and Chuck Berry were always more interesting than the anodyne Bill Haley or Cliff Richard (though it shouldn't be forgotten that even they raised the opprobrium of an older generation at the time), and a tradition of rock 'n' roll bad boys ensued. Punk, in many ways the ultimate culmination of the bad boy stereotype, could thus become, in the words of the Slits, "another marketing ploy" for businesses trying to ensnare a style-conscious, rebellious youth. Punk was also sold as a lifestyle choice—punk clothing, punk records, punk movies, and punk magazines had quickly filled a consumer void in the wake of its first explosion. Now, the "spirit of punk" was ripe for exploitation and made its entreaties to a wider demographic of resistant buyers who might be persuaded to buy into punk as "outsider art."

Some Product

The graphic language of punk, then, was applied to makeup, fashion accessories, youth magazines, soft drinks, interior design, textiles, and jewelry: there was little in the way of merchandise that couldn't be sprinkled with a little subcultural cachet. Punk's long battle for "authenticity" herein collided with a wider public recognition of its base symbols. Many punk designers already knew this, of course, and a self-aware and knowingly contrary subculture made great play of the juxtaposition. The debut Buzzcocks album being packaged in a bag labeled "product," or Flipper's *Generic Flipper*, with its cover simply stating the word "ALBUM," are just two examples, with Public Image Ltd's self-marketing as a corporate business entity furthering the conceit.

As the original punks matured, marketeers found new ways to target their goods to that consumer group. Beyond the punk records, clothing, artwork, and books, other niche businesses popped up to satisfy the demand for punk ephemera and novelties—such as Aggronautix, a Phoenixville, Pennsylvania company that produces " . . . Throbbleheads— a punk rock version of the ever-popular bobblehead doll that runs rampant throughout American culture." The company designs and manufactures polyresin effigies of punk icons such as GG Allin, Milo of the Descendents, the Dwarves, Tesco Vee, and Jello Biafra.

Some strategies echoed earlier models by identifying punk product with a "rebellious consumer," if such an entity could ever be anything but oxymoronic. Others were largely nostalgic or comedic in nature. Punk scrubbing brushes and ransom note fridge magnets hold little specific connection to the user group as products in themselves, but they make an ideal gift for the old punk in your life— especially one retaining a sense of identification with punk as both a visual and philosophical token of "difference," however deeply the ensuing years had sucked them into the rat race.

Perhaps the ultimate irony, or the ultimate sell-out, depending on perspective, occurred in 2008. John Lydon—formerly Johnny Rotten, lead singer of the Sex Pistols—signed a contract to appear in a series of television and magazine advertisements for Country Life butter, a product manufactured by Dairy Crest Ltd. and undergoing a rebrand, moving away from the term "English butter" to "British butter" in the process. The ads were based on the slogan "It's not about Great Britain, it's about Great Butter," with Lydon appearing dressed in tweeds as a traditional English gentleman, offering an amusing comic interpretation of national identity. The ads helped lift sales of the brand by more than 85 per cent, and Lydon, who had completed the journey from most despised man in England to cherished uncle, later credited the fee earned with providing him the opportunity to fund a Public Image Ltd reunion tour the following year.

CASH FROM CHAOS

02 03
04 05
01 | 06 07

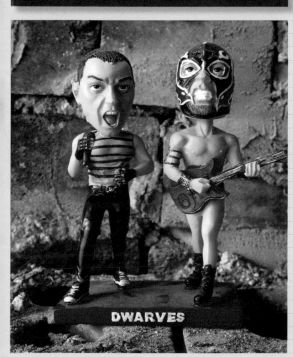

The Bright Lights of America

After spending a decade on the hardcore underground, Pittsburgh's Anti-Flag signed to major label RCA for their seventh album, *For Blood and Empire*, in 2006. The group's overtly political songwriting was accompanied on their album releases with booklets of essays by band members alongside extracts from historians and political commentators, together with stencils and posters drawing on their powerful graphic design. Common themes explored include the ongoing War on Terror, international human rights, and the global economic crisis, together with outspoken support for activist groups such as Greenpeace, Amnesty International, PETA, and Democracy Now!, marking them as key representatives of a left-leaning, progressive punk movement.

Similarly radical and outspoken, New York's Leftöver Crack are renowned for their critiques of religion, capitalism, and authority, and their antagonistic lyrical and graphic messages. Following contractual difficulties with Epitaph offshoot Hellcat Records—who were inflamed by the band's choice of debut album title, *Shoot the Kids at School* (subsequently issued as *Mediocre*

Generica)—the group moved on to Jello Biafra's Alternative Tentacles for their follow-up, *Fuck World Trade*, in 2004. Unsurprisingly, the album was banned in multiple chain stores including WalMart, Best Buy, and Music Land due to its controversial name and subject matter—particularly its front cover, which features a photomontage of George W. Bush, Dick Cheney, and Rudy Giuliani pouring petrol on the World Trade Center during the 2001 attacks.

Unsurprisingly, this critique of global capitalism was mirrored across the subculture in the early twenty-first century as economies began to collapse and the dark underbelly of international politics became more exposed. Following a number of releases on their own Bluurg label, Citizen Fish, a UK ska-punk group formed by Dick Lucas of the Subhumans, released a split album with Leftöver Crack in 2007. Building an international reputation as a danceable political punk outfit, the group developed a typically reflective and personal interpretation of the consumer crisis on their album *Goods*, released on the Alternative Tentacles imprint in 2011.

01
Artist Anti-Flag
Title Die for the Government
Format LP, 12-inch
Label New Red Archives, USA, 1997
_ Design by Alex Submachine and Keriann "The Sneetch" Martin.

02
Artist Anti-Flag
Title The Bright Lights of America
Format LP, 12-inch
Label RCA, Europe, 2008
_ Design by Rob Larson.

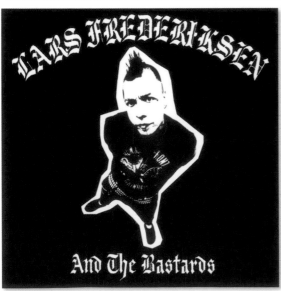

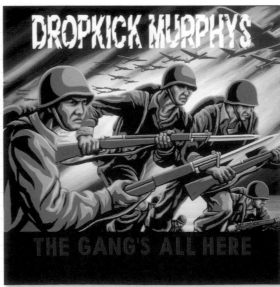

Art Attacks

Inspired by punk, drawing cultural references or conceptual cues from its "attitudes" and identities, or commenting on punk itself, many contemporary artists have established their practice through a relationship to the subculture. The range of sophisticated visual codes and references developed through the different phases and subgenres of the movement have resulted in a powerful visual vocabulary—a kind of graphic shorthand—that can be discerned by those inside and outside of the scene. Those same codes might be used by lifestyle branders seeking to tap into an audience demographic embedded within the notion of the "outsider," but they can also provide inspiration for a more philosophical and intelligent visual art practice.

A number of artists with a background in graffiti and street art have drawn directly from the subculture—the pseudonymous UK activist Banksy has established a worldwide reputation for his public critique of duplicitous values in our societies, often drawing iconic elements from punk in the process. Los Angeles-based street artist Shepard Fairey, creator of the Obey Giant sticker campaign and subsequently the 2008 presidential election Barack Obama "Hope" poster, drew directly from the skateboarding and punk scenes of the 1980s. Fairey's screenprinted reappropriations of classic punk images draw direct parallels between the Obey campaign and punk iconography.

Dexter Dalwood, a former member of Bristol punk group the Cortinas, has built a reputation as a high-profile contemporary British artist, creating paintings that depict imagined and constructed interiors or landscapes, as memorials or descriptions of famous historic people, places or moments. His *Room 100, Chelsea Hotel* depicts an imagined reinterpretation of the infamous location where Nancy Spungen met her untimely death, allegedly at the hands of boyfriend Sid Vicious in 1978.

Others, like painter Paul Harvey, draw on the concept and ideology of punk itself for their visual expressions—as a critical commentary on figurative painting and conceptual art. A similar critical approach inspired Danish artist Knud Odde, a self-taught musician and painter, who developed his practice from the punk underground and art scene in Copenhagen in the late 1970s as a member of the "Young Wild" group of painters. The group set out to react against gallery conventions and the ruling paradigms of minimalism and conceptual art in order to reawaken the art of painting. Later, Odde incorporated a number of punk-related portraits in his work, including Patti Smith, Lou Reed, and Mark E. Smith of the Fall.

PUNK ART

01

_ *Room 100, Chelsea Hotel* by Dexter Dalwood, renowned British contemporary painter and former member of Bristol punk group the Cortinas. "It has to be a subject that has been in my thinking. It has to be personal to me. I try to evoke things that are not obvious. It was to do with the idea of Sid in New York and the Chelsea Hotel, the quicksand of history and success. I like to record moments in history. I've always liked art that features little bits of all the things I'm interested in." (Dexter Dalwood)

02

_ *Don't Forget Your Scarf* by Banksy, 2009, oil on board.

03

_ Banksy, London, 2010.

04

_ *Punk Victorian* by Paul Harvey, 2004, acrylic and gold leaf on canvas. Harvey projects photographs—in this case singer/songwriter Anna Page—onto canvas, which he then traces and paints to create complex compositions. Harvey is a member of the Stuckists, associated with the work of Billy Childish among others, a radical and controversial art group, and also has a background in punk as a musician, playing guitar in UK punk outfit Penetration.

05

_ *Poly Styrene*, portrait of X-Ray Spex singer by Chris Bell, who also plays drums in the Briefs.

06

_ *Burning in Water* by Marco Palumbo-Rodrigues, of the Gaggers and the No Front Teeth label, acrylic, emulsion, enamel, gloss, shellac, and oil on hardboard, 2011. The painting is named after a song by Moving Targets.

07

_ *Mark E Smith II*, portrait by Knud Odde, 2001. "After a pause of some twenty years, I went to see the Fall play again in 2001, and was stunned by how exciting they still were. Alas, I made some paintings." (Knud Odde)

```
         03
01    04  05
02  |  06  07
```

So, what does the future hold for the "No Future" generation(s)? Punk's lifetime has already extended well beyond the wildest predictions of its early champions and its critics, encompassing fashion, design, art, media, writing, photography, politics, and of course, music. Some former (and current) participants in the subculture have become prominent activists, politicians, artists, writers, musicians, and educators—with many citing punk as a formative experience.

Punk always balanced a positive message within its provocative rhetoric, offering up the potential that we have to destroy in order to create—"No Future" could be read as both a nihilistic outburst and a call to arms for more affirmative action. That libertarian and progressive aspect of the movement has helped to shape and found social and political activist groups, do-it-yourself cooperatives, and a worldwide network of support and communication channels.

Another impact of the evolution of the subculture has been the development of a self-sustaining international underground economy centered on music, fashion, publishing, and design. For some, aspects of this "alternative capitalism" model of "punk" lifestyle can be seen as counterintuitive to the original ideology and ethos of the subculture, while others are happy to be able to access a vibrant network of live gigs, records, events, and commercial outlets for punk "products" that form a central part of their personal self-image and identity.

Whatever your opinion, it is certainly the case that punk has refused to die, demonstrating an astute and adept ability to modify and adapt in respect to its wider context. Punk graphic design and art still have currency and credibility, and the phrase "Punk Is Dead: Long Live Punk!" has become an aphorism for a debate that endures.

Penetration, led by Pauline Murray, were the northeast of England's most important and challenging punk-era band, immediately receptive to the sea change in the UK capital but never constrained by any notion that punk could only be a wall of noise, unpunctuated by melody or harmony.

> "Punk was a life-changing experience. The music, words, clothes, and the attitude were very liberating. Anything was possible. It opened your eyes and mind to respond to the world in a different way. It was a creative time when people discovered and utilized their talents—writers, photographers, artists, poets, musicians, and the audience were included. It felt like you had turned your back on the old established ways and were entering unchartered territory. It was a unique movement—and people still try to analyze this. Primal, yet intelligent."

Pauline Murray, Penetration

Tesco Vee specialized in confronting concepts of decency throughout his tenure as main man of the Meatmen and coauthor of *Touch & Go* fanzine and its associated record label, an enterprise that was subsidized initially by teaching elementary school.

> "Roughneck street-level noise had been 'round since real gone cats loosened some tubes, slicked up their dos and scaled down their attack to a gritty and wondrous sound, and twenty hence here was a sizable and necessary backlash aimed at the bloated prog fucks and what the '70s had become musically and they called it . . . punk rock . . . which of course was but one handle for this groundswell of cacophonous crash 'n' burn, and I got swept up in it an' rode that rat rod o' rock 'n' roll mayhem via my zine and label Touch & Go for four years. It felt new. It felt fresh. And most of all, loud and dirty. American hardcore was our middle-class reaction to all these UK rumblings, and provided all of us of minimal talent and maximum spirit an outlet for whatever was popping in our collective, creative craniums. I was lucky enough to cover it first hand both as scribe and protagonist. I was there in person for both the Midwest and [Washington] DC happenings. It was a special and important time in music history, one that still resonates, and that can never come again. And I thank Satan I was there to witness it first hand!"

Tesco Vee, the Meatmen and *Touch & Go* fanzine and label

Former bass player with first-generation UK punk band the Adverts, Gaye Black has recently been behind the "Beyond Punk" exhibitions, which feature both original and contemporary work by those involved in the punk scene.

> "When Signal Gallery suggested I curate a show for them I thought it would be interesting to bring together punk musicians who were also producing visual art. The punk movement was like no other, bursting with originality and enthusiasm and an 'anything goes' ethos, with music, artwork, and fashion interlinked. Bands designed their own record covers, decorated their own clothes, and fanzines burst forth. That kind of freshness and creativity has never been replicated."

Gaye Black, the Adverts

Milo Aukerman, lead singer with Californian hardcore stalwarts the Descendents, pursued a career as a research biochemist. However, he has little time for pretentious academic reviews of punk, here reacting to an article entitled *Is Punk the New Jazz?* in *The Chronicle of Higher Education*.

> "Jazz caters to the intellectual elite, an increasingly diminished faction, and therein lies its demise. Punk, almost by definition, is for the pinheads/outcasts/ normal Joes, that is, the masses. In that sense, it has more in common with pop music than anything else, and I don't see that genre of music going by the wayside anytime soon. Punk is inclusive, anyone can do it; that's why it will always be around. As long as there's some kid with an electric guitar who wants to make some noise, and doesn't really care if he gets paid to do so, we will have punk. The genre will likely cycle in and out of popularity, and there will no doubt be times when there are no hard chords on the radio,' but that doesn't mean punk has disappeared. Whenever punk goes underground and then reemerges in some reenergized form, it serves to demonstrate that, in music, the desire for popularity is always trumped by a more visceral urge that requires nothing more than a warm body and a loud electric instrument . . . I am referring to THE NEED TO ROCK."

Milo Aukerman, the Descendents

NO FUTURE?

_ *Pretty Disobedient*,
screenprinted poster
by Shepard Fairey based
on the "boredom buses"
image originally
appropriated and adapted
by Jamie Reid for the Sex
Pistols in 1977, 2001.

_ *Vicious Subversion*,
screenprinted poster by
Shepard Fairey, based on
a 1977 portrait of Sex
Pistols' bassist Sid
Vicious by photographer
Dennis Morris, 2001.

_ Film still from
the animated movie
Persepolis, 2007.
The film, based on an
autobiographical graphic
novel by Marjane Satrapi,
centers on the story of
a young girl coming of
age during the Iranian
Revolution.

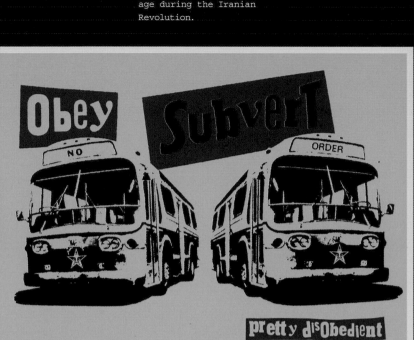

INDEX

Page numbers in italics refer to the illustrations.

PICTURE CREDITS

Record covers appear © their respective labels. Every effort has been made to acknowledge the pictures, however the publisher welcomes any further information so that future editions may be updated.

The publisher would like to thank the following people and organizations, especially Russell Bestley, Alex Ogg, Josef Loderer, Chuck Warner, Candy Wall and Anne Poole, for access to their collections. Without them this book would not have been possible.

Courtesy Ace Records Ltd. www.acerecords.com: p30 (06), p31 (11), p63 (15), p63 (15), p95 (07).

Courtesy of The Advertising Archives: p213 (05).

Design by Keith Breeden (Assorted Images): p89 (04).

Chris Brief: p217 (05).

Hugh Brown: p89 (03).

Courtesy of Jefe Brown: p208 (02).

Camera Press/Caroline Coon: p42 (01).

Roger Crimlis: p13 (03), p21 (08, 11), p24 (12, 13), p45 (05), p49 (04), p54 (03, 04), p55 (02, 05, 06), p91 (10).

© Dexter Dalwood courtesy Gagosian Gallery: p216 (01).

Ben Tecumseh DeSoto: p9 (04), p197 (01).

Dizzy Detour: p64 (02, 03), p65 (05).

Courtesy of Discharge: p173 (07).

Sarah Dryden: p213 (07).

Courtesy and © Karen Duckworth / www.karenduckworth.co.uk: p8 (02), p9 (03).

Enemy Ink, Orlando, Florida USA: p201 (02), p215 (07, 08).

David Ensminger: p69 (06, 07), p71 (03-06), p184 (01), p185 (06, 07), p186 (01), p187 (09), p189 (selected images), p190 (01-03), 190 (05, 06), 191 (07, 08, 11), 192 (03, 08), 195 (08), 203 (10).

Courtesy of Shepard Fairey/OBEYGIANT.COM: p219 (01, 02).

© Catherine Faux: p33 (01).

Danny Fields: 27 (01).

© f-stop fitzgerald inc. 2012. All rights reserved: p89 (05).

Design by Malcolm Garrett: p105 (05); Design by Malcolm Garrett. Photograph by Jill Furmanovsky: p49 (05); Design by Malcolm Garrett (Accompanying Images). Photograph by Jill Furmanovsky: p105 (09); Design by Malcolm Garrett (Aesthetic Images): p105 (06); Design by Malcolm Garrett (Agreeable Images). Photograph by Jill Furmanovsky: p105 (07); Design by Malcolm Garrett (Appetent Images). Photograph by Chris Gabrin: p105 (08); Design by Malcolm Garrett (Assorted Images): p109 (01-04); Design Malcolm Garrett and Linder. Illustration by Odilon Redon: p99 (09).

Getty Images/Howard Barlow/Redferns: p7 (01); Kevin Cummins: p8 (01); Estate Of Keith Morris/Redferns: p17.

© 1973 H.R. Giger, All Rights Reserved. Courtesy of www.HRGigerMuseum.com: p195 (09).

Peter Gravelle: p7 (02), p47 (01-05), p50 (02), p57 (06), p59 (01), p79 (02-04).

© Gary Grimshaw: p14 (01), p15 (06, 07).

Design: Geoff Halpin. Art Direction: Michael Ross: p85 (08).

© Paul Harvey: p217 (04).

John Holmstrom: p23 (03-05).

Courtesy of Sean Jefford: p208 (01).

Barry Jones: p56 (01-02), p57 (03-05, 07).

The Kobal Collection/2.4.7. FILMS/Courtesy Marjane Satrapi: p219 (03).

Peter Lloyd: 109 (04).

Dennis Loren Collection: p14 (01, 02), p15 (06, 07), p21 (09, 10), p25 (15), p69 (04, 05, 08), p185 (05), p189 (selected images), p210 (01).

Gary Loveridge: p25 (17), p33 (02), p37, p39 (02), p40 (10), p42 (01), p45 (04), p48 (02, 03), p61 (04, 07), p62 (11, 12), p65 (06), p79 (05), p80 (01, 02), p82 (01-04), p83 (07, 08), p87 (18), p91 (11), p96, p101 (20), p113 (06), p123 (02).

Mike Malignant: p31 (07), p40 (12), p64 (01), p65 (04), p67 (13), p99 (10).

Manchester District Music Archive: p105 (05).

From the collection of Andrew Matheson: p29 (01).

Jo Mirowski: p209 (08).

Steve Mitchell: p19 (03, 08), p20 (02), p25 (14), p98 (01).

Knud Odde / www.knudodde.dk: p217 (07).

Marco Palumbo-Rodrigues: p210 (01-06), p211 (07, 08), p213 (06), p217 (06).

Courtesy of Pest Control Office: p216 (02), p217 (03).

© Raymond Pettibon. Courtesy the artist and Regen Projects, Los Angeles: p189 (selected images).

Courtesy of PunkDistro.de: p135 (06), p144 (04), p204 (01-03), p205 (04-09), p209 (07).

Anna Raposo: p141 (02, 03), p160 (03), p161 (06, 07), p174 (06), p179 (11), p181 (01), p202 (04), p203 (07, 08).

Jamie Reid, courtesy Isis Gallery UK: p38 (01), p39 (03-06), p40 (07-09), 11), p41 (13-15), p73 (02-06), p75 (01-05).

Rex Features/David Dagley: p59 (02); Everett Collection: p29 (02); Sheila Rock: 59 (03); Ray Stevenson: p55 (01).

Alan Rider / adventuresinreality.co.uk: p109 (01).

Greg "Stainboy" Reinel • stainboy@stainboyreinel.com: p201 (01, 02).

Rockpopmem.com: p13 (01), p18 (02), p19 (04, 06), p43 (03, 04), p81 (03).

Håkan Sandsjö: p146 (13,14), p147 (15-18).

© Peter Saville: p49 (07, 11).

© Skydog / Marc Zermati, www.skydog.fr: p20 (01), p21 (11), p33 (01-03).

© Winston Smith / www.WinstonSmith.com: p197 (02, 05), p201 (05).

Stolper/Wilson Collection, London: p59 (04, 05).

Luk TAM89: p127 (02, 03), p151 (03), p206 (01, 02), p207 (03-07), p209 (05).

Design by United Artists, based on sleeve design by Malcolm Garrett (Arbitrary Images). Montage by Linder: p49 (04).

Arturo Vega / ramonesworld.com: p27 (01-04, 06).

Andy Wake: p49 (05).

Per-Åke Wärn: 127 (01).

All other images from private collections.

Russ Bestley is a Principal Lecturer in Graphic Design at the London College of Communication. A keen interest in punk during his teenage years led to his involvement in the movement as a fan, roadie, sound engineer, technician, musician, collector, designer and writer. He has co-authored and designed a number of books, including *Visual Research* (AVA Academia 2004, 2nd edition 2011), *Up Against the Wall: International Poster Design* (RotoVision 2002) and *Experimental Layout* (RotoVision 2001), and has contributed articles to magazines and journals including *Eye*, *Zed*, *Émigré*, *The National Grid*, *The Oxford Encyclopaedia of the Modern World* and *Punk & Post-Punk*. His PhD thesis, *Hitsville UK: Punk Rock and Graphic Design in the Faraway Towns*, 1976-84, led to a number of publications, a website www.hitsvilleuk.com, and exhibitions at the Millais Gallery, Southampton, British Film Institute, London, Rebellion Punk Festival, Blackpool and the Post-Punk Symposium, Leeds. He lives in Portsmouth and runs very long distances for fun.

Alex Ogg is one of the UK's most prominent historians of punk and independent music. He is the co-editor of the academic journal *Punk & Post-Punk*, as well as the author of UK punk history *No More Heroes* and the first comprehensive document of UK independent labels, *Independence Days*. Other books include *The Hip Hop Years*, accompanying the BAFTA-nominated documentary series on which he served as consultant, as well as biographies of Radiohead, Rick Rubin and Russell Simmons of Def Jam, a guide to rap lyrics and *Paid In Full*, surveying the indigenous UK hip-hop culture. Forthcoming books include one on America's premier punk band, Dead Kennedys. As well as journalism for *The Times*, *Etapes* (*France*), the *Sunday Herald*, *Classic Rock*, *Record Collector*, *The Quietus*, *Vive Le Rock* and *New York's Big Takeover*, he has contributed to more than 30 music encyclopaedias and written dozens of CD or DVD sleevenotes. These include the liner notes for *Pillows & Prayers*, which received a Mojo award for best catalogue release. His guest lectures include appearances at universities including Leeds, Birkbeck and Central St Martin's, as well as the National Film Theatre, Pushkin House and Rough Trade East. He supports Scunthorpe United.

The authors would like to thank our collaborators in the development of *The Art of Punk*, without whose valuable advice and support the book would not have been possible. Josef Loderer, Chuck Warner, David Ensminger, Luk Tam, Andrew Matheson, Mick Farren, Marco Palumbo and Steve Mitchell all played a substantive role in shaping the book in your hands. Also, our thanks to Mario Panciera, Brian Young, Tom Arnaert, Ana Raposo, Roger Sabin, Marcus Gray, Ian Noble, Paul Luce, Kev Bradshaw, Tony Credland, Chris BCT, Andy Thompson, Tony Gunnarsson, Peter Craven, Christian Lloyd, Ged Babey, Rich Levene, Aggro Culture, Don J Whistance's Clash website, Archive 45 and all the Pompey Punks for their insight and critical feedback on the book's content and writing. Thanks to Gary Loveridge, Trygve Mathiesen, Tim Pittman, Cameron Ross, Roger Crimlis, Barry Jones, Henrik Poulsen, Håkan Sandsjö, Dizzy Detour, Mike Malignant, Perry Goble, Candy Wall, Anne Poole, Dennis Loren, Micha at Punk Distro, Paul Cooper, Ben DeSoto, Mish Harrington, Teal Triggs, Mick Mercer, Rick Poynor, Sarah Dryden, Per-Åke Warn, Karen Duckworth, Gordon Wilkins, Marc Littell, Elle Font-Merde, Brad Castlen, Simon Grigg, Dan Heskamp, Gregor "Hayfever," Shaun Jefford and Jefe Brown for supplying images, artwork, and artifacts to broaden our scope; and the artists, designers, and musicians interviewed, who provided a story to tell behind their extraordinary visual work—Jamie Reid, Peter Gravelle, Marc Zermati, Malcolm Garrett, Winston Smith, John Holmstrom, Arturo Vega, Jo Mirowski, Knud Odde, Dexter Dalwood, Banksy, Paul Harvey, Chris Bashford, Jennifer Egan, Steve McGarry, Bill Smith, Roger Huddle, Jill Mumford, Hugh Brown, Joly MacFie, Jim Phelan, Knox, Jello Biafra and Alan Schneider at Alternative Tentacles, the Stern brothers, Dick Lucas, Mike Magrann, Marjane Satrapi, Pauline Murray, Gaye Advert, Tesco Vee and Milo Aukerman. Banksy images courtesy of Pest Control Office. Alex Ogg would like to thank Dawn Wrench, and his boys Hugh and Laurence Wrench. Russ Bestley would like to thank Sarah for sharing the punk obsession and contributing a key critical voice to the project. Josef Loderer would like to thank Alexander Magrutsch, Andreas Kuttner, Lurker Grand, Orlando Altermatt, Boris Nicolaj Bühler, H.R. Giger, and Marco Palumbo.

Special thanks should also go to Paul Palmer-Edwards for his practical skills, critical voice and enduring patience, together with his willingness to go above and beyond the call of duty in the pursuit of design perfection, and to Katie Greenwood for her dedication to the task as permissions editor. The punk movement has always engendered a spirit of cooperation and collaboration, and the willingness of these stalwarts of the punk community to contribute, debate, critique and advise stands as an exemplar of that philosophy in action.